W9-CRQ-026

$1.700.

Photo No. 1. Palace of Sayil. The magnicence and beauty of the Puuc arquitecture it is posible to admire it in this picture. Photo courtesy of the writer Luis Ramírez Aznar from his book "PUUC".

PROFR. GUALBERTO ZAPATA ALONZO

AN OVERVIEW OF THE

MAYAN WORLD

WITH SYNTHESIS OF THE OLMEC, TOTONAC ZAPOTEC, MIXTEC, TEOTIHUACAN, TOLTEC AND AZTEC CIVILIZATIONS

MERIDA, YUCATAN, MEXICO

1985

FIFTH EDITION IN ENGLISH

1ra. Edición: 1985
© Producción Editorial Dante, S.A.
   Calle 59 # 472
   Mérida 97000, Yucatán, México

Colección: sueste

ISBN: 968-7232-19-6

Impreso en México
Printed in Mexico

Acknowledgement

I sincerely wish to thank Ronald Aplin and Cheryl Mochalski, two graduates of the University of Wisconsin —Green Bay—, for their work in the translation and general revision of this text. Without the assistance of these fine people, this book could not have been published in this way in its English version.

The Author

TABLE OF CONTENTS

5

PROLOGUE

When I first met Professor Gualberto Zapata Alonzo, and became aware of his characteristic tenacity and irrepressible passion for delving into the bottomless depths of what is still largely the unknown past of the great Maya people, he was compiling the complicated parts of the first Spanish edition of his fascinating book "Una Visión del Mundo Maya". Meticulous in both his actions and his speech, Don Gualberto was selecting photographs, drawings, maps...

Since then, I have had the privilege of appreciating his diligence, his profound knowledge of the history of pre-Hispanic cultures, and his undoubted capability for consultation, all without false vanity. Proffesor Zapata has been. for many years, a professional researcher. His deductions and inferences, analyses and theses have not been obtained from sitting at far-removed library desks or limited to the study of valuable pre-Columbian texts written by eminent scientists. He has more than once visited each of the sites where the great culture of the "ancient Maya" flourished; and he has poured his great enthusiasm and passion into each hieroglyph, each stone and each architectural motif that his profound knowledge might indicate or that would give him the opportunity of discovering some new vista ... His research is done in situ and his studies are based in the "fields of facts".

No one can have a higher opinion of the fascinating talks -which frequently become learned lectures- on the various archeological sites, particulary in Yucatán, than the lucky foreign visitors who have had Don Gualberto as their tourist guide.

I have always admired the researcher. More so the one that goes out into the field, because it is there, in the "fields of facts" that inspiration is actually realized.

7

Proffesor Zapata is not content with his enormous historical and scientific knowledge -- much less with only drinking from the fountains of knowledge provided by scholars of the Maya culture. He continues to scan the vast horizon of our ancient history, convinced that in every corner of the crumbling and destroyed religious or hierarchichal centers and cities built by these incredible pre-Hispanic educators, lies the key or the secret that might allow us to reach newer and more surprising heights ...

When I found him on my selfsame path of editorial efforts, selflessly and with unbridled interest, trying to publish all that he had been able to accumulate in many years of responsible labor, I warned him -- more as stimulation than pessimism -- on how tortured and rough it was to walk this highly- esteemed but under-paid path.

But, as has already been said, Don Gualberto is irrepressible in his passion for espressing views and promoting responsible discussions that will lead to the desired goals. With considerable economic sacrifices, he undertook his first venture in publishing, a Spanish book entitled "Una Vision del Mundo Maya", which summarized the Olmec, Totonac, Zapotec, Mixtec, Teotihuacan, Toltec and Aztec cultures, in a highly professional, clear and attractive edition. He was duly compensated, for his work was warmly received by both the learned and the uninitiated. It is a readable and knowledgeable work, avoiding the pitfalls of novelization or distortion of historical facts.

Nothing could have been more appropiate or stimulating ...

Listening to the positive advice of those better informed, Proffesor Zapata prepared a second edition this time in English, which vastly surpassed his hoped for success. We present, for review by the professionals, an easy and fluent book by one who offers the results of his research, analyses, critiques, logic and realism.

8

You, dear reader, interested in the history of ancient man, avid to learn more about the extraordinary knowledge of the Maya educators, and hoping that researchers may overcome their concerns and reach incontrovertible proof, will find in this edition of "An Overview of the Mayan World" a real text on the subject.

And you shall agree with me on the capability and proffesionalism of Don Gualberto ...

LUIS A. RAMIREZ AZNAR.

INTRODUCTION

The authors of works on the ancient cultures of the Americas, always encounter difficult and complicated problems when trying to detail the history of the American civilizations. These problems arise because of the fact that upon the arrival of the Europeans in the New World, the oldest civilizations had already disintegrated, leaving as proof of their existence only buildings in ruins, idols made of a variety of materials, ceramics, and many reliefs, some of which are carved with hieroglyphics, among other things. Some ancient cultures left behind codices whose meanings were unknown With only these objects as proof of their existence, it is difficult to unravel the mysterious past of these peoples.

Unfortunately, the majority of the conquistadors were poorly educated, and in accordance with the thinking of their time, they felt that little or nothing that they encountered in America was important enough to merit their investigations. Rather than study these once great civilizations, they tried to destroy everything which lay in their path. It is because of this attitude and the actions of the conquistadors that the investigators of today have a very limited base from which to work, and why their conclusions are, for the most part, of a hypothetical nature.

The investigations of the more recent cultures such as the Mixtecs and the Aztecs, especially of the latter, is better defined and complete because these civilizations were at their high point at the time of the Spanish conquest.

Some of the histories of these cultures were passed down from generation to generation among the indigenous people from the time of the collapse of the civilization. However, these historical facts suffered many revisions over time, and as a result, evolved from truth to myth. Still other histories, which have survived the passage of time, are full of contradictory facts which only add to the researchers' problems.

All of the above reasons account for the discrepancies which are found between the data provided in the books of one author and those of another.

It is truly admirable to see how human ingenuity rises above these obstacles to open paths to the history of these cultures. Because of the tenacity and perseverance of many researchers, a bit more of the mystery of the past of our ancestors is revealed in each new investigation.

Hundreds of books on archaeology have been written, more than seven hundred of which deal with the Mayan culture. The authors of some of these books have been outstanding archaeologists and anthropologists, while others have been professional engineers, architects, doctors, professors, and so on. Others have simply been gifted writers who were motivated to write because of the interesting and intriguing aspects of the Mayan culture. Because of their desires to write something worthwhile in the study of these people, they have dedicated most of their lives to this intensive field of investigation with true love and passion.

Some authors have written several volumes dealing with all of the aspects of the Mayan culture; others just one book. On the other hand, some authors have concentrated their writing in one specific area of the Mayan culture, such as their architecture, mathematics, chronology, ceramics, language, and so on.

After so many works have been written on the subject of the Maya, it would seem unnecessary to write another. It was this idea that made me resist my desire to write on the subject for quite some time. It was, in part, my experience gained in constant visits to many Mexican archaeological sites, both as a tourist guide and as a curious observer, and the many analytical studies which I had made over the years, which led me to believe that I could indeed write such a work.

One experience was of major importance in my decision to write this work. In September of 1976, I was invited by Professor Larry McWilliams, the Coordinator of Instruction at the Jefferson County School of Lakewood, in Denver, Colorado (United States), as well as the other directors of the school, to take part in a conference on the Mayan culture, along with seventy other professors. I accepted their invitation to this international event, which was held from the 11th to the 15th of October, 1976. I wrote a work, in accordance with the desires of my hosts, about the origin of the American Man, which outlined the evolution of the Meso-American cultures in general, and the culture of the Maya in particular, since the conference was focused primarily on the

Maya. Fortunately, my presentation was well-received, and was praised by the organizers of the event; this reception gave me the stimulation I needed to publish the materials which I have writen in the form of a book, with some modifications and pertinent elaborations.

Another reason for my decision to write a book was because of the fact that the majority of the visitors to the archaeological zones of Mexico, many of whom make this trip only once, cannot memorize nor absorb all of the explanations of the tourist guides, no matter how well these explanations are delivered. The visitor generally leaves confused by the number of names of cultures, places, dates, facts, etc., that have been discussed. Many of these visitors, enthusiastic about all of their newly acquired knowledge, buy thick books full of details and technicalities, which they read avidly upon their return home, only to lamentably cast them aside to be forgotten in some corner of their libraries. These works are written for those who wish to expand their knowledge of the subject, not for those who only want to have a clear, general concept of the ancient cultures presented in a simple manner.

For this reason, I had to modify my original work and employ an easier and more accessible language in the writing of this one, eliminating, whenever possible, the complicated technical terms, and mentioning only the most important facts and historical figures in a necessary chronological order. I left out the superfluous details so that the reader will not lose interest because of an excess of minor details.

One of the most complicated areas of study of the Mayan culture is that of chronology, which I did not eliminate from this work because it is very important and quite fascinating. I feel that the way in which I present the Mayan chronology will make it relatively easy to understand. I advise the reader who is not interested in this theme to skip this part of the book and continue with the following chapters.

Another of my intentions was to explain the historical facts of these cultures thoroughly, but without lengthy explanations, so that the reader would not have to resort to consulting other texts for clarity. This does not mean that I believe that the other volumes of written work are unnecessary; on the contrary, I feel that the material presented in this book should serve as a base for the general public, from which they can complement their knowledge with more extensive works.

I believe that this book will prove to be of little use to the scholars and the authorities of Meso-American archaeology; the only new concepts that these people will find published within are some personal conclusions which I have included. These conclusions are of a truly hypothetical nature in that they do not have a firm basis for the explanation of some of the varied problems that the study of the ancient cultures have posed, as is well-known by all of the scholars in this field.

This book is a product of my personal effort. I hope that it will be of some use to those who consult it. I have faith that it will serve as the incentive for others who are avidly interested in the ancient American cultures in the unraveling of the mystery of our origin.

The Author.

PART ONE

CHAPTER ONE

ANTECEDENTS OF THE AMERICAN INDIAN

The origin of the Maya, like the origin of the rest of the groups that populated the American Continent, is unknown to us. One is able to fill page after page with information, citing and commenting on investigative studies, without arriving at satisfactory conclusions because use of the available information revolves around hypothesis.

One of the most popular theories of the origin of the American Indian states that millennia ago the race came from Asia across the Bering Strait of Alaska either by way of the Diomedes Islands (whose formation served as a ladder), or the Aleutian Islands. It is thought that these groups arrived at different times and in different migratory surges. This theory is strengthened by the fact that the indigenous groups of the Americas, especially the Maya, are born with the Mongolian spot at the base of their spine. This circle, dark at birth, fades as the child grows older and, at about nine years of age, it totally disappears. This fact, along with the very similar facial characteristics between the Asian people and the indigenous American groups, supports the theory which is stated above.

Another important fact which is worthy of mention is that the stature of the Japanese race is shorter than that of the other Mongolian peoples; this fact, combined with likenesses in facial characteristics and their other morphological traits, makes the appearances of the two races so similar that many times they are easily confused. The majority of the Japanese also possess the Mongolian spot; perhaps the Japanese people were part of the later migratory groups to the Americas.

D. Ignacio Magaloni Duarte quotes the investigator and traveler James Churchward as saying "...that a Mexican Indian and a Japanese can understand one another without the aid of an interpreter, and that forty percent of the Japanese language has Mayan idiom roots..." [1]

1).— Magaloni Duarte Ignacio. **Los Educadores del Mundo.** B. Costa — Amic, México City, 1969; page 57.

15

Scientists know of the presence of the first inhabitants in the Americas because of the stone tools and other objects which these early tribes left behind, such as knives, scrapers, arrow and spear heads, and carved bones. Excavations in various parts of the Americas have uncovered the skeletons of different animals, most of which are extinct today. These animals (the mastadon, the mammoth, the ground sloth, the horse, the rhinocerous, and others), also came to the Americas by crossing the Bering Strait; they (arrived, however, at the end of the last Ice Age.

Stratigraphic and Carbon-14 studies have been the key sources for calculating the time of arrival and establishment of these groups in the Americas. Some scientist calculate that the appearance of man in the Americas occurred between the years 15,000 to 20,000 B. C., while others place the date at 35,000 B. C., in accordance with new findings.

When artifacts are found in excavations and scientifically analized, they are classified according to the following eras:

(a) Sandia Cave ——— This comprises the area of New Mexico, parts of Colorado and Texas (The U. S. of North America) 18,000 to 13,000 B. C.

(b) Clovis ——————— Area of New Mexico. In this period the tips of the stones have a special characteristic and are similar to those found Alaska to the north, and the actual Mexican Republic to the south. Period from 13,000 to 10,000 B. C.

(c) Folsom Complex— Comprises an extensive area from Canada to Texas in North America and Mexico, Central and South America, Period 10,000 to 8,000 B. C.

Many human skeletons have been found in the Valley of Mexico; for example, the Jawbone of Xico, Rock of the Baths Man (Peñón de los Baños), and Tepexpan Man, among many other fossils. A skeleton of a mammoth was found very near to the remains of Tepexpan Man. By the spear found on the mammoth's bones, it appears that it was hunted by man. When the Carbon 14 method was used to date carbonized vegetable matter located into the skeleton of the mammoth, it was found to be 11,300 years old.

This date is very close to that which was established previously by Dr. Helmut de Terra using the Stratograph method.[3]

The archaeologists of the Autonomous University of the state of Guerrero, Mexico, published in June of 1976, a report which detailed the finding of the remains of a 30.000 year old mastadon and ground sloth in Apaxtla de Castrejón.

Archaeologists of the Institute of Paleontology of this same University found vestiges of fauna of the Quarternary Age in an extensive area in which many ruins are also found. These paleontologists were able to determine the origin of the most remote groups that inhabited that area, which today comprises the cities of Iguala and Tierra Caliente in the state of Guerrero. Scientists of the Autonomous University of Mexico (U.N.A.M.) have confirmed the findings of these paleontologists.

Other scientific investigations have discovered a Mylayo-Polynesian influence in the Americas; this influence is manifested in the existence of anthropological and linguistic similarities, and similar practices and customs such as the use of the hammock, blowguns, war clubs, hanging bridges, dances which employ masks, and others.

Strong linguistic and ethnographic similarities exist between the people of Lagoa Santa in Brazil and the inhabitants of Mylasia.

There are some investigators who believe that the American Indian originated on this continent, although this theory is not widely accepted because of the fact that remains of evolutionary man have not been found in the Americas. However, the American Continent is vast and much of it unexplored... perhaps new investigations will reveal surprising truths.

3).— Canto López Antonio, **Apuntaciones Sobre Mesoamérica**, Mérida, Yucatán, 1973; page 4 — 5.

CHAPTER TWO

MESO-AMERICA

"Meso-America" is a relatively new scientific/anthropological name which is used to designate the area where various cultures developed, each with its own well-defined and distinctive characteristics. The Meso-American area comprises a little more than half of Mexico extending from a line in the north which approximates the 23rd parallel in the east, bends south to about the Lerma River, and then ends at the Sinaloa River in the west, an area which encompasses all of the central, south, and southwest of Mexico. Also mentioned in the Meso-American area are Guatemala, Belize, the western part of the Honduras, El Salvador, Nicaragua, and part of Costa Rica. [1]

For the purpose of their studies, scientists have divided Meso-America into six archaeological regions in the following manner:

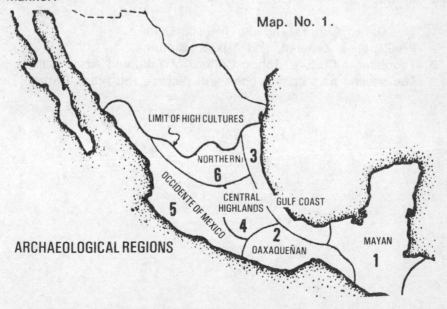

Map. No. 1.

LIMIT OF HIGH CULTURES

NORTHERN 3

6

OCCIDENTE OF MEXICO

CENTRAL HIGHLANDS   GULF COAST

5

4   2

ARCHAEOLOGICAL REGIONS   OAXAQUEÑAN

MAYAN

1

1).— González B. and Guevara R:, Op. Cit.; page 23.

1. The Maya Region — This region comprises the states of Yucatán, Campeche, Quintana Roo, Chiapas, and part of Tabasco in Mexico. Outside of Mexico it encompasses the Central American countries already mentioned.
2. Oaxacan Region — This region comprises the Mexican states of Guerrero, Puebla, and Oaxaca.
3. Gulf Coast Region — Encompassed in this region are the states of Veracruz, Tamaulipas, Puebla, and part of Tabasco.
4. Central High Plains Region — This region encompasses the Valley of Mexico, Toluca, Morelos, Tlaxcala, Hidalgo, and part of Puebla.
5. Western Mexico Region — This region is comprised of the Mexican states of Michoacán, Guerrero, Colima, Nayarit, and Jalisco.
6. The North Region — This region is comprised of the area in Mexico just south of the northern border of Meso-America.

In order for the reader to become better aquainted with the evolutionary process of the different Meso-American cultures, the oldest culture and those which stemmed from it, will be described first, then the second oldest culture and its branch cultures, and so on, in chronological order from the oldest to the most recent, as follows:

1. The Olmec Culture and the Totonac Culture.
2. Pre-Zapotec, Zapotec, and Mixtec Cultures.
3. Teotihuacan Culture, Toltec Culture of Tula, and Aztec Culture
   The second part of this book will discuss the Maya Culture.

CHAPTER THREE

a). The Olmecs   b). The Totonacs

a). The Olmecs

Some historians affirm that it was the Aztecs who gave the name "Olmec" to the cultureless tribes that lived in a region which encompassed the southern part of the state of Veracruz and part of Tabasco. These tribes (the Olmecs) were not related in any way to the famous culture that existed in the same area at a much earlier date, about a millennium before Christ. The Aztecs called the Olmec country "Olmán", which in Nahuatl means "the land of rubber" because rubber trees are abundant in that area. After, researchers have called also at the legendary creators of this culture the Olmecs.

In 1871 an enormous human head weighing several tons, was found in Tres Zapotes, Veracruz. The scientists who analyzed it at that·time thought that it had come from another continent. Later, other stone heads were found, along with many other objects which had similar characteristics; through these discoveries scientists learned that the heads and the other objects were originally of a culture which had existed in that region many years ago. [1]

The Olmec territory runs parallel to the coast of the Gulf of Mexico and is approximately 200 kilometers long and 50 kilometers wide. It is watered by the Grijalva, Tonolá, Papaloapan, and Coatzacoalcos rivers.

The most important Olmec centers were La Venta (the best known of the centers), Tres Zapotes, El Cerro de las Mesas, and San Lorenzo.

The fertile land of this region is covered with dense vegetation which would have supported a greater abundance of wild game and fruits and vegetables in Olmec times. The Olmecs also had long shorelines which provided them with a variety of seafood.

No one knows for certain the origin of these people, nor

1).— **La Aventura de México,** Ayala Anguiano Armando, General Director Vol. 1, No. 2, Publicaciones AAA, S. A., México City, 1966; page 18, "Los Misteriosos Olmecas".

the time of their arrival in that area. It is believed that they arrived on the coast of the Gulf of Mexico in approximately 1500 B. C., and that they later established themselves in a place called "Tamoanchán", the location of which still remains unknown.

The cultural manifestations of the Olmecs have helped us to learn something of their mysterious past. In this respect, their fabulous ceramics, which are extraorinarily realistic, have played an important role, along with their monoliths, some of which represent enormous, detached human heads, with animated facial expressions, negroid lips and noses, and oriental eyes. On these heads are carved helmets similar to those used in the North American sport of football.

Two enormous stone heads were found in Tres Zapotes, five in San Lorenzo, and four in La Venta; a total of eleven have been found altogether. The majority of these heads measure 2.46 meters high and weigh more than thirty tons. Blocks of rock weighing more than fifty tons were also transported to this area. It is thought that these monoliths possibly came from the rock quarries of San Martín Pajapan, Veracruz, a distance of 130 kilometers. [2]

D. Ignacio Marquina states that one of the colossal heads of Tres Zapotes is carved from a single block of gray basalt rock, and that it weighs about ten tons. It is possible that this rock was taken from the bed of a nearby river or stream, since the next nearest source is sixteen kilometers distant, a distance which would make the transportation of such a heavy stone very difficult. [3]

Recently, another stone head was found on the Gobata Ranch, owned by Mrs. Concepción Fernández Sedas, and located some fourteen kilometers from the town of Santiago Tuxtla. It measures eight meters in circumference, 3.5 meters in height, and weighs more than twenty tons. (The information provided on the weight of this monolith suggests that it was poorly calculated; another head which weighs thirty tons is only 2.46 meters high. However, the circumference of the latter was not specified.)

The Olmec sculpture called the "Wrestler" or "Ball Player", which was found in Uxpanapan, Veracruz, has been considered a masterpiece of the artists of that era.

2).— La Aventura de México, Ibid, page 24.

3).— Marquina Ignacio, **Arquitectura Prehispánica,** 1964; page 393. Editor. Instituto Nacional de Antropología e Historia de México.

The majority of these artistically carved monoliths can be found in the Museum of Tabasco Park which is located on the outskirts of the city of Villahermosa; others can be seen in the Museum of Archaeology in the same city, and still others are located in the patios of the Museum of Jalapa, Veracruz.

The manner in which these enormous monoliths were transported in Olmec times remains a mystery, although it is suggested that they were placed on rafts which were moved by means of rollers.

Olmec influence has been identified in different parts of the Mexican territory and even outside of it.

The writer and archaeologist Wolfgang Cordan, who died while taking part in explorations in Central America, shows by means of photographs taken on the Monte Alto Farm in Guatemala, the discovery of some colossal Olmec heads.[4] These heads are believed to be older than those found at La Venta, Tres Zapotes, and San Lorenzo because of the roughness of their carving.

In spite of the fact that these heads have a facial expression which is very distinct from those found in the Olmec region, these heads are still used to reinforce the hypothesis that the Olmec, if they were not of Maya origin, at least lived in the Maya region. Human figures of ceramic, jade, serpentine, and other materials which were found in the Olmec territory have a typical form distinctive to that of the Maya. The shape of the heads of these figures is almost always elongated, which leads one to believe that cranial deformation was practiced. Many of the faces of these figures seem to be those of children with oriental eyes, some of which have mouths that resemble the mouth of the jaguar, an animal which the Olmec considered to be sacred and possibly a diety. Some experts believe that the jaguar represents a sun god; others believe it to be the god of water.

A sculpture found in Portrero Nuevo, Veracruz, shows a woman mating with a jaguar. [5] Perhaps this is a symbolic form which demonstrates that the Olmecs believed themselves to be descendent from this animal, or that they had inherited from it its courage, agility and cunning.

On a slab of rock which was found in the Olmec zone, a carved relief shows the profile of a man with a hooked nose and

4) — Cordan Wolfgang. **Secret of the Forest,** Doubleday and Co. Garden City, New York, 1964; Photos 51 and 52.

5) .— **La Aventura de México,** Op. Cit; page 18.

a long beard which seems to be false. His physique is completely different from the other human representations found in that area which further complicates the study of the origin of these people.

The fact that Olmec influence has been found in other cultures in Mexico, especially in the culture at Monte Albán, and because the Olmec culture is the oldest of the Meso-American cultures, Dr. D. Alfonso Caso, an outstanding Mexican archaeologist, arrived at the conclusion that the Olmecs represent the Meso-American mother culture.

b) . The Totonacs

After the collapse of the Olmecs, which occurred at the beginning of the Christian Era, a new culture emerged: the culture of the Totonacs. Their territory was just north of the Olmec region, parallel to the coast of the Gulf of Mexico, in the state of Veracruz.

Little is known about the Totonac culture. Some experts believe that they were a mixture of the Nahua and Totonac peoples.

Historians disagree on the date of the phases of this culture; some cite the Totonacs' first phase as extending from 200 to 650 A. D. and the second from 650 to 1000 A. D., while others cite the first as extending from 600 to 1200 A. D. and the second from 1200 A. D. until the Spanish conquest. In order to arrive at a workable chronology, it would be more convenient to divide the culture into three phases: the first phase being from 200 to 650 A. D., the second from 650 to 1200 A. D., and the third from 1200 until the time of the Spanish conquest.

From their beginning, the Totonac culture had a strong Teotihuacan influence; later it absorbed Mayan influence. The Totonacs were also influenced by their neighbors to the north, the Huastecs, and finally, by the Cholultecs, whose influence was especially strong in Cempoala, the place which served as their capital in the final phase of their culture.

The Totonac masonry constructions are not as impressive as those of other cultures, with the exception of the Pyramid of the Niches at El Tajín, their first capital. This pyramid —certainly very original— has a square base which measures 35 meters on each side and is 25 meters high. It consists of seven superimposed structures that decrease in size from bottom to top. There are niches in all of the seven structures; in total, there are 364 niches. Because this number approximates the number of days in the year, it is believed that the pyramid bore a relationship to their calendar.

Pieces of green rock (diorite and serpentine) and basalt have been found in excavations of several Totonac areas. Some of these pieces are in the form of a horseshoe and are called "yokes". They are delicately carved with a variety of motifs, most of which represent animals. Other pieces were found which were given the name "palmas"; their use is unknown.

One of the peculiar characteristics of Totonac ceramics are some little smiling faces which are so finely detailed that no other Meso-American culture was able to imitate them. [6]

Very little is known about their religion. They adored Tajín, the god of thunder and rain; they named their capital after him. They also worshiped Quetzalcoatl, as did other cultures.

6).— González B. and Guevara R., Op. Cit.; pages 83 — 85.

CHAPTER FOUR

a). The Pre-Zapotecs and Zapotecs   b). The Mixtecs

a). The Pre-Zapotecs and Zapotecs

The Pre-Zapotec culture was the next oldest culture following the Olmec. This culture is also known by the name of "the Culture of Monte Albán" (Monte Albán being their primary cultural center). From Monte Albán, they extended their territory to cover a vast area from the Pacific coast to as far north as Cholula, where their very distinctive ceramics· have been found.

A strong Olmec influence can be noted in Monte Albán during its First Phase, which leads experts to believe that there was a close relationship between the two cultures.

Monte Albán is located in the state of Oaxaca, at the high point of a low mountain range that intersects the Valley of Oaxaca. This high part of the mountain range was leveled in order to convert it into an artificial plateau which measures 700 meters from north to south, and 250 meters from east to west. The rectangular plaza of Monte Albán measures 300 meters in length and 200 meters in width, and is 400 meters above the valley floor. This plateau rests 2,000 meters above sea level. [1]

It is said that the first inhabitants settled in this place to protect themselves from their enemies. The city itself was very extensive; explorations of the surrounding area have determined that it covered almost forty square kilometers. The original name of this site is not known, although some historians mention that it was called "El Cerro del Tigre" (The Tiger's Hill).

This culture has been divided into phases as follows: Monte Albán I, Monte Albán II, Monte Albán III, Monte Albán III-A, Monte Albán III-B, Monte Albán IV, and Monte Albán V. The dates of each period are the result of approximate calculations, since the precise dates are not known. This is the reason why authors sometimes give different dates to these periods.

The first period, Monte Albán I, began around 700 to 600 B. C., with the establishment of Monte Albán, and ended in 300

1).— **Guía Oficial de Monte Albán-Mitla,** Inst. Nacional de Antropología e Historia de México, 1962; page 9.

B. C. The construction of the first structures was initiated during this period. Carved in one of these buildings are the well-known reliefs called "The Dancers", whose distinctive forms reveal an Olmec influence. Hieroglyphic writing, numerology, and the calendar appeared during this period. The first tombs, in rectangular form with flat roofs, were also constructed.

It has been concluded that the first inhabitants of Monte Albán arrived there with a culture intact, as no traces of a beginning or formative period have been found.

The following period, Monte Albán, II, began in the year 300 B. C. and ended at the beginning of the Christian Era. The influence of another culture, thought to be that of the Maya of Guatemala, became evident during this period. A change in the existing ceramic style can be noted with the introduction of special four-footed vessels; tombs rich in offerings, some with colored paintings, were also constructed.

A period of transition between phase II and III followed which is noted in only one part of the Zapotec country. The Classic Period then began, and it is divided into two phases; the first is Monte Albán III-A, which lasteds until the year 500 A. D., and the second is Monte Albán III-B which ended around 900 to 1000 A. D.

Mayan influence persisted during the Classic Period; influence of the cultures of Teotihuacan and of the Toltecs can also be observed. Expansive growth of the Monte Albán culture is also noted during this period.

A decadent period followed this prolific phase, and Monte Albán was abandoned for reasons which are unknown. Some investigators suggest that this emigration was caused by the invasion of the Mixtecs, who converted Monte Albán into a burial ground for the interment of their nobility.

Monte Albán IV followed this decadent period. During this period complete dominion of all of the surrounding region was obtained, including the towns of Zaachila, Etla, Mitla, and so on.

The final period, or Monte Albán V, included the era of the dominance of the Mixtec culture. [2]

It is important to emphasize that Monte Albán is noted for the wealth of clay artifacts which have been found there, the majority of which are of good quality, with the exception of those which were made during the decadent period.

2). — Ibid, pages 4 — 5 — 6.

28

Perhaps the greatest number of jewels found at one site in all of Meso-America were discovered at Monte Albán. The richest tomb found in Mexico, (Tomb Number 7), was explored by Dr. D. Alfonso Caso in 1931. It is a multiple tomb, in which the remains of nine people were found. Also found in the tomb were more than 300 objects of gold, silver, copper, jade, shell, pearls, turquoise, and rock crystal, the most outstanding of which is a cup made of a single piece of the crystal. Thirty bones, delicately carved with a variety of motifs, were also found in the tomb; it is believed that these were jaguar, deer, or eagle bones. This tomb was utilized by the Zapotecs in the Third Period, and later by the Mixtecs, who put the above described jewels there.[3]

Explorations have uncovered a total of 153 tombs at this site.

In a place of worship which is situated nearly at the center of the plaza, a mask of dark green jade, which represents the Bat God, was found mounted on a wooden base. This jewel is now in the National Museum of Mexico.[4]

The Zapotec numerology was similar to that of the Maya; it is based on the dot (to represent units of one) and the bar (to represent five), a system which they used up to the number nineteen. We do not know how they wrote the number twenty.[5] This will be more easily understood when Mayan numerology is discussed in later chapters.

The Zapotec writing system was hieroglyphic, and has thus far been impossible to decipher. The significance of only some of the symbols is known. It had been thought to be ideographic in nature; it is now said also to be, in part, of a phonetic nature as well.

The Zapotecs had two calendars, of 260 and 360 days, respectively. Professor Wigberto Jiménez Moreno states that it is possible that the Zapotecs had another of 365 days which they used to identify the position of the day in the month.

Due to the work of the distinguished Mexican archaeologist Dr. D. Alfonso Caso, the different periods of the occupation of Monte Albán, which were previously unknown, have now been determined. His careful explorations and studies over many years have clarified part of the mystery of this historic region.

3).— Marquina Ignacio, Op. Cit.; pages 339 — 352.
4).— **Guía Oficial de Monte Albán-Mitla**, Op., Cit.; page 15.
5).— Iturribarria Jorge Fernando, **Las Viejas Culturas de Oaxaca**, Imprenta Valle, México City, 1952; pages 42 — 43.

b). The Mixtecs

The Mixtec territory comprised part of the states of Oaxaca, Guerrero, and Puebla, and their establishment in this area is calculated to have occurred during the Seventh Century of the Christian Era. The towns that the Mixtecs established were Achiutla and Tilantongo in the central part of their territory, Tututepec in the south, and Coixtlahuaca in the north; these centers were so independent that they were almost separate dominions.

The similarities between the Toltec and Mixtec cultures are attributed to the collapse of Tula in 1156 A. D., when some of the Toltecs from Tula immigrated to the Mixtec territory, uniting with them in Coixtlahuaca and in nearby areas.

According to some historians, the Chichimecs invaded the territory of the Mixtecs in 1173 A. D., forcing the inhabitants to immigrate to Zapotec territory. The Mixtecs took possession of Monte Albán, all of the Zapotecapan region, Tututepec, and Teotitlán del Camino, establishing a hegemony that lasted many years. Later the Mixtecs recovered their lost territory in Puebla and expanded their dominion to as far north as Chalco. [6]

In Achiutla in 1456, the Mixtecs made the imprudent mistake of killing some Aztec traders, and act which resulted in a war. After exhibiting heroic resistance, they were defeated and subjected to servitude, a condition which lasted until the arrival of the Spaniards.

The conquest of the Mixtecs by the Mexicas (Aztecs) was a relatively simple matter, due to the constant conflicts and strife which the Mixtecs had with their neighbors, especially the Zapotecs.

The Mixtecs had the best and the most numerous codices which have been found on the Mexican High Plains. These were made with animal skins (especially deer skin), which were carefully flattened and then coated with a thin layer of lime.

Mixtec writing and numerology was similar to that of the Zapotec.

The Mixtec ceramic is considered to be one of the most beautiful of Mexico and it appears to be strikingly similar to that of South American cultures.

The gold work of the Mixtecs is surprising in its beauty and in the technique employed in its elaboration; they used the method called "lost wax", as well as filigree and hammering. Their clay urns and paintings are truly remarkable.

6).— González B. and Guevara R., Op. Cit.; page 134.

CHAPTER FIVE
CIVILIZATIONS OF HIGHLANDS (Valley of México)

a). **The Teotihuacan Culture**
b). **The Toltecs**
c). **The Seven Nahuatl Tribes**
d). **Ethnic Coincidences Between the Nahua Culture and that of the Indigenous People of Mesa Verde**
e). **The Aztecs**

a). The Teotihuacan Culture

To date, no one has been able to explain the origin of the Teotihuacan culture; all that is known about this culture has resulted from speculation on the part of scientists who have dedicated themselves to the study of the mysterious past of this great civilization. The specialists can base their studies upon the great pyramids of the Sun and the Moon, as well as many other minor structures, ceramics, and painted murals, the most outstanding of the murals is from Tepantitla in which among other things the Paradise of Tlaloc (the God of Rain) is represented.

Investigators are not in agreement as to the date of the beginning of the Teotihuacan culture. Specialist Robert Wauchope, for example, places its beginning around the year 600 B. C., while the archaeologist Pedro Armillas is of the opinion that the urbanization at Teotihuacan commenced around the year 400 B. C. On the other hand, the tourist guide which is published by the Institute of Anthropology and History of Mexico and was researched by the archaeologist Jorge R. Acosta assigns, a developmental date between the years 100 B. C., to possibly 650 or 700 A. D., to this culture, basing this calculation on the types of ceramics found at the site and on Carbon-14 dating tests.

For many years it was believed that the builders of the great pyramids at Teotihuacan were the Toltecs of Tula; this information was included in some textbooks. However, the historian Professor Wigberto Jiménez Moreno made detailed investigations in Tula, and his studies clarified the fact that the indigenous chronicles and other reports obtained after the conquest

31

mention the Toltecs as the inhabitants of Tula, not of Teotihuacan. He also discovered that Tula and Teotihuacan were not contemporaries, but that Tula existed after Teotihuacan. [1]

Teotihuacan was not just a ceremonial center, it was a true city. It had drainage canals, narrow parallel streets, and numerous squares that formed housing blocks which were 70 meters long on each side.

The Teotihuacan people were extremely religious, as were almost all of the cultures of Meso-America. Their supreme god was Tloquenahuaque. Secondary dieties were Tlaloc, the god of Rain, Quetzalcoatl, believed to be associated with Tloquenahuaque; Huehueteotl, the god of the Elderly and of Fire; the goddess Xipe of Fertility, and Chalchitlicue, the goddess of Water. They also worshipped the sun, the moon, and the stars. Some of these gods appear in other, later cultures, conceptualized in a similar manner.

It is believed that their system of government was predominantly theocratic, with the ministerial class controlling all aspects of daily life, especially the economic.

Listed below are the results of a comparison which was made between the dimensions of the Pyramid of the Sun at Teotihuacan and the Egyptian Pyramid of Cheops: the base of the Pyramid of the Sun is 225 meters per side, while the base of Cheops is 226.5 meters; the height of the Pyramid of the Sun (including a rough calculation of the size of a temple which once rested atop the pyramid, and which no longer exists) is 75 meters while the height of Cheops is 144.32 meters; Cheops was constructed in 2650 B. C. and the Pyramid of the Sun at Teotihuacan in 100 B. C. [2]

In their third phase, or florescent period, the Teotihuacans extended their influence in different directions reaching northwest to La Quemada, and northeast to La Huasteca and eventually incorporating Tajín. To the west, their influence spread to the state of Michoacan and Oaxaca, and to the southeast through Chiapas. The Teotihuacan influence can be seen in the Mayan region as far south as Honduras, their most marked traces and influences, however, are found in Kaminaljuyú, Guatemala.

1).— Acosta Jorge R., and Martínez del Río, Dr. Pablo, Guía Oficial de Tula, Instituto Nacional de Antropología e Historia de México, México City, 1961; page 7.

2).— Guía Oficial de Teotihuacan, I.N.A.H. de Méx. México City, 1965, pages 34 — 35.

b). The Toltecs

It has been established that the name "Toltec" does not refer to a race, but refers instead to a culture, and that the meaning of "Toltec" can be variously expressed as "artist", "craftsman", "constructor", or "civilizer". Because of its significance, this term has been applied to other cultures, among which were the Olmec and the Teotihuacan, a policy which has created some confusion. Taking this into consideration, it is prudent to clarify the fact that the Toltec culture which is discussed in this section is that of Tula, the famous Tollán. Tula is located in the state of Hidalgo, approximately 80 kilometers north of México City.

It is known that the Toltecs were of Nahua-Chichimeca origin, and that they arrived in the Valley of México led by Mixcoatl, who was also called Totepeuh. They arrived at Acolman and Teotihuacan by the year 900 A. D., after the cultural collapse of the Teotihuacan. The Toltecs took control of the region and established their capital in Culhuacan, which is situated near the "Cerro de la Estrella" (the Hill of the Star). Culhuacan was a strategic location for their capital, as from there the Toltecs were able to conquer the Otomis, with whom they were later to live side by side.

During the wars of conquest, in the town of Cuahuanahuac (today's Cuernavaca), Mixcoatl met a woman called Chimalma, by whom he had a son. The baby was named Ce Acatl Topiltzin. Mixcoatl was assassinated before the birth of the child, and the mother died during childbirth; the grandparents took charge of raising and educating the child, teaching him the religion of his ancestors, which included the adoration of Quetzalcoatl (a practice which was inherited from previous cultures).

An usurper took possession of the dominions of Mixcoatl upon the death of the latter. These were subsequently seized by Topiltzin, who was aided by the sympathetic Toltec-Chichimecas.

Later, pressured by the Olmecs, the Toltecs moved their capital, first to Tulancingo, and finally to Tula.

The people of Tula rapidly reached a high cultural level and were outstanding in the arts and sciences. They used the knowledge of other cultures, especially that of the descendants of the Teotihuacan artists who had settled in nearby areas, to augment their own thinking. They constructed masonry houses, temples, and palaces, some of which were decorated with reliefs representing people, animals, and other motifs.[3]

One of the most notable temples of Tula is called "Tlahuiz-calpantecutli" (Morning Star or Star of Venus). On the upper platform of this temple rest the gigantic idols called "atlantes", "caryatides", or "telamones", which measure five meters in height. These idols were carved with precision and perfect craftsmanship, and at one time they served as columns to support the beams of the roof, which have since collapsed.

The Toltecs cast various objects in metal, which they finished with great care. They made writing paper, wove fabric of colored cotton, and made beautiful and complicated feather headdresses from the plumes of rare birds. They also attained a remarkable knowledge of astronomy.

Toltec ceramics are known by the names of "Coyotlatel-co" and "Mazapa". The former is believed to be inherited from the Teotihuacan culture; the latter is purely Toltec. Aztec ceramics were found in excavations of Tula, a discovery which revealed that the Aztecs temporarily occupied this site after it was abandoned by the Toltecs. It is also known that the Aztecs transported various carved rocks and other objects from Tula to their capital at Tenochtitlan.

The remarkable progress of Tula was due to the prudent and wise government of Topitlzin, under whose mandates the inhabitants witnessed great progress in all areas. The government also encouraged the people to practice the cult and the worship of Quetzalcoatl.

Topiltzin tried to restrict and eventually eliminate human sacrifices because this practice did not please a portion of his subjects, especially those inclined to favor the god Tezcatlipoca over Quetzalcoatl. The dissensions which resulted from his efforts to restrict human sacrifices provoked such a strong friction among the people that they forced Topiltzin to emigrate to the southeast. He passed through the states of Tlaxcala, Puebla, and Veracruz. From Coatzacoalcos, in the latter state, he headed toward the Yucatán Península.[4] This event occurred in the year 987 A. D., and coincided with the arrival of the famous Kukulkán (plumed

3) .— Jiménez Moreno Wigberto, Miranda José and Fernández María Teresa, **Historia de México**, Editorial E. C. L. A. L. S. A., Constitución 18, Librería de Porrúa, México City, 1967; pages 100 — 101.

4) .— Ibid, pages 103 — 104.

serpent) among the Maya; for this reason, it is thought that Kukulcán was actually Topiltzin. Since Topiltzin is believed to have been an enemy of human sacrifice, however, there is little possibility that he (Topiltzin) was the same Kukulcán, because, according to the reports of the Indians of the Yucatán Península, it was Kukulcán who introduced the practice of human sacrifice to the Maya.

Another version of Topiltzin's exile says that he threw himself into a fire, at which point he was converted into the planet Venus. It is said that before throwing himself into the fire he promised to return again from the East. Topiltzin was remembered by the natives for many years, and after a time, he came to be worshipped and adored as the god Quetzalcoatl. Upon the arrival of the Spaniards, the indigenous people believed that Cortez was actually Topiltzin (Quetzalcoatl), a fact which greatly influenced their reaction to the Spaniards. This was especially true of the Aztecs, who helped the Europeans in their conquest of México.

After Tula was abandoned by Topiltzin, there came a period which saw a rapid succession of chieftains and general cultural decay, along with a number of natural calamities, among these prolonged droughts. All of these factors served to drastically impair the living conditions of the Toltecs.

In 1156 A. D., Huemac, the last of the Toltec chieftains, was forced to move the Toltec capital to Chapultepec as a result of pressure exerted by his enemies within the tribe. These enemies, in turn, were forced to leave Tula by several invading Nahua tribes. The displaced Toltec peoples headed in different directions. One group returned to their old capital, Culhuacan. Others went to Cholula, where the historical Olmecs governed. This Olmec culture was not related to the legendary Olmec culture of La Venta and Tres Zapotes, but were rather of the Nahuatlized Popoloc-Mixtec origin. The Toltecs were accepted as refugees and were submitted to difficult living conditions which they endured with patience and stoicism, only to later rebel and expel the Olmecs from Cholula. Because of this, the inhabitants of Cholula of that time are called "Cholultecs". (5)

5).— Ibid, page 104 — 106.

c) . The Seven Nahuatl Tribes

The Yucatecan historian Profr. Don Antonio Canto López relates in his book entitled **Apuntaciones Sobre Mesoamérica (Anotations on Meso-America),** which is based on information gathered from the Boturini Codex, the Ramirez Codex, (also known as **The History of the Mexicas by Their Paintings),** the Florentine Codex, the works of Don Fernando de Alba Ixtlixochitl, the **Mexican Chronicles,** by Fernando de Alvarado Tezozomoc, **Annals of the Federal District, of Chimalpahin,** and **History of the Affairs of New Spain,** by Fray Bernardino de Sahagun, among other sources, that the last Nahua tribes that invaded the Valley of Mexico were made up of the Xochimilcas, Chalcas, Tepanecs, Acolhuas, Tlahuics, Tlaxcaltecs, and Aztecs or Mexicas. Canto also states that the place of origin of these tribes was Chicomoztoc, the "place of the Seven Caves". For some, Chicomoztoc is considered to be an actual site. However, for others, it is a mythological and allegorical place, supposedly situated in the northwestern part of Mexico in Aztlan ("the land of herons and of whiteness"), a place that has never been actually located. There are those who think Chicomoztoc was located in New Mexico in the Valley of Las Casas Grandes (Valley of the Big Houses), near Chihuahua; others believe it is found on an island in the lake of Chapala, or in the lagoon of San Pedro Mexticacan in the state of Jalisco, while still others identify Chicomoztoc as Culhuacan, today Culiacán. Canto indicateds that some contemporary specialists locate Chicomoztoc in the plains region of Ixtlahuaca in the state of Mexico.

The pilgrimage of the Nahua tribes to the south probably commenced at the beginning of the Tenth Century A. D. The Aztecs, through the counsel of their god Huitzilopochtli, became separated from their brothers, delaying their arrival to the Valley of Mexico. [6]

Canto also notes that the accounts of this pilgrimage are a mixture of myths, legends, and historical facts which have to be carefully studied in order to distinguish the absurd and improbable from the accurate.

Other authors consider Aztlan and Chicomoztoc to be situated in two different places. For example, Professors Wigberto

6) .— Canto López Antonio. Op. Cit.; pages 43 — 45.

Jiménez Moreno and María Teresa Fernández state that Aztlan is situated on the lake of Mexcaltitlan on the coast of the state of Nayarit, and that the Nahua left there around 1111 A. D. In another part of this same work (**Historia de México**, or **The History of Mexico**) they state that Chicomoztoc, is found between Tula and Jilotepec (perhaps this was another place with the same name). [7]

Since the wanderings of these tribes lasted many years and included constant migration from place to place, it is logically possible to conclude that Aztlan and Chicomoztoc were very distant from the Valley of Mexico.

Professor Canto López concedes that the seven Nahuatl tribes arrived at the Valley of Mexico, and that each one occupied a place of its own preference and convenience. The Chalcas settled on the shores of a small lake which they called "Chalco". The Xochimilcas settled on the shores of another lake which still retains the name of these first settlers. The Tepanecs established themselves in Azcapotzalco, and the Acolhuas settled on the shores of Texcoco Lake. The Tlaxcaltec tribes, having arrived at a later date, had to settle outside of the Valley of Mexico, first in, Tlaxcala and then later in Cuahunahuac (today, Cuernavaca). The Aztecs, having been separated from the group, arrived last, when all of the territory had been already occupied.

Some historians fail to mention all of these Nahuatl tribes. They only cite the Acolhua, Tepanec, and Otomi immigrations. Others also cite the barbaric tribes who originated in the south of Texas and the Bolsón de Mapimí, and migrated to the territory which is now called Meso-America. One of these groups, the Pames, infiltrated the Chichimec army which was captained by the famous Xolotl, and which arrived in the Valley of Mexico in the 13th Century. This tribe, as well as others, scattered inside and outside of the Valley of Mexico. The descendants of the Toltecs of Tula also formed different domains in and around the Valley of Mexico. They still led a life full of conflict, fighting among themselves a considerable part of the time.

The reader will recall that in the introduction of this work I spoke of the difficulty involved in reconstructing the history of the Meso-American people from the available information. The paintings and other informational sources which remain only give

7).— Jiménez M., Miranda, and Fernández, Op. Cit.; page 100 — 115.

a general idea of some important historical passages, but they alone cannot give an accurate historical account. At the base of the problem is our lack of specific knowledge. Some of the written histories that are based on these fragments of information can be very near the truth, or they can be filled with inaccurate hypothesis.

d). Ethnic Coincidences Between the Nahua Culture and that of the Indigenous People of Mesa Verde

In October of 1976, I had the opportunity to visit the fascinating archaeological site at Mesa Verde. It is located just a few kilometers from the small, picturesque town of Cortez, Colorado (United States). This area has been converted into a beautiful national park by the United States government.

My family and I decided to make this trip with the encouragement of our good friends Mr. and Mrs. Wayne Gangwich, who had repeatedly invited us to visit them. We had only a faint idea of the history of this area, and the booklets and pamphlets about the ancient culture at Mesa Verde which the Gangwiches sent us were most intriguing.

It was a pleasant surprise when the owners and the manager (Mrs. Dorothy Wayt) of Cortez Travel Service informed us that they had made special arrangements to have Gilbert Wenger, archaeologist and park chief at Mesa Verde, act as our guide. I had met Mrs. Wayt previously when she and a group of her clients were in the Yucatán and had engaged me as their guide to the Maya ruins.

Mr. Wenger, a sincerely kind man, put aside his multitude of daily responsibilities and spent most of an entire day explaining, in great detail, the history of Mesa Verde's culture. Wenger guided us through the large area of cliff dwellings, answering our many questions in an enthusiastic and informed manner as we went along.

We were continually surprised and amazed by the hundreds of groups of masonry buildings made from stones, cut in small blocks and mortared into place. Some of these constructions were as much as four stories high. The floors of these buildings were originally made of wood. However, due to exposure to the elements and time, very little of them still exist. The buildings, for the most part, are constructed within the hollows and caves on the face of an enormous canyon which is several kilometers long.

38

The builders took advantage of the caves' ceilings, using them to serve as the roofs of their houses. Some of these dwellings are square, others rectangular, while still others are round. One peculiarity found in these dwellings is that while some were built on the floor of the canyon, others were constructed in lofty, multilevel caves which can only be reached by long, wooden ladders.   Photos numbers 2, 3, 4 and 5.

Photo No. 2. The Bolcony House constructed in 1200-1278 A. D. Anasazi Culture Mesa Verde National Park, Colorado, U. S. A. Photo courtesy of the archaeologist Gilbert R. Wenger, Chief of the park.

It is almost inconceivable that the indigenous people of this area were able to accomplish an architectural work of this type on the face of a cliff without adequate metal tools; to date, no metal tools have been found anywhere at Mesa Verde.
Minor constructions are located on the upper level, that is, on the Mesa which is 700 meters above the floor of the Mancos Valley. Only the foundations of these dwellings still exist because, in part, vandalism has destroyed them. Other ruins were destroyed by modern agriculturalists who plowed the earthen mounds which contained some of the ruins.

Photo No. 3. The Cliff Palace, constructed in 1175-1275 A. D. Anasazi Cultu-re Mesa Verde National Park, Colorado, U. S. A. Photo courtesy of the archaeologist Gilbert R. Wenger, Chief of the park.

Photo No. 4. The Long House, 1175-1280 A. D. Anasazi Culture, Mesa Verde National Park, Colorado U. S. A. Photo courtesy of the archaeologist Gilbert R. Wenger, Chief of the park.

Photo No. 5. Anasazi Culture, Mesa Verde National Park, Colorado Spruce Tree House Ruin, again, dates A. D. 1175 to 1275 (3rd largest ruin in park) Housed about 160 persons in it's 110 rooms and 8 kivas Classic Pueblo Period. Courtesy of Gilbert R. Wenger.

We were fortunate enough to see this park in the autumn, when the leaves of vegetation were turning colors, giving the impression that the whole region was an enormous flower garden, and the ground an endless carpet embroidered with colors.

According to archaeologists, Mesa Verde was occupied by Indian farmers at the beginning of the Christian Era, sometime between the years 01 and 450 A. D. These people are given the name of "Basket Makers" because of the high quality of the woven baskets that they made.

The inhabitants of the second period (450 to 750 A. D.) are called "Modified Basket Makers". During this period, the art of making pottery arose, houses with roofs were built, and the use of the bow and arrow began.

By the year 600 A. D., most of the constructions were built in the open air, on top of the plateau.

In approximately 750 A. D., the people of Mesa Verde began to show a tendency to live in compact living groups. They utilized diverse building materials, including adobe, along with

41

wooden beams and stone blocks, which they used until they started using masonry. The caves were partitioned into planned sections to better fit the needs of the people.

Circular chambers, called "kivas", which were built inside of natural caves, are commonly found in these housing centers. The kivas were apparently ceremonial chambers, many of which are connected by underground tunnels.

This period ended around the year 1100 A. D. Kivas were in general use until the end of the 13th Century. (8)

The 12 th and 13 th Centuries are known as the "Great Classical Pueblo Period" at Mesa Verde. During this period, hundreds of units called "pueblos" were built on the plateau and later, in the caves. The most important of these pueblos is called the "Cliff Palace" which has 220 chambers and 23 kivas; enough space for 250 people. (9)

The year 1276 A. D. marks the beginning of a 24-year drought. This seems to be one of the main reasons why the site was abandoned. The inhabitants of Mesa Verde emigrated to the south of New Mexico into the territory of the Hopi Indians in Arizona, and later to the Rio Grande area, never to return.

The historians Wigberto Jiménez Moreno and María Teresa Fernández state the following with respect to the indigenous tribes of North America: "...As to the Nahua, this group belongs to the Nahuatlana family of Yuto-Aztec that, together with the Tañc-Caigua, make up the group Taño-Aztec. The Yuto-Aztec family had a very large geographical distribution. Parts of this family who had a similar language, populated eleven North American states (Nevada, Utah, Colorado, Wyoming, Texas, New Mexico, Arizona, California, Oregon, Idaho, and Montana), and a large portion of western Mexico..." (10)

Mesa Verde is situated in the southwestern corner of the state of Colorado, where the borders of Utah, Arizona, Colorado, and New Mexico join.

Most historians agree that the Nahua race was related to the indigenous people of the southwestern United States, who later entered Mexico through the states of Sonora, Chihuahua, and Sinaloa, and dispersed throughout Mexico. Although I do not know

8) .— Watson Donald, **Indian of Mesa Verde,** Mesa Verde Museum Ass'n., Mesa Verde National Park, Colorado, 1961; page 156.

9) .— Wenger Gilbert, Chief Archaeologist at Mesa Verde Nat'l. Park, verbal information.

10) .— Jiménez M., Miranda, and Fernández, Op. Cit.; page 86.

enough about the ethnic similarities between the Nahuatl and the Mesa Verde tribes to know if they were the same people, there are enough coincidences to make me believe that Mesa Verde may have been the legendary Chicomoztoc, the place from which the Aztec came.

It is true that at Mesa Verde there are numerous caves with interior buildings, but perhaps only seven of them were considered to be most importants;one will recall that "Chicomoztoc" means "the seven caves" in the Nahuatl language.

There is also the possibility that the Nahuatls did not belong to the ethnic group of Mesa Verde; they may have only lived with them for a period of time before continuing their pilgrimage into Mexico. If so, perhaps they set off in a large group prior to 1276, when the area was totally abandoned, since it has been calculated that they left Chicomoztoc sometime in the 10th or 11 th Centuries, finally arriving in the Mexican highland, as will be seen in the following section of this chapter.

It should also be mentioned that near Mesa Verde there is a valley called "Montezuma" (a name which is similar to the one used by one of the Aztec emperors), and located a few kilometers from this valley are some ruins called "Aztecs".

e). **The Aztecs**

Upon leaving Aztlan, the Aztecs began a long pilgrimage, settling in many places along the way which, due to a variety of circumstances, they later abandoned. They finally arrived in the Valley of Mexico and settled in Coatlicamac, where they fought with scattered groups of Toltecs for the land.

The Aztecs were always guided by Huitzilopochtli, their god and counselor, whose will was transmitted to their priests, who in turn interpreted his will for their subjects.

The Aztecs celebrated the end of their calendaric cycle of 52 years with an important ceremony that involved the igniting of a new fire for the advent of the next cycle. It was during this early time that they changed their name to "Mexicas".

In Coatepec, near Tula, they built an artificial lake for the breeding of aquatic animals in order to improve their food supply. It is well know that the Aztecs preferred to live in areas where there were lakes.

They lived happily at Coatlicamac for some time, but apparently some sort of natural disaster destroyed the site, and they were forced to abandon it. One group went to Tula, and the rest forded lake Texcoco, arriving at Chapultepec in 1267 A. D. In this region, they engaged in bloody struggles with their neighbors, being forced, as a result, to change their residence on several occasions. After many moves, guided by their leader Tenoch, they finally arrived at a small island in the center of Mextliapan lagoon ("Mextliapan" means "the Lake of the Moon"). It was here that they saw an eagle devouring a serpent on top of a nopal cactus. According to Aztec mythology, this was a sign for them to establish their city there. [11]

Some historians mention the year 1325 A. D. as the date of the founding of this city; however, recent investigations calculate its founding to the year 1345 A. D.

The first of the Aztecs' constructions were rudimentary, using adobe and palm for their temples and living quarters. Because they were restricted to the land of this island, they engineered their famous floating gardens (chinampas) for their horticultural needs. These gardens consisted of earth-filled rafts or floats.

The Aztec people were paradoxically both deeply religious and fervently warlike. They audaciously used intrigue to lure their neighbors into combat, provoking wars in which they acted as mercenaries, and extracted profits so that in each conflict they always came out ahead, gaining some piece of land or some other political advantage. Seeing that they were firmly established in their territory, the Aztec rulers attempted to extend their dominion, never ceasing to wage wars of conquest. To succeed in these conquests, they made use of the help of roving traders who served as spies. These spies were taught well to observe and report the organization, customs, economy, and military power of each neighboring town so that later, when the Aztecs thought it was convenient, they could attack and conquer them.

Nearly all the males were educated from childhood in the art of war, and as adult warriors they were rewarded in accordance with the number of prisoners they captured. They also believed that death in combat meant that their spirit would go to dwell in "the paradise of Tlaloc".

11).— Martínez Marín Carlos, **Los Aztecas,** I. N. A. H. de Méx., México City, 1965; pages 5 to 9.

The Aztec weaponry consisted of the bow and arrow, the spear, the "macana" (a wooden club with sharply filed rocks imbedded into it), and the spear thrower. For their own protection they carried shields, and wore quilted cotton breastplates and wooden helmets.

One of their emperors, called Tizoc, was considered to be moderate in the number of his wars of invasion, and it is said that for this reason alone he was poisoned. He had been in power for only five years.

Another emperor by the name of Ahuizotl was a man of totally different qualities. He tried to extend his dominions in all directions, reaching the states of Veracruz, part of Guerrero and Oaxaca, and the coast of Chiapas. He even declared war on the Huastecs.

The Aztecs allowed relative independence for the dominated regions, but the conquered people remained economic subjects, being forced to pay heavy tribute to the Aztecs.

In 1487, while governed by the same Ahuizotl —one of the most bloodthirsty Aztecan emperors —a dedication of the Main Temple of Tenochtitlan was arranged. It was to be an event in which 20,000 people were sacrificed, the majority of whom were prisoners captured during the wars. The chiefs of enemies and friends alike were invited to witness the horrendous ceremony, the idea being to impress them with the power of this Aztec chieftan. [12]

The human sacrifices practiced by the Aztecs involved opening the chest of the victim in order to tear out the heart. The heart was then offered to their gods. This was a common practice among the Aztecs. In order to obtain victims for the sacrifices when they ran out of real war prisoners, the Aztecs organized "guerras floridas" (simulated battles) with the friendly neighbors, and used these mock prisoners as sacrificial victims. They practiced human sacrifice because they thought it was necessary to feed the sun and their gods with human blood.

Ahuitzol died in an accident while trying to escape a deluge. He was succeeded in power by Moctezuma Xocoyotzin who, at the outset, appeared to be a modest and humble ruler. Later, however, there was a noticeable change in his character, as he did a complete about-face, becoming haughty, arrogant, and tyrannical.

12).— Jiménez M., Miranda, and Fernández, Op. Cit.; page 128.

Some consider him to have been like an Eastern satrap. His vanity reached such proportions that he changed his elaborate clothing four times a day, never wearing the same thing twice. After each change he made a gift of the discarded costumes to his most dedicated collaborators. He did the same with his cups, plates, vases, and other eating utensils, which where made of the finest ceramics and precious metals, such as gold.

During his reign, Moctezuma tried to extend his domain, suffering consecutive humiliating defeats by the Tlaxcaltecs. Shortly after his last defeat, Moctezuma heard of the arrival of the Spaniards. Even though extremely vain and proud, he was intimidated by the presence of the foreigners. He became even more so when he learned that Cortez had managed to defeat his enemies the Tlaxcaltecs, something he was never able to accomplish. Moctezuma confused Cortez with the god Quetzalcoatl, and invited him to his palace in order to honor him. Fearing an ambush, however, Moctezuma surrounded himself in the palace, guarded like a hostage, and sent out orders to his people to submit to the Spaniards. The Mexicas, tired of the presence and the demands of the foreigners, and of the cowardice of their ruler, rebelled, attacking the palace and wounding Moctezuma in the fray. The Spaniards no longer considered Moctezuma to be useful, and killed him.

After the murder of Moctezuma, Cortez and his soldiers succeeded in fleeing the city, protected by the shadow of night. But because of the great difficulty they encountered, several of their men were lost.

Upon the death of Moctezuma, Cuitlahuac was made the new emperor. He tried to obtain help from his neighbors but unfortunately for the Aztecs, he died in 1520 from small-pox, brought from Cuba by a Negro. He was succeeded by Cuauhtemoc ("Cuauhtemoc" means "the descending eagle"), who organized his army and prepared for the defense of Tenochtitlan.

For his part, Cortez, with the alliance of the Tlaxcaltecs and Totonacs (who hated the ruling Aztecs), gained control of the areas surrounding the city, and prepared for the siege of Tenochtitlan. On August 13, 1521, after many bloody battles, the greatest empire of America finally succumbed. At this time it was renamed by the Spaniards as "La Nueva España" (The News Spain).[13]

13).— Ibid, pages 222 — 223.

46

Once established in Tenochtitlan, the Spaniards destroyed all of the Aztecs' temples and palaces, and with the stones of these buildings they built the present-day city of Mexico. By doing this, the Spaniards attempted and accomplished the eradication of the native religion ad customs.

Very little escaped the widespread nature of this destruction, since all that remains are some of the bases (some of which are carved), on one side of the Metropolitan Cathedral and in the Plaza of the Three Cultures.

Recent excavations in the center of Mexico City by those working on the construction of the subway system, have uncovered a great number of objects of the Aztec culture, including stones carved with interesting reliefs, and the bases of some Aztec buildings.

The organized life of the Aztecs was relatively short. The period from their foundation in 1345 until their conquest covers a time span of only 176 years. During this time they accomplished great material and cultural progress, and witnessed a remarkable expansion of their territory.

At first the Aztec government was directed by the priests, since all of their activities revolved around their religion. Later, power was transferred to non-religious leaders, and the Aztecs founded a kingdom.

To mitigate the pressures exerted by their enemies, the Aztecs asked the lord of Culhuacan that his grandson, Acamapichtli, govern them.

There were a total of eleven Aztec emperors (including Cuitlahuac whose rule was ephemeral) who governed in the following order: Acamapichtli, Huitzilihuitl, Chimalpopoca, Izcoatl, Moctezuma Iluicamina, Axayacatl, Tizoc, Ahuizotl, Moctezuma Xocoyotzin, Cuitlahuac, and Cuauhtemoc.

During the beginning of the Mexica reign, the Aztecs were reduced to a state of submission by the Lord Azcapotzalco. It was the fourth king, Izcoatl, who cleverly gained for them their independence with the help of Netzahualcoyotl, the dethroned king of Texcoco.

The Aztecs were polytheists, as was the case with almost all of the Meso-American cultures, hence they worshiped different gods, the most important being Huitzilopochtli the god of war. Quetzalcoatl, plumed serpent of the quetzal bird, represented several concepts; the god of Wind, the god of the planet Venus, and the god of Wisdom. Tezcatlipoca was the god of the Night Sky. Tonatuih represented the Sun. Huehueteotl was the god of Fire and of the four cardinal points. Tlaloc was the god of Water and the god of Vegetation (the Rain God). Xipe Totec was the god of Planting Time and of the Fields. Tloquenahuaque was the lord that is always near. These are but a few in a complex pantheon. Some of these dieties were inherited from other, older cultures such as the Teotihuacan culture.

The Aztec writing system was at first hieroglyphic, to which they lated added ideograms, and finally, phoneticisms.

Their numerology was a base-20 system which utilized symbols different from other cultures. The exception to this was the dot which they used to represent one. The Maya, Olmec, and Zapotec numerologies did the same.

The Aztecs attained advanced astronomical knowledge. They used two calendars: one a ritual calendar that consisted of thirteen months of twenty days each (a total of 260 days) which they called "Tonalamatl"; the other was the civil calendar consisting of eighteen months of twenty days, and one more month of five days, making a total of 365 days. This calendar was called "Tonalpohualli". Both of these calendars were similar to the Mayan calendar as will be seen in later chapters. The Aztec century or "Xiumolpilli", was the result of the combination of the Tonalamatl and the Tonalpohualli, and it contained fifty-two civil years, "Xiumolpilli".

Other historical sources state that the "Tonalpohualli" was the Aztec's ritual calendar, and that it has been confused with the "Tonalamatl" which means "paper of the days", and which was the book in which the Aztecs recorded the "Tonalpohualli" and the period of 365 days called the "Xiumolpilli".

END OF PART ONE

PART TWO

CHAPTER ONE
SOURCES OF INFORMATION

a) . **Bishop Diego de Landa.**
b) . **Chronicles of Chilam Balam,** and **Relación de Cabildos y Enco-
menderos (Relations of Town Councils and Landowners).**
c) . **Codices.**
d) . **Popol Vuh; Annals of the Cakchiqueles.**
e) . **Explorers, Authors, and Institutions.**

a) . **Bishop Diego de Landa.**

Our knowledge pertaining to the ancient Maya has come
from many different sources of information. One of the most
valuable of these was bequeathed to us by Diego de Landa, the
second Bishop of Yucatán, in the form of his famous **Relación
de las Cosas de Yucatán (Report of the Things of Yucatán)**.
Bishop Landa was a great observer, and in the above mentioned
work he describes the customs of the Maya that he encountered
upon his arrival in the Yucatán Peninsula.

Landa explains in detail how the men, women, and children
were dressed, how they were educated, what and how many times
a day they ate, how they prepared their food, and under what
social organization they lived (i.e. their form of government,
system of commerce, laws of the region, form of punishment for
offenders, religious and secular ceremonies, etc.)

As a result of careful investigations among the learned
Mayan chieftains of the Decadent Period, he recorded the most
outstanding historical passages of their ancestors, as well as
their sciences, arts, etc. He described the most important
Yucatecan forest animals, song birds, reptiles, mammals, and
flora; he also described the most important characteristics of the
marine fauna.

One of the most valuable descriptions that Landa left us
was that of the function of the calendar which was in use during

the Decadent Period, and of another system of dates, called the Short Count, which will be described in greater detail in the chapters which follow. He carefully copied the twenty hieroglyphs corresponding to the Mayan months, noting the phonetic pronunciation and significance of each. He also detailed the religious ceremonies which the Mayas practiced on certain days of the month.

To compare the Julian and Mayan calendars, he copied a complete Mayan calendaric year, later inserting the names of the months of the European calendar in order to demonstrate the relationship which existed between the two systems. Apart from the calendar hieroglyphs, Landa copied other glyphs in an attempt to perceive a Mayan alphabet which, in reality, had never existed

In Landa's report, it is mentioned that one of his best collaborators in the compiling of his information had been Juan Cocom. Landa mentions that Cocom was a man of great reputation, and was very intelligent, sagacious, and wise. Cocom told the Bishop a great deal of the history of his Mayan ancestors, and showed Landa a book belonging to his grandfather, who was the son of the Cocom who was killed in Mayapán, as will be discussed in later chapters. On this book was painted a deer; Grandfather Cocom told his grandson that the Mayan religious worship would end when the "big deer" arrived in the land of the Maya; the cows brought by the conquering Spaniards were incorrectly interpreted to be these "big deer".

Thanks to Bishop Landa, investigators have been able to interpret the content or significance of many of the surviving glyphs. Dr. Sylvanus G. Morley, renowned North American archaelogist, asserts, and with just cause, that Landa's report is the equivalent of the Egyptian Rosetta Stone.

b. The **Chronicles of Chilam Balam,** and **Relations of Town Councils and Landowners** .

After the conquest, because the Spaniards were eager to rapidly convert the Maya to Christianity, they taught the Maya to read and write the Spanish language. In this way each literate Maya automatically became a transmitter of the Catholic religion. These first Mayan students, with the pretext of practicing their writing at home, smuggled sheets of paper, which were in very short supply, into the waiting hands of their chiefs and priests, some of whom could boast of understanding the very complicated hieroglyphics of their ancestors.

The Maya realized that by combining five vowels with some consonants, they could write what they wanted phonetically; the system seemed very easy to them. It was in this manner that they wrote part of their history, prophecies, chronology, religion, medicine, astronomy, divinations, and even current events, all in the Mayan language, using the sounds of the Spanish letters.

There were sixteen of these **Chronicles,** eight of which have been identified and analyzed; the whereabouts of the other eight Chronicles is unknown. Each one was named after the place in which it was found. The most important Chronicles are those of Maní, Tizimin, and Chumayel, which were combined and designated by the name "Matichu".[1]Although some parts of these writings contradict archaeological information, they have been of great value in substantiating important historical details which would have otherwise remained unknown.

Another source of information is the **Relations of Town Councils and Landowners,** which was also written after the conquest.

When the king of Spain learned of the existence of the beautiful, artistically-worked stucco and masonry buildings which lay partially in ruin in different areas in the Yucatán Peninsula, he became curious, and wanted to know the history of these constructions. He offered sizeable rewards to his authorized representatives in the Yucatán, for information of this nature; the collected reports of these representatives comprise the **Relaciones.** Some of these were of great value in reconstructing the history of the Mayan area.

c). **Codices.**

Another important source of information can be found in the three surviving codices. These are written with hieroglyphics and drawings (some in color), and are artistically elaborated.

For writing, the Maya invented a paper which was very similar to our own, using the bark of a tree called "copo", or the Yucatán elm. After the white part of the bark was finely ground, they mixed it with gums from the cedar tree, and from another

1).— **El Libro de los Libros de Chilam Balam,** Barrera Vásquez Alfredo, and Rendón Silvia, Fondo de Cultura Económica, México City, 1948; page 12.

51

tree of this region called "pich" in Maya. The mixture thus obtained was probably pressed between two wooden rollers to produce long strips of paper, which were finally given a fine coating of lime. This paper was used to record their sciences, projects histories, and other works. They folded it in the form of a folding screen or accordian so that it was easier to handle.

Bishop Landa says that the paper was made from the roots of trees.

The longest of the codices is the Tro-Cortesiano or Madrid Codex. It measures 7.15 meters long, is 24 centimeters high, and has a page width of 13 centimeters. It has 56 leaves or folds, or 112 pages. It is divided into two parts: one was found in Extremadura, Spain, and the other in Madrid, between the years 1860 and 1870. According to specialists, it is a divination textbook which helped the priests foretell the future (predict).

In one section of this Codex is a table which shows the signs of the zodiac. Detailed among these symbols are the scorpion, the tortoise, and the rattlesnake; the other signs are represented by hieroglyphics.

The next longest codex is the Dresden Codex which was found in Vienna, Austria, in 1739. It was taken to Germany by the director of the Royal Library of Dresden. It is 3.5 meters long, 20 centimeters high, and has a page width of 9 centimeters. The Codex has 38 sheets or folds, or 76 pages. This Codex is concerned with astronomical information; found among its pages is a table which shows 59 solar eclipses over a period of 33 years. Another chart plots the rotation of Venus through its orbit with such exactness that experts say the Mayan were off by only 14 seconds.

The shortest codex is only a fragment, and is called the Perez Codex. It measures 1.45 meters in length, 24 centimeters in height, and has a page width of 13 centimeters. It has 11 leaves or folds, or 22 pages. The contents of this Codex are basically concerned with ritual. [2]

In addition to these, there is talk of a new codex, located in New York; up to this time its authenticity as a genuine Maya book remains debatable.

Dr. Morley is of the opinion that these codices could be part of a Mayan encyclopedia, the remaining volumes of which have been lost.

2).— Morley Sylvanus G., **La Civilización Maya,** Fondo de Cultura Económica, México City, 1975; pages 265 — 267.

d). **Popol Vuh; Annals of the Cakchiqueles.**

Other important documents which were found after the conquest are the **Popol Vuh** and the **Annals of the Cakchiqueles,** both of which were written in the Mayan Language, using the phonetics of the Spanish system of writing.

The **Popol Vuh** represents the most notable writing of the Guatemala Mayas, and is written in the Quiché dialect. It deals with religion, cosmology, mythology, migrations, and the history of the Quichés. The beauty, lofty style, and elegance of the Quiché language have indeed made the **Popol Vuh** a work of great literary value.

For its part, the **Annals of the Cakchiqueles** deals with the history of the Cakchiqueles, describing events that occurred during and after the conquest.

e). **Explorers, Authors, and Institutions.**

In 1839, John L. Stephens, traveler, diplomat, and amateur archaeologist, visited the Mayan zone with his English friend, Frederick Catherwood, a famous artist and architect. After visiting more than forty of the larger Mayan ruins, usually on muleback, Stephens wrote his famous works, entitled **Incidents of Travel in Central America, Chiapas, and Yucatán,** which was published in 1841, and **Incidents of Travel in Yucatán,** which was published in 1843. Both works were printed in two volumes, and contain information of great archaeological value, both in Stephen's descriptions and Catherwood's masterful drawings.

Another distinguished pioneer of the exploration of the Mayan culture was the Englishman Alfred Maudslay. The results of his extensive explorations between 1881 and 1894 are five superbly edited volumes, with photographs of buildings, stelae, drawings of hieroglyphic inscriptions, and many maps, which have served as a basis for extensive investigations.

Another notable investigator, sent by Harvard University, was Teoberto Maler. Maler was a native of Germany who later became a naturalized Austrian. He came to Yucatán where he was introduced to the adventure of exploring; he visited many unknown places in Yucatán, Campeche, and Quintana Roo. He was accompanied by natives who abandoned him in times of difficulty. Maler was an honorable man, devoted to the Mayan culture; at the time, he defended the monuments against vandalism. Without his efforts, important information would have been lost.

Ernst Forstemann, also a German, produced distinguished work in the investigation of the hieroglyphics of the Codices, and we owe much of our understanding in this domain to him.

Alfred Tozzer, proffesor of achaeology at Harvard University, made the first ethnological study of Central America, living for some time among the Lacandon Indians. He taught some of his more advanced students the technique of archaeological investigation.

The Carnegie Institute of Washington made excavations in Chichén Itzá from 1924 to 1939, extracting highly valuable data which contributed to our understanding of the Mayan culture. Their work was not limited solely to excavations of ruins, as they undertook studies in many other important fields such as ethnology, anthropology, history, medicine, and epidemology.

The Hacienda Chichén Itzá, now converted into a picturesque hotel, was used as a center for these studies. A small medical clinic was established in this hacienda in the jungle that not only served to protect the health of the workers at the excavation site, but also was used to ease the lot of the country folk in the region who lacked medical services at the time.

In 1932, I took over as director of the Federal School in the village Chan Kom, which is located twelve kilometers from Chichén Itzá. I was substituting for my good friend Profr. Alfonso Villa Rojas, now a Doctor of Anthropology, who had done brilliant cultural and material works in Chan Kom, and who had joined the Carnegie Institute in their investigations. I was lucky enough to witness part of these investigations, and helped to convince the Chan Kom parents to allow their children to conduct periodic graphic studies in order to know their physical development. At this same time, Carnegie was restoring the complex called "El Mercado" (The Market) at Chichén Itzá.

Other centers of investigation were the University Museum of the University of Pennsylvania, the Middle American Research Institute of Tulane University, the National Institute of Anthropology and History of Mexico, the British Museum, and the Chicago Museum of Natural History.

It would be unjust not to mention another of the greats of Mayan archaeology. The learned archaeologist J. Eric S. Thompson dedicated almost all of his life to extensive studies and investigations. He wrote many books, outstanding among them **The Rise and Fall of the Maya Civilization.** Unfortunately for all of archaeology, Thompson died recently, leaving a great void that will be difficult to fill.

As one can see, there are many people and institutions that have been dedicated to the study of this culture. Thanks to their perseverance and patience, we have been able to unravel many mysteries of the ancient Mayan culture.

Currently the Mexican government is doing restoration work in Coba, and in Konhunlich, Quintana Roo. The distinguished Yucatecan archaeologist Víctor Segovia Pinto, is in charge of the work in Konhunlich, and no doubt the results of his explorations will produce important new discoveries.

CHAPTER TWO

ARTISTIC/RELIGIOUS SIMILARITIES BETWEEN THE MAYA AND ASIAN AND MIDDLE EASTERN CITIES

I am including here part of an article originally published on June 11, 1976, in a daily Yucatecan newspaper,   written by the anthropologist Carlos Villanueva C., entitled "The Mayas New Historical Vision". Villanueva cites a legend which states, in part" ...and then the Naiki tribe constructed an enormous ship and put to sea, passing by Nuku Hiba and continuing their trip to the East, finally arriving at Tefiti, a great country, rich in...'

"This legend comes from the Naiki tribe of the island of Hiba Oa, one of the Marquesas Islands in Polynesia... myths and legends speak of a great country to the east of the Pacific... without a doubt, it (this legend) is in reference to America."

In another part, this article states, "...From the early dates of the first cultures of Ecuador, or some 3,000 years before Christ in the Period of the Concheros, in Valdivia, an area near the coast, a new element appeared in South American cultures, with new forms of ceramic identical to that of the Jomon culture of Japan... the Jomon were composed of bold sailors, and their Asiatic influence covered a huge area that extended from Polynesia to Australia.

"Great navigators reached as far as America, utilizing the Kuro-Shivo current to cross the Pacific, producing a cultural-commercial transplant. This link was not lost until the time of the great cultural advances of South and Central America."

The author continues, saying that Asiatic influences are common in Meso-America. As an example, Villanueva cites the Corbelled Mayan arch, which was used by the Maya as early as 300 A. D., and which can be seen in most Mayan temples. This arch is also found extensively in India, Pakistan, and Southeast Asia. The stelae of Copán and Quiriguá, as well as other religious-artistic manifestations in the Maya zone of Guatemala, are very similar to those of Indo-China and Indonesia. There are also similarities between the temples of Tikal ín Guatemala and the pyramid of Baksei Chan Grong in Angkor, Cambodia.

"In India, within the temples of Ajanta, are found representations similar to those of the Temple of the Cross at Palenque, in the Mexican state of Chiapas. This same foliated cross has surprising similarity to the religious symbols carved in Java, and in Angkor in Southeast Asia.

"Many artistic-religious representations, like the doorways of the Mayan temples which take the form of the faces of mythological animals, appear related to those found in Java. The carvings of Atlantes of the Mayan culture also appear in India, in the province of Sanchi, around the year 100 B. C.

"In Uxmal, Copán, and Chichén Itzá are found bas-reliefs of mythological serpents with human figures emerging from them. Lotuses and flowers, also from which human faces emerge, are similar to the Hindi figures called 'Makaras', found principally in Amaravati, and apparently carved in the Second Century of our era.

"The murals of Bonampak and Piedras Negras are surprisingly similar to the Hindi and to Eighth and Ninth Century murals found in Java. The serpent, like the phallic cult, is found in all areas of India, being thought of as the synthesis of the universe.

"The Mahabarata and the Ramayana, sacred books of India, speak of the expulsion of a tribe of men called 'Mayas', and of a Hindu divinity who bore the name of 'Maya'.

"One passage speaks of a tribe called 'Nagas', which inhabited India, and which was already in decline at the time of the writing of these books. Ninety percent of their language resembles the Maya of this (Yucatán) region.

"It is undeniable that the permanent trace of an Asiatic contact in American lands persisted across time; it mixed and continued on to form part of the same cultures of the (American) Continent.

"Independent of their hereditary culture and of the observations which were produced in their autonomous development, the Maya society yielded in passing to an influence from beyond the sea..."

Not long ago, in a conversation I had with Mr. Villanueva regarding the extraordinary similarities between the cultures of the Americas and of Asia, the anthropologist mentioned a very unusual incident which occurred in the Mexican state of Chiapas. Villanueva was commissioned in 1973 to do an anthropological study in the above mentioned state, along with a team of investigators, among whom was Yutaka Yonome, a man of Japanese descent, who at that time was an accomplished student at the School of Anthropology and History in Mexico City.

Having finished their work in Chiapas, the group headed toward the Guatemalan border, making use of public buses in their travel. It was aboard one of these above mentioned buses, while passing by the Chiapan city of Comitán, which is located on the shores of the Montebello Lakes in the Tojolabal district, when the strange incident occurred. A group of local people, who were also riding the bus, began to speak among themselves in the Tojolabal dialect of the Mayan language, and their conversation seemingly fascinated Yutaka, who, surprised with the conversation, took out his notebook and began to write in Japanese. When questioned by Villanueva, the Japanese scholar stated that he was understanding parts of the conversation, and that he had written some of the words used by the Tojolabal in Japanese.

Unfortunately, as their studies were concerned with other matters, the party was unable to pursue any of the linguistic aspects of Mayan in the state of Chiapas, much less its linguistic variations such as Tojolabal.

The Tojolabal zone encompasses all of the communities situated around Comitán, and extends all the way to the Pacific coast. The Tojolabal dialect is still spoken throughout the area; it is also, unfortunately, among the many Mayan dialects which are gradually being lost due to the passing of time and to the intrusion of the colonial language of Spanish.

Another Surprising Case

Another similar case was related to me by a Colombian by the name of Alberto Sánchez, who frequently guides groups of tourists in South America. Sánchez has a great interest in the ancient cultures, and never misses an opportunity to learn something new in this field.

Sánchez informed me of the existence of a tribe called "Colorado", or "Red", which can be found in Ecuador. The tribe is virtually extinct today, with only five hundred people remaining who speak the Colorado dialect, which is similar to Japanese.

Sánchez tells of one memorable occasion in which a Japanese tourist whom he was guiding managed to hold a brief conversation with one of these surviving Colorados; when, in telling the story, Sánchez observed a look of doubt on my face, he very seriously reiterated that the incident happened just as he had described it, and lamented the fact that he had not had a tape recorder to record the event.

In addition to this story, Sánchez told of the Chibcha tribe, who live on a high plateau (2,800 meters above sea level) in the Colombian Andes, near Bogotá. This tribe, which today is disintegrating because of the isolation in which they live, also employ a dialect which is phonetically similar to the Japanese language. Sánchez explained that many of the people of the tribe in both past and present times, have Japanese like names to their villages, such as Facatativa, Zipaquirá, Monoquirá, Gachancipá Tocancipá, Tobabitá, and Chiquinquirá, to name just a few.

The morphological characteristics of the Chibcha tribe, which was virtually decimated by the Spanish during and after the Conquest, are also similar to those of the Japanese; they exhibit a rather short stature, oblique eyes, projecting cheekbones, straight hair, etc.

The late Colombian archaeologist Ezequiel Euricochea took a great interest in this tribe, and was to attempt to locate a common base between the language of the Chibcha tribe and Japanese; unfortunately, Professor Euricochea died before he was able to realize his goals.

As the reader may have noted at the beginning of this chapter, quoted from the article by the anthropologist Carlos Villanueva, a ceramic style identified as belonging to the Jomon culture of Japan has been found precisely on the coast of Ecuador, in Valdivia. If this finding can be verified, we may finally have proof of the existence of some form of contact between the two races.

Other Coincidences

We have other reasons to believe in the reality of a cultural contact between the Maya and the Asians. One of these can be found in the late Carlos Echánove Trujillo's description of his final visit to Copán, in this description, Echánove observes the strikingly Asiatic influence which is found on two of the stelae of Copán.

A Chinese-looking face is found on one of the stelae, with thin, lank whiskers which give it the look of a Mandarin from the Country of the Sun, while the other, the famous stele B, exhibits a head crowned with a headdress of decidedly Asiatic influence. The most impressive part of this stele, in Echánove's opinion, are the two elephant heads which adorn both sides of the upper part of the monolith (Photos 6 and 7).

Photo No. 6. A figure on one of the stelae of the Ceremonial Patio, Copán, Honduras whose physical appearance and dress are of marked Asiatic influence. Photo by D. Carlos Echánove Trujillo from his book "Esas Pobres Ruinas Mayas Maravillosas".

Photo No. 7. The corner of one of the stelae of the Ceremonial Patio, Copán, Honduras, which represent two elephants heads. Photo by D. Carlos Echánove Trujillo from the same book.

Echánove ends his description with the following comment: "The discussion is already old as to whether or not Copán exhibits proof of Asiatic influence, as do Palenque and other sites in the Mayan area. Archaeologists such as Tozzer, Spinden, Means, and Morley try to use Stele B to argue that it (Copan) does not. Spinden was... the first to identify these disquieting representations as the heads of two blue macaws. For me, with all due respect to these specialists, these heads are really the representations of the heads of elephants. Not only are the forms of the heads, and the proportions and designs of the eyes convincing, but so also are the tusks of the snout, which appear stylized on both sides of the trunks...", and finally asks this question: "Which group is right: those who affirm or those who deny the Eastern Asian influence among the extraordinary Maya?." [1]

After carefully analysing the excellent photographs taken by Echánove, one finds himself inclined to agree with his point of view; the figures in question are undoubtedly elephants.

In light of the above information, it seems highly probable that a Hindu people from the Orient emigrated to the Mayan area during the Classic Florescent Period, bringing with them the concept of the elephant. It is further possible that, for reasons unknown to us today, the Maya came to associate their god of rain, Yum Chaac, with this animal, and that this is the reason that the god is represented with a nose very similar to the trunk of an elephant.

More Coincidences

We find related information in a book published by the Yucatecan author Don Ignacio Magaloni Duarte in 1969, entitled **Educadores del Mundo** (Educators of the World.) Duarte tries to prove that the Maya once lived in the Far and Middle East (Japan, China, India, Egypt, Greece, etc.), places which seem to have exerted strong cultural influences on the Maya. Magaloni also maintains that the Maya language is in fact the mother language which is being looked for by contemporary philologists, as many root words in the Maya language are equal to those of other languages of the world.

"Millenia ago", says Magaloni "some Mayan tribes arrived in India. These tribes were first called 'Nagas', and later "Dañavas" Their capital city was Nagapur. The historian Valmiki (4th Century B. C.) notes that in ancient times a race of people had arrived and settled in regions of Tibet; these were given the name Naga-Maya. This is historical, not a myth or legend. This same race later took its civilization to Babylonia, Acadia, Egypt, and Greece."

To confirm by comparison that Naga and Maya are a single language, Magaloni gives some examples. The Maya and Naga

1).— Echánove Trujillo Carlos A., **¡Esas Pobres Ruinas Mayas Maravillosas!**, B. Costa-Amic. México City, 1973; pages 167 — 168.

63

numbers are similar in their pronunciation, and the same in their written form, from one to ten as shown below: (2)

	Maya	Naga		Maya	Naga
1	Hun	Hun		•	•
2	Ca	Cas		• •	• •
3	Ox	Ox		• • •	• • •
4	Can	San		• • • •	• • • •
5	Ho	Ho		——	——
6	Uc	Usac		•	•
7	Uac	Uac		• •	• •
8	Uaxac	Uaxax		• • •	• • •
9	Bolom	Bolam		• • • •	• • • •
10	Lahun	Lahun		═══	═══

   Magaloni also demonstrates similarities in architectural relationships between the constructions of ancient America, and those of the East and Middle East, especially the concept of the pyramid.

   With regard to domestic artifacts, Magaloni uses photographs to illustrate the similarities between the Mayan and Oriental styles. For example, there are pictures of a Babylonian bowl with Mayan ornamentation; an Assyrian vase with the same type of serpentine design as is found in reliefs in Mayan temples; a vase of the city of Ashur, Assyria which shows the stylized Mayan rattlesnake (also on this vase are rosettes, with a sort of hanging fringe which is very similar to the border of the east, south, and west cornices of the Nunnery Quadrangle of Uxmal; photos 8, 9

2).— Magaloni D., Op. Cit.; page 81.

and 10 a Mayan corbelled arch, found in similar form in the tomb of Agamemnon in Micenas. The same arch is found in the Palace of Agamemnon (Door of the Lions), and a gallery with a Mayan arch can be seen in the Cyclopian ruins of Corinth (ancient Greece). Photos 11, 12 and 13.

Solar Cosmogliph

México.   Egipto.

Creation Ideogram

Creta.   México.

Photo No. 8. Babylonian Bowl with Mayan ornamentation (Greek line), Taken from the book "Los Educadores del Mundo" by Ignacio Magaloni

Compare the idiogram of the creation which is found in Mexico with that of Crete and Egypt; the solar cosmoglyph is similar in both cases.

James Churchward, traveler and relentless investigator says: "...a notable fact is that we find Mayan words in all of the languages of the world. In Japan, 40% of the Japanese language has Mayan roots. In India, a great portion of the spoken languages come, without a doubt, from the Maya, and all of the European languages are permeated with Maya, especially Greek, the alphabet of which is made up of Mayan words. A Mexican Indian

Photo No. 9. An Asyrian vase with the type of serpentine design as is found in reliefs in mayan buildings. From the same book "Los Educadores del Mundo".

and a person from Japan can understand each other without the use of an interpreter. There are many common roots in both languages".[3]

In an attempt to reaffirm these cultural connections, and as a consequence of his investigations, Magaloni writes the foilowing:

"We can prove that Jesus was in Himalaya for a long time. In a text that still exists in the Monastery of Hemis in Leh, Cachemira (adjacent to Tibet), we find the inarguable historical facts as to how and where Jesus spent his time during his historical absence. This text states, in part, that:

" 'When Jesus left his homeland, he first went to Egypt, where he studied the ancient 'osiriana-maya' religion. From Egypt, he went on to India, where, in many cities, including Benares and Lahore, he studied the teachings of Budda Gautama (who had studied the Mayan religion). Later, he entered the monastery of

3).— Magaloni D., Op. Cit.; page 56 — 57.

Photo No. 10. Vase from the city of Ashur, Asyrian with the stylized rattlesnake. From the same book.

Himalaya, where he studied the Maya and their cosmic sciences. After twelve years, he became a Teacher.' "

The author (Magaloni) states that we cannot forget this important historical fact; Christ learned Maya.

There are many temples and monasteries in India and Tibet that still have in their possession writings which refer to Christ during that period of time. There are also Eastern legends about him. One notable fact is that none of these texts call him Christ; he is always called Jesus. In the monastery of Lassa in Tibet, there is a text which states the following: "Jesus became the most proficient Teacher ever in this land". Today, the name Jesus is more revered in this monastery than in any sect of Christian priests. [4]

When Christ was crucified, his last words were HELI LAMAH ZABAC TANI. These words do not exist in any language of the old or new world other than Maya. In Maya, the ritual idiom of Christ (a historically proven fact), each of the words has a significance, claims Magaloni. The phrase formed with all words

4) .— Magaloni D., Op. Cit.; page 75 — 76.

Photo No. 11. Mayan arch in the Cyclopean ruins of Corinth in ancient Greece. From the same book "Los Educadores del Mundo".

joined. is magnificently coherent in Maya, and worthy of the crucified Master. In the Spanish-Maya dictionary of Ticul (a city in the Yucatán), the significance of these words can be found:

HELI   now, finally, already
LAMAH   to submerge or immerse oneself
SABAC   smoke, vapor, steam, or pre-dawn
TANI   in front or in the presence of

The phrase, thus organized, translates:

"Now I immerse myself in the pre-dawn of your presence".[5] Most people believe that this phrase, translated from the Hebrew, signifies: "God, why hast thou forsaken me?", but the above Mayan phrase seems more acceptable.

The book to which I am referring consists of 204 pages, and contains observations and experiences gathered during the au-

5).— Magaloni D., Op. Cit.; page 80.

Photo No. 12. Mayan arch in the tomb of the Agamemnon in Micenas, ancient Greece From the same book.

Photo No. 13. Mayan arch in the Palace of Agamemnon (Door of the Lions). From the same book.

thors's extensive studies. It gives the impression that the similarities are not purely coincidental, and that it is possible to conclude that the Nagas, or Mayas, were civilized groups which came from India to Yucatán, passing through China, Japan, and across the Bering Straight, especially since the Maya culture is relatively recent compared with cultures of the Far and Midle East.

THE MAYAN COUNTRY AND PERIODS OF THEIR CULTURAL EVOLUTION

CHAPTER THREE

a). **Dimensions of the Mayan Territory**
b). **Periods of Their Development**
c). **Probable Causes of Their Cultural Collapse in 925 A. D.**

a. **Dimensions of the Mayan Territory**

The country of the Maya had an area of approximately 325,000 square kilometers. It comprised almost half of the state of Chiapas, a little more than half of the state of Tabasco, and all of the states of Campeche, Yucatán, and Quintana Roo in Mexico; outside of Mexico it comprised almost all of Guatemala, a small section of El Salvador, part of Honduras, and all of the new country of Belize in Central America.

b. **Periods of Their Development**

Some years ago scientists felt that man was present in the Mayan territory around 3000 years B. C., especially in Honduras, Guatemala and nearby areas. It also thought that man ceased being nomadic and built villages in 800 B. C. Later scientific investigation, revealed this date to be an earler one of 1500 B. C.

Recently, the results of a 1976 British archaeological expedition were published. The major discovery of this group was that of the oldest Mayan ruins of the lowlands of Central America. A partially burned piece of wood, uncovered at the site, was subjected to the Carbon-14 dating test. The results of this test indicated that the burned remains dated back to the year 2500 B.C., as opposed to 1500 B.C., the date which had been previously postulated. Among the findings at this site were jewels, tombs and small constructions of clay and plaster (the quality of this plaster indicates that the lime which was used to make mortar was discovered at a much later date. This will be discussed at greater length later in this book).

Another expedition to this same area, sponsored by Cambridge University and the British Museum, and with financial

Map. No. 2

FIRST CLASS ▲
SECOND CLASS □
THIRD CLASS ●
FOURTH CLASS 0

GOLFO DE MEXICO

YUCATAN

DZIBICHALTUN
T-HO
IZAMAL
CHICHEN ITZA
OXKINTOK
MAYAPAN
YAXUNA
UXMAL
COBA
KABAH
SAYIL
LABNA
TULUM

QUINTANA ROO

LAGUN OF CHICHAN KANAB

S. ROSA XTAMPAK
EDZNA
HOCHOB
PPUSTUNICH

CAMPECHE

LAGUNA BACALAR

BECAN
DZIBANCHE
RIO BEC
KALAKMUL
EL PALMAR
RIO HONDO

NAACHTUN
CHOCH QUITAM
LA HONRADEZ
UAXACTUN
TIKAL
NAKUM
NARANJO
BENQUE VIEJO

TABASCO

JONUTA
USUMACINTA RIVER
PALENQUE
TONINA
PIEDRAS NEGRAS
YAXCHILAN
BONANPAK
POLOL
TZIMIN KAX
SEIBAL
LUBANTUN
PUSILHA

CHIAPAS

BELIZ

GOLFO DE HONDURAS

CARIBBEAAN SEA

GUATEMALA

PUERTO BARRIOS
QUIRIGUA
MOTAGUA RIVER
COPAN

REPUBLICA DE HONDURAS

CAMINALJUYU

PACIFIC OCEAN

Map No. 2 of the Mayan Archaeological Zone.

aid from North America, began field work in 1978. At the present time they are excavating the site where the Maya celebrated their religious ceremonies, a task which is estimated to require several months for completion. The Project Directors for this expedition are Dr. Norman Hammond, a former professor of archaeology at Bradford University in northern England, and Bonaghey, an archaeologist from the York Archaeological Trust of England, who is in charge of the work near Orange Walk, Belize. Their investigatory team consists of twenty English and North American specialists — archaeologists, artists, surveyors, project developers, and museum personnel.

Another report that has caused a sensation among students of archaeology detailed the finding of a stele in the ruins of Copán by a group of North American and Honduras archaeologists. According to the specialists that worked on this exploration, this stele dates back to the year 750 B.C. This information was provided by Charles Cheek.

This same publication (March 13, 1978) states that twenty scientists did research in the Great Plaza in Copán, and that one of these scientists, French archaeologist and Project Director Claude F. Baudez, indicated that were deciphered more than two hundred hieroglyphs. He later submitted his work to foreign and national experts for study.

We do not know how accurate this translation of the date glyphs is, nor do we know of the quality of the carvings; the brief publication does state, however, that two human forms can be discerned, carved in relief —legs, torsos, and heads— in similar form to the figures found on the stelae throughout the Mayan zone of Mexico and Guatemala.

Prior to the discovery of the above mentioned stele, the oldest known date stelae were: a) "La Placa de Leyden" (The Plaque of Layden) which bears a date glyph corresponding to September 15, 320 A.D.; b) Stele 9 of Uaxactun, Guatemala, with a date of April 9, 328 A. D.; and c) Stele 29 in Tikal, found by the University of Pennsylvania archaeologists between 1956 and 1966, and bearing an inscription which corresponds to July 6, 292 A. D.

As the reports regarding the recently discovered stele mentioned above are very brief, the reader should delay forming his final opinion until more substantial information is available.

Dated stelae, along with pottery shards, were the basic elements scientists used to classify the various periods of development, and they also served as a basis in the calculation of the ages of surrounding buildings.

Not long after its discovery, the Carbon-14 dating method was used extensively in determining the age of animal and vegetable remains. The system has been an invaluable tool to researchers, as they are now able to date buildings more accurately by using the Carbon-14 test on organic materials found within the ruins, and even on the wooden door lintels and cross-beams which were employed in the construction.

The date carved on the recently discovered Copán stele was more than likely executed prior to the construction of the surrounding masonry buildings, although other known stelae and their surrounding buildings generally parallel each other in time (as an example, the sapodilla wood lintel of the Pyramid of the Magician in Uxmal was dated at 569 A. D., a date which corresponds exactly to the Puuc Style of architecture which was employed in the building's construction).

Perhaps there are some who might hesitate to accept this line of reasoning; How could a civilization with such an advanced knowledge of the art of sculpture lack a similar knowledge in the art of stone masonry? Despite the logic of this argument, we find an example of such a culture in the Olmecs, who were masters in the art of sculpture, but never built any masonry edifices of any consequence. It is possible that a lack of knowledge of the fabrication and implementation of lime, a basic and irreplaceable ingredient in the production of mortar, was the underlying reason for this paradox.

Regardless of such speculation, this stele, which is still undergoing the process of analysis, is the only presently known monument of its kind with such an ancient date inscription.

We do not know whether the Maya of that time built their monuments to commemorate events which had occurred in the past, and as such, inscribed them with the dates of the events which they intended to commemorate, or if instead they inscribed them with the stele's date of construction. This theme will be discussed in greater detail in the chapter of this book which deals with chronology, in the section which refers to the "Secondary Count".

After these commentaries, we consider it necessary to make the description of new discoveries which came to radically change our earlier knowledge about the origin of man in the country of the Maya. These discoveries were the finding of the piece of a tusk and the molar of a mastodon, the fibula of a bison, and the hoof of a small horse from the Plaistocene period. These findings, along with bones of other prehistoric animals, were all excavated from Chamber No. 6 "Huechil", in the interesting cave of Loltun. This cave is located 7 kilometers from the village of Oxkutzcab, and 110 kilometers south from the city of Merida, capital of the state of Yucatan. Loltun is a Mayan word meaning ston flower.

The archaelogists of the National Institute of Anthropology and History of Mexico, made these excavations. They determined these new discoveries were from the same era as various implements of stone, wood and bone that were found. This indicates that man and animals co-existed at least 8000 year B. C., and possibly earler.

Various experts classify and subdivide periods of the Mayan cultural evolution, in different way. One of the best known, and widely accepted classifications, is that of the English archaelogist, J. Eric S. Thompson. In particular, his analysis of time from the Classical period to the final collapse of the Mayan civilization.

Taking into account the new discoveries and the fact that agriculture began approximately 2500 years B. C., a new classification in the following order, might be appropriate:

FIRST PERIOD: **Pre-Maya** From 8000 B. C. to 2500 B. C.

SECOND PERIOD: Formative or **Pre-Classic** — 2500 B.C. to 200 A.D.

THIRD PERIOD: **Classic,** subdivided into three parts:
Early Classic	200	to	625 A.D.
Florescent Classic	625	to	800 "
Decadent Classic	800	to	925 "

FOURTH PERIOD: **Toltec Influence**   925   to 1200   "

FIFTH PERIOD: **Mexican Absorption**   1200   to 1540   "

We know very little about the formative period because we lack historical information to help us in our research. The information we have was the result of stratigraphic exploration and the analysis of specialists in this matter. Now we have the help of carbon 14 radioactive, that works only in organic matters, as we previously mentioned. Archaeologist analized very carefuly all of the objects found in the excavations: stone implements, clay, wood and other materials. These findings are all related so that we might know when these artifacts existed in a particular place. In this maner they could determine the development of evolution of the culture that started approximately 2500 years before Christ.

It was at this time the Mayans started to make huts of straw or palms, developed agriculture, and fabricated implements of hard stone. They also began to work in ceramics and created religios rites or ceremonies. Soon, they devised a system of writing, numerology, the calendar, and discovered how to extract by fire the lime from limestone and mix it with white earth for making mortar. This ability to make mortar created the beginning of architecture. All of this advancement constituted the foundation of the Classic period.

During this brilliant Classic period, the Mayan rose their highest level of culture. They built the most beautiful buildings, created the most notable sculptures, and made the best ceramics, all with great elegance. They obtained extremely important knowledge in astronomy creating a perfect calendar with astonishing precision, etc.

c. Probable Causes for Their Cultural Collapse in 925 A. D.

According to various sources of information, the Mayan culture began to decline sometime around the year 800 A. D., so that by the year 925 there was a general paralysis of activities; it was as if the Maya had disappeared from the cultural scene. They ceased construction of buildings, stelae, etc., for approximately fifty years. This cessation of activities or decadence, is indicated in part, by the last carved dates which have been found: in Copán, the final date is that of the year 800 A. D.; in Edzná and Piedras Negras, 810; Oxkintok, 849; in Tikal, 869; in Chichén Itzá, 889.

D. Rafael Girard, another devoted archaeologist, did explorations primarily in Guatemala, and came to the conclusion that it was the invasion of the Pipil Indians, an ethnic group of Nahua origin, which triggered the decline of the Mayan culture.

76

The Mayan cultural collapse has also been attributed to the loss of crops over successive years, due to the depletion of soil nutrients and to prolonged droughts. This could account for the decline of one section of the Mayan territory, but certainly not all of their realm. The drought theory makes even less sense when one considers the fact that regions like Chiapas in Mexico, Copán in Honduras, and Quiriguá in Guatemala all had extremely fertile valleys and fields that were watered by several rivers.

Historians also mention epidemics as another possible cause of the decline. While an epidemic could occur in isolated sections of the Mayan area, it is doubtful that it would encompass all of their territory.

Earthquakes have also been suggested as a possible cause for the collapse, but these natural phenomena are localized to some areas in Guatemala, and to the isthmus of Tehuantepec. Earthquakes in the Northern Yucatán are so slight that they can scarcely be noticed.

I am inclined to agree with those who think the collapse was caused by a rebellion of the working class against the nobles.

We can probably assume that in the beginning, the priests and nobles combined the principles of religious belief and terror to keep the working class in line. This was accomplished by cleverly making use of certain natural phenomena, which they could accurately predict; phenomena such as eclipses, hurricanes, prolonged drougths, excessive rains (that which prevented burning off the jungle for field preparation), etc. These phenomena were designated as punishment from the gods by the Mayan priests, who explained that the gods had to be appeased by the construction of great temples and palaces. The priests tried to prove their connection with the gods through these predictions, boasting that they were heavenly messengers.

However, it is also possible that the well-armed and tightly-controlled army was used to apply pressure on the work forces.

It is possible that some of the more ambitious rulers continually demanded greater constructive endeavor, as well as additional comforts and luxury, and applied pressure to their people in order to obtain them. This situation may have provoked a local rebellion, which later spread to other areas. After many conflicts, with frustrations and failures, we can surmise that the rebels finally triumphed, and that some of the nobles and priests were consequently put to death or imprisoned.

The triumphant rebel chiefs were not able to agree on a new distribution of power, and it is possible that this motivated an internal war which culminated in the partial destruction and abandonment of the ceremonial centers and a general paralysis of cultural activities

After some years of stagnation, the Post-Classic period marked a cultural renaissance of the Maya, only in the northern part of the Yucatan Peninsula.

In Chichén Itzá, the Post-Classic Period coincided with the arrival of the Toltecs of Tula. Upon their arrival, the Toltecs imposed their architecture and parts of their religion upon the Maya. Among these, most notable was the idea of human sacrifice. For their part, the Mayan surrendered to the Toltecs their language, writing system, and some of their customs.

Most historians agree that the Toltecs came as conquerers and took possession of a portion of the northern part of Yucatán by force. They set up their camps in Chichén Itzá, which was to be the area of their most profound cultural influence.

Due to the circumstances which existed at that time, and the long distance between Tula and Chichén Itzá (over 1,700 kilometers), it does not seem feasible that the Toltecs would have occupied this metropolis in this way. Without adequate means of transportation, it would have been impossible to mobilize such an enormous army in order to defeat a densely populated Mayan state.

How many weapons and meals were needed to traverse such a long route? How many wide rivers were there to ford, marshes to cross, insects and poisonous animals to be dealt with? Apart from these natural obstacles, the Toltecs had to go through numerous countries and other populated regions. The inhabitants of these areas would not have permitted such a well-armed militia to cross their territory, as it would have posed a threat to their domestic peace and safety.

My theory is this: suppose that in Tula, two rival factions were engaged in a power struggle, the loser of which would be forced to leave. Undoubtedly, this exiled group would have been composed of civilized people with advanced scientific knowledge, Being a small and unarmed party, they would not only have obtained permission to cross frontiers but would have received help and hospitality over the course of their long journey.

Upon their arrival in the Yucatán, they attempted to live with various Mayan groups that they encountered in passing, but were accepted only as temporary guests. They continued their journey until finally reaching Chichén Itzá, where they worked hard to convince the inhabitants and rulers that they should be allowed to remain there permanently.

The combination of the two technologies produced a rapid and explosive cultural development which caused deep and profound shock waves to engulf the rest of the people of the peninsula. These other groups began to fear the new culture, imagining pressures and possible aggression. Chichén Itzá, for its part, did the same by beginning its own military preparations. Perhaps this may be the reason for the many war scenes represented in murals and reliefs.

The most important war mural is found in the second interior chamber of the Temple of the Jaguar. In this mural can be seen disorderly huts of straw or palm, in front of which are women wearing ankle-length skirts with tucked-in blouses and doing their household chores. The clothing of these women is similar to that which is used today by the women of Tehuantepec, Campeche, and other regions in Mexico. Rapidly marching soldiers, with shields and lances, are depicted below and in front of the women; their short skirts are reminiscent of the style worn by ancient Roman warriors. In another section of this mural, other soldiers are apparently on the attack.

This scene has been interpreted as the Toltec conquest of Chichén Itzá, an idea which is not acceptable for the following reasons: a) all of the warriors are short and of the same stature, and dressed alike (it is known that the Toltecs were tall); b) the lances which the warriors carry are pointed down, not at other people; c) in an earlier reproduction of this mural, which was made when it was in better condition, none of the combatants are seen wounded, impaled, or thrown to the ground; and the fact that the women are depicted as placidly going about their chores, and show no signs of uneasiness or fear, certainly suggests to us that this is not a combat scene, and even less is it the conquest of Chichén Itzá. It could well have been the ceremony of Ek Chua, the war god, or a practice or training session.

Perhaps because of limited space, the artist has things slightly out of proportion in this mural, since the people are almost the same size as the huts.

In speaking of the Toltec culture, I mentioned that Topiltzin immigrated to the Yucatán Península in this same period, or sometime around the year 987 A. D. Although the Toltec informational source mentions him as a solitary immigrant, it is possible that he came with a large following. It is possible that he was not the Kukulcán-Quetzalcoatl that Bishop Landa tells us about, as Topiltzin fled Tula, under pressure from his enemies, precisely to avoid human sacrifice, and Kukulcán is believed to have introduced sacrifices to the Yucatán.

Some studies do not accept this pacifistic theory of the Toltec arrival because they allege that the Aztecs, with similar transportation problems, managed to dominate a rather extensive territory. Bear in mind, however, that the Aztecs were extending their domain out from their capital, using the conquered countries as stepping stones, while the Toltecs were abandoning their homeland to immigrate to another area.

Mural from the interior of the Temple of the Jaguars. The above portion shows a Mayan village, and below, a battle or a war dance. Photo taken from the Official Guide of Chichén Itzá by I. N. A. H. of México.

CHAPTER FOUR

a). Writing   b). Language

a). Writing

Without a doubt, the Mayan culture can be considered as the most brilliant of the American continent, and as one of the most notable of the world in its time. These considerations can be easily verified through the analysis of their difficult and complex writing system, as well as the many other great realizations of their advanced culture. Communication through the use of the written word is generally accepted as one of the most admirable manifestations of any culture.

The Maya possibly began their writing at the beginning of the Formative Period, and it gradually evolved until its perfection sometime in the Early Classic Period. Maya writing is original and very complicated. Eight hundred and sixty-two different characters have been discovered in the three codices previously mentioned (Dresden, Peresiano, and Tro-Cortesiano), and in the temple carvings, columns, and stelae; hence, the Maya had no alphabet as we know it. Imagine the mental capacity of the Mayan intellectuals who were able to memorize hundreds of symbols more complicated than those used by the oriental civilizations!

There has been a great deal of discussion over the subject of the Mayan writing system, and previously, the system was thought to be of a ideographic nature. Several modern investigators, however, suggest that the system is also phonetic. One of these investigators, the engineer Héctor M. Calderón, in his interesting book entitled **Clave fonética de los jeroglíficos mayas**, published in 1972, tries to demonstrate the phonetic approach to understanding the Mayan writings through detailed analysis.

As is mentioned previously, it has been possible to find out the meaning and pronunciation of some of the glyphs through the records of Bishop Landa. However, we are still ignorant as to the reasoning behind the different signs, and because the Mayan writing system is not related to any other known form of writing, we are still unable to understand the meaning of many of the glyphs.

The longest carved writing is found on the steps of the Hieroglyphic Staircase of Copán, Honduras, on which are found 1,688 glyphs. Since this stairway was badly deteriorated upon discovery, it was difficult to distinguish the number of steps, let alone the number of glyphs carved on the sides. However, from September to November 1946, Raúl Pavón and his three assistants (the Campechean artist Hipólito Sánchez and the two young Hondurans Miguel Angel Ruiz and Dante Lazaroni), photographed and sketched the existing 1,688 glyphs and concluded that at one time there had been 63 steps of ten meters in width, and that the number of glyphs to be found in Copán had once totaled 4,658. [1]

(The next longest engraved writing appears to be the one in the Temple of Insciptions in Palanque).

One peculiarity of Mayan writing is in the fact that they used different signs to represent the same thing. For example, the day "Kin' has four different glyphs. For the period of one "Katun" (20 years) there are three different signs. For one "Baktun" (400 years) they used two.

Numbers were represented by images of human heads. The numbers 1, 15, 18, and 0 could be represented in five different head glyph variations each; 5, 8, 9, and 13 could be represented in six, and so on. The curious day "Ahua" had more than twenty variations.

Unfortunately, Bishop Landa, motivated by his religious fanaticism, took a negative attitude toward the Mayan writing and ordered twenty-seven Mayan books to be burned in the atrium of the church in the village of Maní, Yucatán, on June 16, 1561. Landa believed that the burning of the books was the best way to eradicate the native religion, which he considered to be filled with evil spirits and demons.

b). Language

According to recent studies, it is known that the Mayan language, in its original form (between 3000 and 2500 B. C.), was only one language; over the years it was regionalized into twenty-three dialects within the Mayan zone, and two more in the Huastec,

---

1).— Proskouriakoff Tatiana, **Album de Arquitectura Maya**, Fondo de Cultura Económica, México City, 1973; page 12.

Potosin, and Veracruz areas.

The archaeologist Eric Thompson says, in reference to the Mayan dialects, that, "...In favor of a fair degree of unity is the fact that the language was practically the same throughout the lowland area, for the differences between lowland languages and dialects 1000 to 1500 years ago must have been less than they are today, and there seems to be little doubt that a Chol would have understood a Yucatec, or a Tzotzil a Chorti, certainly as easily as a Neopolitan understands a native of Turin".[2]

Thompson also says that if a language map was made of the places where the different Mayan dialects are spoken, it would be impossible to delineate exact zones, as the changes are so progressive and gradual that it is often difficult to determine the place where one dialect stops and another begins.

Tozzer, who is mentioned by Morley, in speaking from the point of view of a lexicographer, states that the Mayan language is distinct from other languages which are spoken in Mexico or Central America, and, because of this fact, has no affiliation with any of them. Nevertheless, some authors maintain that Zapotec is a near relative to the Mayan language.

The Mayan language has a sweet musical sound, and is basically monosyllabic. Listed below are some examples of monosyllabic Mayan words which are used for various parts of the human body.

Maya Pronunciation	English Translation
pol (pronounced like "pole" in English)	head
uich (weetch)	face
ich (eetch)	eye
ni (nee)	nose
chi (chee)	mouth
yak (yahk)	tongue
coh (koh)	tooth
cal (kahl)	neck
tzotz (tsots)	hair
tzem (tsem)	chest
nak (nahk)	stomach
puch (pootch)	back
ka (kah)	hand
pix (peesh)	knee
ok (oak)	foot
choch (chotch)	bowel

2).— Thompson Eric. Op. Cit.; page 91.

83

It is prudent to explain that among the twenty-three dialects that are spoken in the Mayan territory, the Yucatec encompassed the largest area (more than half the Yucatan Peninsula), while the others were confined to smaller zones.

In alphabetical order, the different dialects are:

1. Aguatec	13. Pokonchi
2. Cakchiquel	14. Pokoman
3. Chol	15. Quiche
4. Chontal	16. Rabinal
5. Chuh	17. Solomec
6. Chorti	18. Tojolobal
7. Ixil	19. Tzeltal
8. Jacaltec	20. Tzotzil
9. Kanjobol	21. Tzutuhil
10. Kekchi	22. Uspantec
11. Lacondon	23. Yucatec
12. Mam	

The Potosin and Veracruz dialects are spoken outside of the Mayan zone, as is mentioned previously.

CHAPTER FIVE
MATHEMATICAL ASPECTS

NUMEROLOGY

The discovery of symbol for zero —the written representation of NOTHING— is considered to be one of the most notable events of mankind. Originally, the Maya were credited with discovering the concept of zero in America. Lately, however, controversies have arisen in respect to this idea.

It is now thought that the Olmecs created the symbol, and introduced it into the Mayan area. This opinion is based on the fact that an Olmec stele of Tres Zapotes bears the carved inscription corresponding to the year 31 B. C., which is earlier than the oldest date found in the Mayan territory of 292 A. D. in Tikal, Guatemala.

It is very probable that the Olmecs introduced some basic mathematical concepts to the Mayan territory, which the Maya then perfected into their fantastic vigesimal (base twenty) system. The system was later refined to such an exact form that they were able to institute their famous Long Count, the high point of Mayan chronology.

Before going further, it should be explained that the Maya used two written numbering systems and 24 representations of zero; 12 were found in the Codices, 8 in the Inscriptions and five more in the form of heads. One of the numbering systems consisted   of 20 faces in profile, each one representing a different number from 0 to 19. Difficult enough, but remember that some of these faces had as many as six written variations, complicating the system even more.

It is possible that the Maya used this complicated system in order to keep secret certain knowledge that was intended only for the priests and nobles and not for the townfolk.

The other system was much simpler.

Apart from the signs for zero, the Maya used the dot to represent units of one, and the bar to represent units of five. Their system was trinomial and vigesimal, functioning by use of multiples of twenty. They were able to count to infinity (millions, billions, etc.) in a form similar to our own decimal system. The

85

Maya, however, wrote the values vertically, one above the other, and read from top to bottom, while in our system, we write the place values (ones, tens, hundreds, etc.) from right to left, and read from left to right, horizontally.

In the Mayan system, the bottom line represented units from zero to nineteen. The next line above was for units of twenty, while the third line represented units of four hundred (20 x 20), the fourth represented units of eight thousand (20 x 400), and so on up successively.

For clarity, we are going to use the following table as a key for understanding their system:

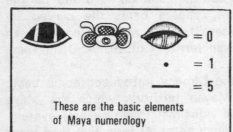

				= 0
			•	= 1
			——	= 5

These are the basic elements of Maya numerology

4th row is for writing multiples of **8,000**
3rd row is for writing multiples of **400**
2nd row is for writing multiples of **20**
Ist row is units, 0 to 19

Numerical value of the positions from the bottom to up.

Occasionally, especially in date carvings on stelae, the dots and bars were put in vertical form (:II) without affecting the numerical value.

Though the system used by the ancient Maya for addition, subtraction, multiplication, and division is unknown, they undoubtedly had one. Some years ago, the engineer Héctor M. Calderón —mentioned in the chapter on Mayan writing— spent considerable time studying drawings and reliefs common to various cultures that had mathematical operations, especially multiplication. He arrived at the conclusion that the Maya, in order to carry out their operations, utilized boxes or counting boards (boards marked off in squares). Instead of the dot and bar, they used seeds to represent ones and sticks to represent units of five. (39)

To reinforce his theory, Calderón states, "... Thousands of years after the Maya used the counting board system for multiplication and division, the Arabs took it back to Europe." (Taken

The following symbols, when in position on the bottom or first row, are read thusly:

• = 1		= 6		= 11		= 16
•• = 2		= 7		= 12		= 17
••• = 3		= 8		= 13		= 18
•••• = 4		= 9		= 14		= 19
—— = 5		= 10		= 15	

To write 20, they put a completion symbol in the units line and put one dot in the 20's line

•   one time 20

+ 0 = 0

= 20

(The Zero symbol is placed in the bottom row so that we will know the dot in the 20's row. The units are "completed".)

•• 2 times 20 = 40

+ 0 = 0

= 40

—— 5 times 20 = 100

+ 0

= 100

•••• 4 times 20 = 80

—— + 5

= 85

12 times 20 = 240

+ 19

= 259

• one time 400 = 400

+ 0

+ 0

= 400

—— 5 times 400 = 2,000

+ 0

+ 17

= 2,017

•••• 4 X 400 = 1,600

18 X 20 = 360

+ 18

= 1,978

• one time 8,000

• " "   400

• " "   20

• " "   1

= 8,421

NOTE: Only by figuring the value of each position we are able to write quantities we want.

from an arithmetic of Johaan Widman published in Germany in 1589). He then provides two multiplication tables, noting that they are none other than the Pythagorean Theorem, which was already in use in Babylonia, and which the Babylonians had certainly gotten from India. In the following paragraph of his book, he states: ". . . Still more convincing are four examples of how they did multiplication in the 15th Century, according to the examples in an arithmetic published in Treviso, Italy in 1478". [1]

Calderón summarizes, and shows in a quick and simple way, that it is possible not only to carry out the four basic operations in the Mayan vigesimal system, but also to extract the square roots and cubes, using only sticks and seeds and the counting board. Not content with these conclusions, he then tries to ascertain the unit of linear measurement used by the early Maya, based on the average of the dimensions of the most important buildings at various archaeological sites.

I believe that Calderón has found the key to the Mayan mathematical system.

So that you will have an idea of the system Calderón explains, we are going to add three quantities — 539 + 1,045 + 2,148 = 3,732 — using his system. I have tried to simplify the explanation, taking into account the fact that most people are not quite familiar enough with the Mayan numerology to follow his explanation.

As you can see, our counting board has three horizontal rows and five vertical ones, making a total of 15 squares. The vertical boxes are marked left to right, A to E. The horizontal boxes are numbered 1, 2, and 3. The separate boxes to the left (without letters) are used only to indicate the value of the positions of the Mayan numbers, and the last row to the right (also without letters) to note the partial totals in Arabic numerals.

The quantities below in Arabic numerals are equivalent to those quantities written in Mayan numerals which are to be added.

The first step is to take all the sticks and seeds from row 1, from boxes A, B, and C, and place them in box D. Next, we do the same in rows 2 and 3. All the sticks and seeds, from all of the horizontal rows, are now grouped together in column D; the

1).— Calderón Héctor M., **La Ciencia Matemática de los Mayas,** Editorial Orión, México City, 1966; page 59.

Positions Values		A	B	C	D	E	Totals
400	1	•	• •	—	•••]	○○○○	.3,600
20	2	•̄	═	• • ═	••••• ═	○	120
0-19	3	•••• ═	—	• • •	••••• ═	• •	12

539 + 1,045 + 2,148 .... = 3,732

0—19 box has five sticks (representing a total of 25) and seven seeds, or a total of 32 units; the 20's box has four sticks (4 x 5 x 20 = 400) and five seeds (5 x 20 = 100), making a total of 500, and the 400's box has one stick (5 x 400 = 2000) and three seeds (3 x 400 = 1200), or a total of 3200.

The only thing left to do is to rearrange the sticks and seeds in the boxes so that no box has more than nineteen of the units which it represents (identical to our own decimal system, in which we add units up to nine, and go to two places with units of ten or more).

Column E. Since there are 32 units in the 0—19 box, one unit of 20 (or four sticks) is removed from the bottom row of column D and is placed, as one seed, in the 20's box of colum E. We now have twenty-six units of 20's (or 520) in the 20's box. We leave six units in the 20's box of column E (in the form of one stick and one seed, and representing a total, as such, of 120) and move the balance of the units, now represented by one seed with a value of 400, into the 400's box of column E, making a total of four seeds and one stick, or nine units of 400 (3600), in the 400's box.

In the final column, the process is converted to Arabic numerals, and the equation is represented as 3600 + 120 + 12 = 3732.

It was not necessary for the Maya to go to these extremes when making their calculations, as they used the dot and bar system with the same ease with which we use our own.

Perhaps it appears to you that this system is difficult and cumbersome; in reality the opposite is true. The above description is a little long, but it is necessarily so in order to be able to understand the process, which, when mastered, becomes very simple and practical. All that you really need to do is to put the sticks and seeds together in column D, and calculate their value.

The other mathematical operations will not be described, as such a description would deviate from the purpose of this book.

CHAPTER SIX

CHRONOLOGY — CALENDARIC SYSTEMS

a). Generalizations   d). The Long Count
b). The Tzolkin   e). Dating of the End of Period
c). The Calendar Round   f). The Short Count

a). Generalizations

The Mayan system of chronology is one of the most complicated that the world has ever known. Its significance is magnified when consideration is given to the ancient time period in which it was invented.

The Mayan calendar evolved in various stages, beginning with the "Tzolkin" or religious year. This early calendar was followed by the Calendar Round, which soon obtained its ultimate perfection in the form of the famous "Long Count". The Long Count later underwent two abbreviations; the first was called "Dating of the End of Period" by chronologists, and the second, which was an even more abbreviated dating system than the first, was called the "Katun Round", or "Short Count".

The Maya had such a preoccupation with marking the passage of time that they constructed slabs of stone upon which they artistically carved bas-relief scenes representing important people; after each period of twenty years, they would inscribe the date upon these decorated slabs. These monoliths have been given the name "stelae".

Toward the middle of the Classic Florescent Period, the ancient Maya began to erect stelae every ten years, and ultimately they were erected every five years.

The largest Mayan stele discovered to date is in Quiriguá, Guatemala. This enormous structure is 10.67 meters tall, 1.5 meters wide, and 1.27 meters thick, and weighs sixty-five tons. It is inscribed with the Mayan date which corresponds to 771 A. D.

In Piedras Negras, Guatemala, twenty-eight stelae, marking consecutive 5-year periods, can be found.

The greatest number of stelae can be found in Calakmul, Campeche (Mexico), near the borders of Guatemala, Quintana Roo, and the Yucatán. One hundred and three stelae can be found at this site, seventy-three of which bear carved inscriptions, and thirty which are smooth. Morley suggests that the smooth stelae were at one time covered with stucco, on which scenes and dates were painted, and that because of its less than permanent nature, the stucco deteriorated over the years. This reasoning is logicaly acceptable, as there would be no reason for the Maya to carve a stone pillar without including the corresponding reliefs which would explain the purpose of its creation. [1]

Some of the seventy-three sculptured stelae have dates which are repeated; we are totally ignorant as to the existence of any reason which the Mayan inhabitants of Calakmul could have had for marking the end of one time period several different times.

b). The Tzolkin

It was the archaeologist William Gates who first called the religious calendar of the ancient Maya the "Tzolkin"; the original name is not known.

In order to understand the workings of the calendar, Professor Antonio Canto López, an expert in Mayan chronology, developed two tables which he explains in his book **Apuntaciones Sobre Mesoamérica (Annotations on Meso-America),** a book which has been used as a textbook in the curriculum of the University of Yucatán.

Table One shows the function of the Tzolkin, while Table Two shows the Calendar Round; both are intimately related, as will be seen later.

The Mayan religious year consisted of 260 days, which were divided into thirteen 20-day months.

The first vertical row in Table One lists the twenty days of the Mayan month, which the Maya represented with glyphs. Immediately following this row are thirteen vertical columns which correspond to the thirteen months of the religious year. There are no names for these thirteen months.

1).— Morley, S. G., Op. Cit. (1966 Edition); page 357.

92

TABLE I

Tonalpohualli and Tzolkin

Nahua	Maya													
Cipactli	Imix	1	8	2	9	3	10	4	11	5	12	6	13	7
Ehecatl	Ik	2	9	3	10	4	11	5	12	6	13	7	1	8
Calli	Akbal	3	10	4	11	5	12	6	13	7	1	8	2	9
Cuetzpallin	Kan	4	11	5	12	6	13	7	1	8	2	9	3	10
Cohuatl	Chicchan	5	12	6	13	7	1	8	2	9	3	10	4	11
Miquiztli	Kimi	6	13	7	1	8	2	9	3	10	4	11	5	12
Mazatl	Manik	7	1	8	2	9	3	10	4	11	5	12	6	13
Tochtli	Lamat	8	2	9	3	10	4	11	5	12	6	13	7	1
Atl	Muluc	9	3	10	4	11	5	12	6	13	7	1	8	2
Itzcuintli	Oc	10	4	11	5	12	6	13	7	1	8	2	9	3
Ozomatli	Chuen	11	5	12	6	13	7	1	8	2	9	3	10	4
Malinalli	Eb	12	6	13	7	1	8	2	9	3	10	4	11	5
Acatl	Ben	13	7	1	8	2	9	3	10	4	11	5	12	6
Ocelotl	Ix o Hix	1	8	2	9	3	10	4	11	5	12	6	13	7
Quauhtli	Men	2	9	3	10	4	11	5	12	6	13	7	1	8
Coscaquauhtli	Kib	3	10	4	11	5	12	6	13	7	1	8	2	9
Ollin	Caban	4	11	5	12	6	13	7	1	8	2	9	3	10
Tecpatl	Eznab	5	12	6	13	7	1	8	2	9	3	10	4	11
Quiahuitl	Cauac	6	13	7	1	8	2	9	3	10	4	11	5	12
Xóchitl	Ahau	7	1	8	2	9	3	10	4	11	5	12	6	13

The days are read by putting the numeral of each vertical column before the corresponding Nahua and Maya name.

Example: 1 Cipactli and 13 Xochitl are the first and last days of the Tonalpohualli. 1 Imix and 13 Ahau are the first and last days of the Tzolkin. (Table developed by Prof. D. Antonio Canto López).

Beginning with the top of the first column to the far left, and numbering each column from top to bottom, the series of numbers from one through thirteen are repeated over and over again until all thirteen columns have been filled, beginning with the number 1. It should be understood that these numbers were not dates, but rather marks which served to pinpoint the position of the day in the month.

The twenty day names of the Tzolkin, alone did not represent days of the month either; they first had to be joined to one of the thirteen numbers, and, therefore, are called "number/names".

When the Tzolkin is filled or completed as shown above, none of the name/number combinations (1 Imix, 10 Oc, etc.) is ever repeated during the entire thirteen months. If you check the form horizontally, you will see that even though the numbers one through thirteen are not in order, they do not repeat; this is because the numbers thirteen and twenty have no common denominators.

A peculiarity found in this table is that in counting horizontally, we find that alternate numbers (that is, every other one) proceed in order, as is hown below:

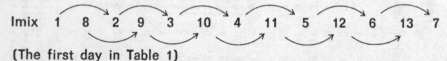

(The first day in Table 1)

It is believed that the days of the Tzolkin represented secondary deities. A Mayan male child born on any of these days adopted a last name corresponding to the day of his birth; the Maya believed that the deity represented by the birthday of the child influenced the course of his existence, and served him as a protector.[2]

Many questions have been raised as to why the Maya used a system of base thirteen in the Tzolkin. It is very possible that each of the thirteen numbers of this religious calendar corresponded to one of the thirteen layers into which the Maya believed the firmament to be divided. This subject will be further discussed in later chapters.

No one knows positively when this calendar first came into use, but it is believed to have surfaced shortly after the invention of numerology.

2).— Canto López A., Op. Cit.; page 150.

I am of the opinion that the Tzolkin was not used to mark the passage of time, but rather as a guide for the arrangement of religious ceremonies which rotated on a 260-day cycle, since the Tzolkin's thirteen "months" of twenty days do not have names; conversely, the months on the Calendar Round were named, as will be seen later in this chapter.

c). The Calendar Round

Sometime around the year 353 B. C. (according to chronologists), the Calendar Round was developed when the Maya discovered the civil year, consisting of roughly 365 days.

It is very probable that while carrying out careful observations, they realized that climate changes, cold and rainy seasons, and other natural phenomena always followed a definite time pattern. Perhaps checking the slow variation from day to day of the position of the sun at sunset gave them the rule for pinpointing the length of the year. The astronomers had only to count how many days it took for the sun to move from the extreme right, or the northwest, to the left, or southwest, and back again to the original starting point, to arrive at a year-length of 365 days.

This same primitive method, based on the observation of solar movement and consequent climate changes, would serve the Maya in determining the equinoxes and the solstices; as the sun swung to its furthest position to the left, the date and position were marked as the solstice we call the Winter Solstice; as it reached the middle point of its migration across the horizon, it would indicate the Vernal Equinox; the position to the extreme right would be that of the Summer Solstice; and finally, the return of the sunset to the middle of the horizon on its way south was indicative of the Autumnal Equinox.

With the advent of the 365-day year, the Maya observed that as time passed, the calendaric year and the natural seasons lost their synchronization; each year, the seasons occurred on later dates than in the preceding year. This time variance was calculated to amount to a period of thirteen days every fifty-two years; this time period (52 years) came to signify a kind of cycle of life to the Maya, much in the way that we consider our own centuries as significant time periods.

Ultimately, it was discovered that the year had more than 365 days. In a most ingenious manner, the Maya adjusted their calendaric year by a fraction close to a quarter of a day, and produced in this way the most exact calendar in the world in their time.

In our own calendaric system, the annual one-quarter of a day is adjusted every four years through the observance of a Leap Year, or a year consisting of 366 days.

In order to demonstrate the accuracy of the Mayan calendar, below is the exact comparison between the Julian, Gregorian, modern scientific, and Mayan calendars:

Julian	365.2500 days
Gregorian	365.2425 days
scientific	365.2422 days
Mayan	365.2420 days

As one can see, the Mayan calendar was inaccurate (by current standards) by only two-ten thousandths of a day! This is an even more remarkable feat when consideration is given to the fact that our scientific calendar, which was recently discovered with the help of modern equipment, contains data which was already known by a Mayan congress of learned astronomers as early as the year 682 A. D.

(The Mayan congress which is mentioned above occurred in the ceremonial center of Copán, in Honduras, which has always been known for its scientific achievements. The meeting served as an opportunity for the Mayan scientists to unify their diverse astronomical knowledge, including, among other things, the discovery of the length of the solar year.

Perhaps the reader would like to know how knowledge of this congress exists when there is no historical basis to use in its certification; J. Eric S. Thompson answers this query in his book **The Rise and Fall of the Mayan Civilization,** saying that on one of the sides of the altars in Copán are reliefs which show sixteen people, all facing the date which is listed above (682 A. D.); these are supposed to represent the Maya scientists who took part in the date-finding discussion. Twenty years later, or in 702 A. D., another altar was dedicated which commemorated the 20th anniversary of the original date computation. On this second altar are carved twenty persons with their faces turned toward the date. Most of these people are depicted as wearing animal masks, a custom which was very common among the Maya, especially

TABLE II

FIRST YEAR OF THE CALENDAR ROUND (THE YEAR 1-IK)

Names of the Months

Names of the Days	POP	UO	ZIP	ZOTZ	TZEC	XUL	YAXKIN	MOL	CHEN	YAX	ZAC	KEH	MAC	KANKIN	MUAN	PAX	KAYAB	CUMHU	UAYEB	Posiciones en el mes
IK	1	8	2	9	3	10	4	11	5	12	6	13	7	1	8	2	9	3	10	0
AKBAL	2	9	3	10	4	11	5	12	6	13	7	1	8	2	9	3	10	4	11	1
KAN	3	10	4	11	5	12	6	13	7	1	8	2	9	3	10	4	11	5	12	2
CHICCHAN	4	11	5	12	6	13	7	1	8	2	9	3	10	4	11	5	12	6	13	3
KIMI	5	12	6	13	7	1	8	2	9	3	10	4	11	5	12	6	13	7	1	4
MANIK	6	13	7	1	8	2	9	3	10	4	11	5	12	6	13	7	1	8		5
LAMAT	7	1	8	2	9	3	10	4	11	5	12	6	13	7	1	8	2	9		6
MULUC	8	2	9	3	10	4	11	5	12	6	13	7	1	8	2	9	3	10		7
OC	9	3	10	4	11	5	12	6	13	7	1	8	2	9	3	10	4	11		8
CHUEN	10	4	11	5	12	6	13	7	1	8	2	9	3	10	4	11	5	12		9
EB	11	5	12	6	13	7	1	8	2	9	3	10	4	11	5	12	6	13		10
BEN	12	6	13	7	1	8	2	9	3	10	4	11	5	12	6	13	7	1		11
IX o HIX	13	7	1	8	2	9	3	10	4	11	5	12	6	13	7	1	8	2		12
MEN	1	8	2	9	3	10	4	11	5	12	6	13	7	1	8	2	9	3		13
KIB	2	9	3	10	4	11	5	12	6	13	7	1	8	2	9	3	10	4		14
CABAN	3	10	4	11	5	12	6	13	7	1	8	2	9	3	10	4	11	5		15
EZNAB	4	11	5	12	6	13	7	1	8	2	9	3	10	4	11	5	12	6		16
CAUAC	5	12	6	13	7	1	8	2	9	3	10	4	11	5	12	6	13	7		17
AHAU	6	13	7	1	8	2	9	3	10	4	11	5	12	6	13	7	1	8		18
IMIX	7	1	8	2	9	3	10	4	11	5	12	6	13	7	1	8	2	9		19

The first day of the year is 1 IK, 0 Pop and the last day is 1 Kimi, 4 Uayeb. The last day of the month Pop is 7 Imix, 19 Pop and the last day of the month Cumhú is 9 Imix, 19 Cumhú.

The above table is taken from the book **Apuntaciones Sobre Mesoamérica** by Prof. Antonio Canto López.

during their religious ceremonies, during times of war, or at times when they were celebrating some important event. [3]   It is believed that each member of this "academy of sciences" came from a different place in the Maya lowlands.

With the discovery of the 365-day year, the Maya were confronted with a new problem: How could they use this calendar without displacing the religious calendar which had been the crux of their existence? Ultimately, they decided to add five 20-day months, and one five-day month, to the 260-day Tzolkin. In this way they developed a calendar consisting of eighteen 20-day months (or 360 days in total), and one month consisting of five days.

The Maya counted elapsed time in their dating system; hence, the first day in the Mayan calendar was numbered "zero", since the day began at midnight, and was completed at midnight twenty-four hours later. This is actually quite logical, since one cannot count a complete day when it has not yet ended.

Table 2 shows the Calendar Round.   In the first vertical column to the left (column one), the twenty day names are listed, beginning with "Ik" and ending with "Imix". At the top of the second column (counting from left to right) is the name of the first month, "Pop" The third column represents the month "Uo", the fourth "Zip", and so on throughout the year, ending with the 5-day month, which is called "Uayeb". The names of these months never change position or order in the Round. The last vertical column, inmediately after Uayeb, lists the numbers 0 through 19, which represent the real dates of each of the months; like the names of the months, the order of these numbers never change. The numbers 1 through 13 are used to number the various months, beginning in the "Pop" column with number 1, and repeating (in order) series of thirteen (always numbering the columns from top to bottom) until all of the months have been completely numbered, ending with the number 1 in the five-day month of Uayeb, in this table. [4]

The groups of thirteen numerals fall into different positions within the various months because of their staggered arrangement; for this reason they are thought of as markers of the position of the number/name within the appropriate month and year, rather than as actual dates.

3) .— Thompson J. Eric, Op. Cit.; page 91 — 93.
4) .— Canto López A., Op. Cit.; page 156.

A date is read on the Calendar Round in the following manner; from Table 2, we will select as an example the last day of the month Imix, which corresponds to the number 7 in the first vertical row in the month Pop. In order to find the date of the month, the horizontal line corresponding to Imix is followed, starting at the number 7, until the last vertical date column (which is numbered 0—19) is reached. In this example, the corresponding number is 19. Thus, this complete date reads 7 Imix, 19 Pop.

Another example follows so that the reader might better understand how a date is read on the Calendar Round. Using Table 2 again, find the day Lamat. Follow the corresponding line horizontally until you reach the 8th column. The number arrived at is 4 in the vertical column of the month Mol. Continue horizontally to the last column; the number arrived at is 6. Therefore, this date is read 4 Lamat, 6 Mol.

Because the last Mayan month only has five days, the year's number/name had to be changed when the new year began. Since the year represented in Table 2 ends in 1 Kimi (see Table), the next year will begin with the day 2 Manik, because this is the day which follows 1 Kimi. Therefore 2 Manik serves as the initiator of the new year, which was as a result, also named "2 Manik". The year 2 Manik ends on the day 1 Chuen, 4 Uayeb; hence, the next year begins with the following day, or 3 Eb, 0 Pop, and ends on 3 Kib, 4 Uayeb. The following year begins on the date 4 Caban, 0 Pop and ends on 4 Imix, 4 Uayeb; the next year will begin once again with the month Ik, but this time with the number 5, or 5 Ik, 0 Pop, and so on.

As can be seen in the examples which are cited above, the days that begin the first four years in Table 2 are Ik, Manik, Eb, and Caban (they are marked with a dash in Table 2 for easy identification). These four days are called "year bearers", because these days begin the years in a successive and orderly way; each year is then named after the day on which it begins plus its corresponding number. (5)

According to the authorities, these year bearers underwent four changes, for reasons that are not entirely known. At the time of the arrival of the Spaniards, the year bearers Kan, Muluk, Ix, and Cauac were used.

"Calendar Round" is the term used to identify this calen-

5). — Ibid. page 157.

dar; the Mayan term is unknown. Due to its unique arrangement, a date on this calendar is repeated only once every 52 years; a person who lived less than 52 years never saw the same date twice.

Professor D. Antonio Canto López developed a cylinder that facilitates the rapid and accurate resolution of many problems of Mayan chronology. Among these problems are: 1) finding the year bearer that corresponds to any date of the Calendar Round, 2) knowing the name of the day that corresponds to any of the 365 positions of a determined year in the cycle, 3) determining the date which ends the Calendar Round, the date of an Initial Series or Starting Sequence, and 4) establishing a Calendar Round date in the Long Count. Canto López, who was an authority in Mayan chronology, called the Calendar Round the "Short Count", while other chronologists use this name for the abbreviated dating system which was in use at the time of the arrival of the Spaniards. Canto López called this latter calendar the "Middle Count" because of the fact that its prescribed cycle of 13 Katuns, each of 19.71 years, amounts to a total of 256.25 years, while a cycle of the Calendar Round has a duration of only 52 years (a markedly shorter period than Canto López' "Middle Count"). This explains his reasoning in calling the shorter cycle (Calendar Round) the "Short Count". Nevertheless, in this work, we will continue using the standardized terms to avoid confusion.

d). **The Long Count**

The name "Long Count" is used to designate the third calendar of the Maya. Because its original name is also unknown, this name was applied to it by Alfred Maudslay in order to identify it in a standardized manner.

Many patient scientists have made contributions toward the understanding of the mechanics of this complicated chronological system which the ancient Maya used with such amazing precision. In 1887, the German archaeologist Hans Forstemann became the first modern investigator to unravel the details of the Long Count system through the analysis of the Codices. In 1890, the North American J. F. Goodman deciphered the time computations of stelae, using as a base for his investigations, the

100

reproductions made by Maudslay; Goodman came to the same conclusions as Forstemann. [6]

It is quite possible that this complicated system was used solely by the astronomer/priests to register important dates, happenings, and notable events in their books and on their stelae; the common people continued to use the "haab" or Calendar Round.

Chronologists say that the Maya used the day as the basic temporal unit of the Long Count, not the year.

The Maya word for "day" was "kin", which meant "sun" or "priest". They called their month "uinal", while the 360-day year was called "tun" The period of twenty tuns was designated as "katún", and the period of twenty katuns was called "baktun". Twenty baktuns was labelled "pictun", and the period of twenty pictuns was called "calabtun". The period of twenty calabtuns was denoted by the term "kinchiltun" and, finally, twenty kinchiltuns was called "alautun". The time periods most often used in Mayan dating were the katuns and baktuns, since the others encompassed longer periods of time than were not necessary for the dates.

To make these time periods more easily understood, the following chart gives the equivalent of each period in days. (As was mentioned previously , the Maya used the day as the primary unite for their computations in the Long Count.)

KIN	1 day
UINAL	20 days or kins
TUN	360 days
KATUN	20 tuns, or 7,200 days
BAKTUN	20 katuns, or 144,000 days
PICTUN	20 baktuns, or 2,880,000 days
CALABTUN	20 pictuns, or 57,600,000 days
KINCHILTUN	20 calabtuns, or 1,152,000,000 days
ALAUTUN	20 kinchiltuns, or 23,040,000,000 days

In the section of this work which deals with Mayan numerology, the function of the vigesimal system is clearly demonstrated. However, it is necessary to note that in this dating system of the Maya, there is one slight variation: in order to arrive at a period of 360 days (Tun), the Maya multiplied the Uinal (20 days) by 18 instead of by 20. The rest of the periods use 20 as their multiplier.

6).— Morley, S. G., Op. Cit. (1975 Edition); page 258.

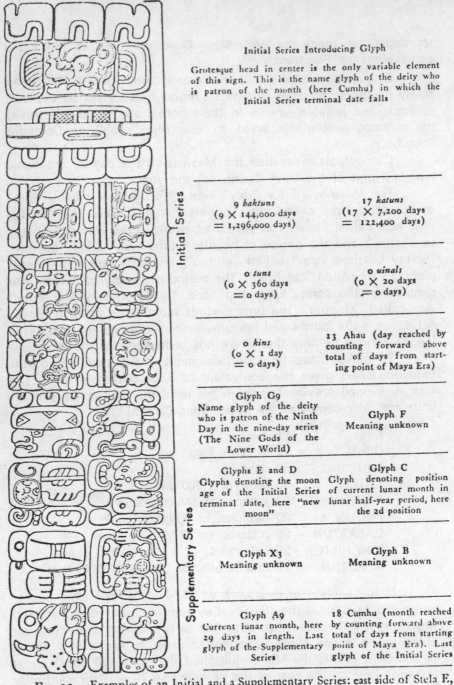

Initial Series Introducing Glyph

Grotesque head in center is the only variable element of this sign. This is the name glyph of the deity who is patron of the month (here Cumhu) in which the Initial Series terminal date falls

9 *baktuns* (9 × 144,000 days = 1,296,000 days)	17 *katuns* (17 × 7,200 days = 122,400 days)
0 *tuns* (0 × 360 days = 0 days)	0 *uinals* (0 × 20 days = 0 days)
0 *kins* (0 × 1 day = 0 days)	13 Ahau (day reached by counting forward above total of days from starting point of Maya Era)
Glyph G9 Name glyph of the deity who is patron of the Ninth Day in the nine-day series (The Nine Gods of the Lower World)	**Glyph F** Meaning unknown
Glyphs E and D Glyphs denoting the moon age of the Initial Series terminal date, here "new moon"	**Glyph C** Glyph denoting position of current lunar month in lunar half-year period, here the 2d position
Glyph X3 Meaning unknown	**Glyph B** Meaning unknown
Glyph A9 Current lunar month, here 29 days in length. Last glyph of the Supplementary Series	**18 Cumhu** (month reached by counting forward above total of days from starting point of Maya Era). Last glyph of the Initial Series

Initial Series / **Supplementary Series**

FIG. 25.—Examples of an Initial and a Supplementary Series: east side of Stela E, Quirigua.

From The Book "The Ancient Mayans" of Sylvanus G. Morley

Sometimes, as many as three sequences or series can be seen in one Long Count date. The first of the three is the "Initial Series" or beginning sequence, which registers the computation of the number of days which have elapsed since the beginning of the Maya Era up to the current date. This sequence consists of ten glyphs which appear in the following order: starting at the top, and reading the double rows from left to right, is the introductory glyph, which is more than twice as big as the others. In the center of this is another glyph, of an average size, which represents the patron deity of the month which ends the date of the Initial Series. This smaller glyph can have as many as nineteen different forms. Moving downward, the first glyph of the top left corresponds to the baktuns, and the first on the top right to the katuns. The next double row of glyphs correspond to the tuns (on the left) and the uinals or months (to the right). Below this row, the next glyph (on the left) pertains to the remaining days in the month, and the glyph to its right represents the day on which the date is registered. Immediately below these is a glyph of one of the gods of the nine levels of the underworld (this will be discussed in more detail in the chapter on religion), and to the right of this is the last glyph, which has yet to be identified. [7]

The "Supplementary Series" follows the Initial Series; it refers to the lunar calendar and consists of six glyphs. Some of the glyphs are preceded by their respective numbers, as is the case in the Initial Series.

The third possible sequence of the Long Count is the "Secondary Count", which will be discussed later.

In order to better understand how the Long Count works, an example is included of one of the most well-known Long Count date carvings; that of Stele E, which is found in Quiriguá, Guatemala. This stele shows 9 baktuns, 17 katuns, 0 tuns, 0 uinals, and 0 kins.   The computation of this stele, converting is into our calendaric system, is as follows:

		In Days
9 baktuns (or periods of 144,000 days)		
9 x 144,000 .... =		1,296,000 days
17 katuns (or periods of 7,200 days)		
17 x 7,200 .... =		122,400 days
0 tuns (360 days) .... =		0 days
0 uinals (20 days) .... =		0 days
0 kins (one day) .... =		0 days
	TOTAL (in days) =	1,418,400 days

7) .— Ibid, page 258.

The last day of this glyph corresponds to the position of 13 Ahua, 18 Cumhú on the Calendar Round. [8]

Before finishing the conversion of this date to our calendar, it is important to note that one of the more serious problems chronologists were faced with when working with the Long Count was the correlation between the Mayan calendar and the European calendar. After long investigations, Goodman concluded that the Mayan Era began in the year 3113 B. C. Juan Martínez Hernández, a Yucatecan researcher, working independently, arrived at a correlation very near Goodman's; it differed by only one day. The archaeologist, J. Eric S. Thompson, who also worked separately, arrived at a date that was within two days of Hernández' conclusions. Because these three researchers arrived at almost the same conclusion, this calendaric correlation has been named the "Goodman-Martínez Hernández-Thompson "Correlation".

Herbert J. Spinden, who also studied this correlation, arrived at a date that differed from that of Goodman-Martínez Hernández-Thompson by 260 years. According to Spinden, the Mayan Era began in 3373 B. C.

Other investigators, one of whom was Escalona Ramos, have done studies and arrived at other correlations between the Mayan and the European dating systems, but none of these have been given much attention.

Since both dates (3113 and 3373 B. C.) are extremely remote, it has been concluded that they do not refer to an actual historical date; the Maya of that time would have had neither writing nor numerology. This date probably marked the origin of the Mayan people or the origin of some important deity.

Once the starting point of the Mayan Era is known, it is easy to convert an Initial Series date to our own calendar. In the case of Stele E of Quiriguá, it has just been demonstrated that it marks a period of 1,418,400 days, which, when divided by 365.2425 (the duration of a year according to the Gregorian calendar), results in the quotient of 3,883.45 years. If the Goodman-Martínez Hernández-Thompson correlation is employed, 3113 (the date of the beginning of the Mayan Era) is subtracted from 3,883.45 years, and we calculate the date glyph to the year 770.45 A. D. Using the Spinden correlation, the glyph would be calculated to represent the year 510.45 A. D.

8) .— Ibid, page 259.

It could be possible that a date of the Initial Series would not total more than 3113 or 3373 years; in this case, the order of the factors is inverted and the number of years on the date glyph is subtracted from either of the two quantities (according to whichever correlation is selected, Goodman-Martínez Hernández-Thompson or Spinden); the difference will indicate the date of the event commemorated in years before Christ.

Secondary Count

Some chronologists suggest that the Maya may have used the Secondary Count (mentioned previously to be a sequence in the Long Count), to adjust the extra fraction of nearly a quarter of a day of each year, in order to compute a date as accurately as possible. However, careful analysis of this question suggests that this is not possible, because the Initial Series, which is the first section of the Long Count, is computed in days, and not in years. In the Initial Series, the Maya marked time as it elapsed, noting the passage of groups of twenty days (uinals), then groups of 360 days (tuns), etc., a system which automatically included the extra one-quarter of a day of each year, with the appearance of an extra day every four years. Our calendaric system is not as automatic. Because of the fact that we use the year as a unit (each year containing 365.2500 days in accordance with the Julian Calendar or 365.2425 in accordance with the Gregorian Calendar), rather than the day, we must account for these extra "quarter-days" by subtracting a full day from every four years ("Leap Year").

This explains why the 360 day tun, which is used in the Initial Series, included neither need for adjustment nor errors. The Maya were not affected in any way by the manner in which their days were grouped; the only thing they were interested in was how many days had elapsed from the beginning of their chronology until the then current date.

People who do not thoroughly analyze the above mentioned problem, easily misunderstand the system; many people ask how it was possible that the Long Count was the most exact calendar of the world at that time since it employed 360-day tuns as years. With the above explanation, these people can now better understand the reason why.

Other experts suggest that the Secondary Count was used when two dates were inscribed on the same stele. They suggest that the Maya made use of part of the Initial Series to begin the date, and that they completed it with the Secondary Count. In order for the reader to understand this point, the following example has been provided: suppose that we date a monument with the year 1950, and in 20 years, we wanted to write on this same monument the year 1970. We might use the first two numbers of the first date (19) and below or to the side we might add the number 70. These experts say that the Maya used this abbreviation because the writing of a date required the use of many numbers and glyphs, and repeating them was a very laborious and involved process.

This conclusion is not satisfactory, however, because the stelae were erected to mark the end of a 20, 10, or 5-year period (as these same experts have noted), and it is illogical to think that they would note the end of two periods on the same monument, when each stele was constructed to commemorate only one period.

If the second sequence of the Long Count, the Supplementary Sequence, corresponds to the lunar calendar, is it not possible that the third sequence or the Secondary Count is related to the Venus calendar? We know that the Maya had very advanced knowledge of this planet and that they considered it very important; they not only knew the exact duration of its orbit, but also of its axial rotation.

It is also possible that the Maya used a system similar to our own for the commemoration of some important event which occurred in the past (such as the date of our independence, etc.): the first date on the monument represents the day, month, and year of the event, while the second date represents the day, month, and year of the commemoration.

Someday, perhaps, this question will be answered.

e). Period-ending Dates

Specialists calculate that by the middle of the Classic Florescent Period, the Long Count was no longer used, perhaps because the writing of a date involved far too much work. The priests, who controlled the knowledge of time dating, would have had to use so much time on one date glyph that they probably

106

opted to simplify the old process with a new system. This system was called "Dating of the End of Period", and it required only three glyphs. The first glyph could be the name of a katún or tun, the second corresponded to the glyph of the Tzolkin, and the third was the position which corresponded to the month.

This method, if used continuously, would indicate the date with exactitude for a period of 19,000 years. The Long Count, which was mentioned previously, would accurately determine the date for 374,440 years, with no date designation or symbol used more than once. Both methods are ample evidence of the admirable excellence of the Mayan chronological systems, as is noted by Morley in his writings.

f). The Short Count

At the end of their Post-Classic Period, the Maya made another, more radical abbreviation of the dating system. This new abridgement has been called the "Short Count", the "Katún Round", or, in Maya, "u kahlay katunob". (Profesor Canto López called it the "Middle Count", as was mentioned previously). Bishop Landa describes it with the name of "uazlazon katún"; however, Morley says that it was properly named "Uazaklón Katún", which he defines as "the war" or "return of the katuns".

Fortunately, Bishop Landa described the function of this Round (although in limited detail), so that today we have an understanding of the way in which it works. He probably copied the Round from the Maya, sketching it without the use of a compass, which makes its form appear to be irregular. Below is a copy of Landa's drawing: for easier understanding, Roman numerals have been substituted for Arabic numerals. The Mayan words for the numbers, followed by the name Ahau, are written on the inside of the Round.

As one can see by this drawing, the Round is divided into thirteen parts, each of which has the symbol of the day Ahau with its respective number indicated in it. Each section represents a period of a katún, or twenty tuns (each tun being 360 days). The experts, in describing the Short Count or the Katún Round, point out that these katuns are not the same as twenty of our years, but were rather of only 19.71 years each. The Katún is composed of twenty 360-day tuns, as compared to our year of 365.25 days, which leaves a difference of 5.25 days per year, or 105 days in a

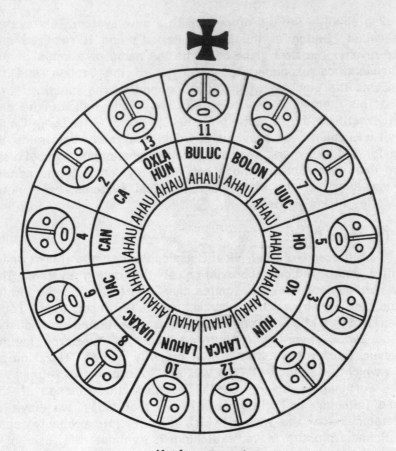

Katúns - Round.

katún; in short, since the Round has 13 katuns of 19.71 years each, the duration of a Round or cycle is 256 1/4 years (13 x 19.71 = 256.23), after which another period of equivalent duration or Katún, begins.

Morley states that the specific katún from which this particular round is counted, is believed to have been the katún of 8 Ahau. The repetition of the sequence began anew after each katún 8 Ahau had been completed.

The Katún Round functioned in a counterclockwise fashion. The reader will note that beginning with the number 2, and counting in a counterclockwise direction, are the even numbers

108

up to 12 (2, 4, 6, 8, 10, and 12), followed by the odd numbers (1, 3, 5, 7, 9, 11, and 13) with the number 13 completing the circle.

Landa says the following with respect to the cross which is seen above the Round in the drawing: "The system that they had for counting their things and making their prophesies with this count was that they had in their temples two idols dedicated to two of these characters (from the Katún Round). To the first (of these idols) which related to the section of the circle above which is the cross, they gave adoration and services and sacrifices in order to cure the plagues of the twenty years (for the first ten years) and in the ten (years) that remained of the first twenty they did nothing but burn incense and pay reverence. (to the other).

"Vervi gratia: the Indians say that when the Spanish arrived in the city of Mérida, in the Year of Our Lord 1541, that it was exactly the first year of Buluk-Ahau, which is the house on which is the cross (here he refers to the cross above the little box), and that they arrived also in the month of Pop, which is the first month of the year. If the Spanish hadn't arrived, they (the Maya) would have continued adoring the idol Buluk-Ahau until the year 51 (1551), which is ten years...[9] (Author's notes of explanation in parentheses.)

According to Landa's description, the cross was placed on the Katún Round in order to mark two events; the arrival of the Spaniards and the first year of the Buluk-Ahau Era ("Buluk" means "eleven", that being the position where the cross is located).

The inconvenience encountered with this system of dating lies in the fact that it does not indicate which period of 256.25 years it represents; it is impossible to determine whether an event belongs to the first period when the Maya started to use this system, the second period, etc. Complicating this situation even further is the fact that it is not known exactly when the Maya began to use this system; it has only been suggested that its use began at the end of the Post-Classic Period. This is the reason why investigations into the Katún Round have been discouraging. A date in this system may have actually been shortened in much the same way that we abbreviate the date January 5, 1977 to read 1—5—77. After hundreds of years had passed, one

9).— de Landa, Bishop Diego, **Relación de las Cosas de Yucatán**, Editorial Porrúa, S. A., México City, 1959 (Eigth Edition); page 104.

would not be able to determine to which century the notation corresponded: 1977, 1577, 877, etc.

To continue with the analysis of Landa's descriptions (since they are the best source of information that investigators have), one can conclude that the Katún Round did not actually function as a calendar, since it only accurately marked the end of a period of 13 katuns, which only ended on Ahau days. It seems that the Katún Round did not indicate any other event aside from those which occurred on this day. In this regard, the Bishop Landa says: "Not only did the Indians count the years and months, as has been previously mentioned, but they also had a certain way of counting time and (of grouping) their things in ages of twenty in (every) twenty years, counting thirteen groups of twenty with one of the 20 letters of the days called "Ahau" without order, (6 even numbers from 2 to 12, and 7 odd numbers, 1 to 13 as appear in the circle...". (10)

In light of this information provided by Landa, it can be deduced that the true calendar in use at the time of the arrival of the Spaniards was the Calendar Round, and not the Katún Round. The Katún Round only served to mark the passage of time in cycles. Indisputable proof of this fact is found in Landa's writings, in which he describes a complete year of the Calendar Round with its eighteen 20-day months, and with the respective names marked with groups of thirteen (as was previously described). Landa makes no mention of the last month of only five days (Uayeb) but instead writes the numbers 1 thorough 5, enclosing each number with a square instead of using the corresponding glyphs. Perhaps he did this because these five days were considered to be ill-fated days, on which the Maya thought that their gods were not protecting them. Landa also inserted the names of the months of the Julian Calendar between the columns of the series of thirteen in order to compare both systems. He did not include in his version of the year of the Calendar Round the dates from 0 to 19. The Calendar Round was continously in use from the time of its invention prior to the Christian Era. The Long Count and the Dating of the End of Period were used only by the priests, who were also the scientists. The common people could not understand these dating systems because of their complexity, and because of the fact that they lacked the priests' education.

10) .— Ibid, page 103.

Thanks to the preceding analysis, we now understand why all of the dates in the indigenous chronicles which cite important events and written in the Short Count always corresponded to the day Ahau. We cannot explain how the Maya noted dates of events that did not correspond to the day Ahau.

CHAPTER SEVEN

ARCHITECTURE

a). **Generalizations**   f). **The Puuc Style**
b). **Architectural Styles**   g). **The Chichén Itzá Style**
c). **The Petén Style**   h). **The Maya-Toltec Style**
d). **The Río Bec Style**   i). **The Serpent in Meso-American**
e). **The Chenes Style**   **Cultures**

a). Generalizations

Their architecture is a material proof of the great intellectual advancement of the ancient Mayas.

"Impossible!", one may say as he looks at the imposing and majestic structures strewn throughout the vast territory; true works of art, of high aesthetic quality and adorned with fabulous relief carvings.

Even more astounding is the fact that these people lacked metal tools, pack animals, and the wheel.

The tools used by the ancient Maya, and other Meso-Americans to create these great works were made of hard stones such as jade, jadeite, basalt, diorite, serpentine, and flint, examples of which can be seen in the Archaeological Museum in Mérida, and other museums, both in México and abroad.

Surely the creators of these works were great engineers and architects, since common people with a low level of education could never have produced them.

In order to draw a parabola or a hyperbola, for example, it is necessary to make various sketches of each, with the objective of finding the points of support, and to sketch each curve section by section; in order to do this, education and intelligence are required. The Maya drew lines more complicated than these, a fact which reveals their good command of geometry.

113

Mayan Stone Chisels

We have mentioned that the ancient Maya invented a paper similar to ours. On this paper they probably drew the plans and elevations of the buildings to be constructed, according to need, or to the desires of Mayan officials. These projects would have been presented for the consideration of these officials for their approval, modification, or rejection of construction.

At this point, a question comes to mind: Where did the Maya establish their educational centers? As a simple, logical deduction, this author believes that at first, classes were held in the open, under the shade of trees; later, large structures of straw or palms were used, and still later, stone edifices.

During that early time, perhaps only the descendants of the nobility and the priesthood were privileged enough to learn the arts and sciences, and in each profession only a few selected participants were allowed to enroll. Owing to the economics of the time, learning a profession may have consisted of one, two, or three related subjects, such that the student finished his work in a short time as an expert in his field, at the expense of other subjects. In other words, the Maya were true specialists and nothing more. It is possible that the most important educational centers were located in specific places according to discipline or category.

As has been noted, Copán, Honduras, was a scientific center of the first order, where the learned men came to discuss academic problems. I believe that in the northern part of the Yucatán Península, Uxmal (the absolutely finest center in terms of pure magnificence of architecture) served as the most important educational center, and that the so-called "Nunnery Quadrangle" was the equivalent of our modern universities. To this center would have come the most distinguished students, the children of the nobility in that district.

Photo No. 14. The Nunnery Quadrangle, Uxmal. Photo by the author.

Although the chambers that make up the Nunnery Quadrangle are small, it is possible that between 12 to 15 students occupied each. Perhaps a different subject or grade was taught in each side.

During the time that these chambers were used as classrooms, they may have been whitewashed to brighten them. In some sections, where these rooms are doubled, the furthest room was also the darkest, and was probably used to store instructional materials and equipment. Perhaps they were also used by the teacher/priest as secluded spots for meditation.

Without doubt, the architectural beginnings owe much to their most important material, which was lime. Without this substance, it would have been impossible to make masonry constructions in the same way as the Maya did.

The greater part of the Mayan territory consists of calcified rock of differing grades and consistencies. Some grades are so hard that carved in cylindrical shape, and hung by a cord, they emit a metal sound when struck, much like that of a bell, as can be verified in the cones found along the base of the "Adoratorio de Venus" Platform at Chichén Itzá. They have been moved near the office at the site to protect them from thoughtless people who have broken some of them in the past. As these cones are of differing size, they produce different tones when struck. Other calcified rocks are of a medium grade, and others are very soft. Probably the medium density rocks are the most appropriate for the fabrication of lime.

Perhaps after accidently burning these rocks for long hours the Maya discovered that the rocks changed into lime, the basic ingredient in the manufacture of mortar. The mortar of the ancient Maya was a mixture of one part lime and three parts white earth, called "sascab" or "sahcab" excavated from some places. To this mixture they added water, and stirred resulting mixture until it attained the desired consistency.

Once mortar was discovered, crude platforms and walls were built, over which were built roofs of straw thatch or palms.

The architecture evolved until the classic Mayan arch was invented. The arch has been given many names: Mayan arch, angular roof, corbel arch, and false arch are all used. This latter name is used because the uppermost which closes the sides functioned as a cap, not as a key, as it does in the Roman arch. The Maya would use slabs and mortar in forming one half arch on one side, supporting it by the weight of the rock and mortar, and then form the other half arch on the other side in the same manner. Once this structure had dried, the cap would then be put in place.

Later, this system was perfected by the use of triangular rocks, in the shape of the high heel of a woman's shoe, as can be seen in the following drawing:

It is not known when lime was first discovered by the Maya, but the discovery must have occurred sometime just before the Christian Era. The present day Maya produce their lime in much the same way as did their ancestors: they cut grown trees, with thick trunks and limbs, so that they will burn for a long time, and carefully pile them in a circular manner, in a diameter directly related to the amount of lime which they wish to make. This is done working from the center outward, leaving spaces between the trunks which are later filled with finer pieces of wood. The quantity of wood generally comprises twice the amount of rock which is to be changed into lime. The rocks are broken into pieces the size of large oranges, and placed in circular form on the wood. A canal is left in the center, in which dry leaves and shavings are placed; these shavings are used as tinder to light the "oven", which burns from the center outward, and from the bottom to the top. This process takes about thirty-six hours. Photos 15 and 16.

Photo 15. Limekiln before it is burned. Photo taken from the book The Mayan Civilization by Sylvanus G. Morley, Plate 62.

Those whose profession it is to make lime are experts, and choose windless nights to fire up the "ovens". These ovens are made in places of sparse vegetation to keep the flames on the rocks.

When the wood has been completely burned, water is thrown upon the rocks which are not well-burned, to assist them in expanding, and thus, in breaking down into lime. This method

Photo 16. Limerkiln after it is burned. Photo taken from the book The Mayan Civilization by Sylvanus G. Morley. Plate 62, the new Spanish edition.

of producing lime is becoming less and less popular, due to the existence of more modern procedures.

It is thought that the corbel or false arch had its beginnings in Uaxactún, Guatemala, one of the most ancient Mayan centers, at approximately the beginning of the Classic Period, or around the year 278 A. D. The technique for constructing the arch was eventually extended to other areas.

b). Architectural Styles

The architectural styles of the Maya are not uniform, although they are founded on the same basic premises. One can see that in each region, the architects tried to highlight their own creations. The experts have tried to classify and name each style; hence, we have the Petén, Río Bec, Chenes, Puuc, Chichén Itzá, and Maya-Toltec styles of architecture. These names come from the areas in which the styles were developed.

c). The Petén Style

The majority of the authors of books on archaeology do not clearly define the Petén Style. Many do so in vague terms, while others simply mention it without description.

The Petén Style is found principally in Guatemala, especially in Tikal, where enormous pyramids are found; Temple V is fifty-seven meters high, while Tmple IV is sixty-nine meters in height. These pyramids are very steep, and consist of superimposed, successively smaller platforms. On the last of these platforms, the Maya built ornamental chambers, topped with enormous combs which are covered with relief work, and in some places nearly twice as high as the chambers themselves. The builders would make the front platforms larger than the ones on the other three sides. Photo 17

Photo No. 17. Temple of Tikal, Guatemala, the Petén Style. Photo courtesy of Professor Robert Turnbull

Some authors affirm that in Oxkintok, a ceremonial center near the village of Maxcanú, Yucatán, there are constructions similar to those at Uaxactún. The glyphs in some of the buildings at Oxkintok are very similar to those used in ancient Petén. In Oxkintok, there was also found the most ancient date in the Northern Yucatán Península: 475 A. D. [1]   This tells us that Oxkintok preceded Chichén Itzá.

1).— Canto López A., Op. Cit.; page 171.

In the Classical Florescent Period, between 625 and 800 A. D., the Mayas built an additional decoration on the roofs of some of their buildings. This has been called a "false facade" when it rests on the front wall of a building, and "roof comb" when it rests on the rear. It seems that these additions served an aesthetic function; that of overcoming a noticeable difference in height between two neighboring buildings a difference which could effect an imbalance in the exterior appearance of the two buildings. Some say that the windows and hollows were used to relieve the force of the wind in times of storm, to diminish some of the weight, and improve the appearance of the buildings. Examples of combs can be seen in Uxmal, in the "Dove House", and in Kabah, in the buildings called "Codzpop" and "Palacio". Photos 18 and 19 The "Casa Colorada" (Red House) at Chichén Itzá has a false facade and comb together.

This additional ornamentation was used in Guatemala, especially in Tikal, so that the buildings might be more impressive.

Photo No. 18. The roofcomb on the Palace at Kabah. Photo by the author.

Photo No. 19. The roofcomb on the House of the Doves, Uxmal. Photo by the author.

d). The Río Bec Style

This style, along with the Petén, belongs to the Classic Period, and is found near the borders of the states of Campeche and Quintana Roo. It is distinguished from the others by its tall towers, on which were constructed the facades of simulated houses. The doors of these houses are decorated to resemble the mouths of enormous monsters, which may represent the God of Rain. Upon these simulated homes are situated richly ornamented combs, and in front of the towers were built stairs which are so narrow that they are impossible to climb. The entire scene, when viewed from a distance, gives the appearance of pyramids, with temples in the upper portion. An example of this style can be seen in Xpuhil, Campeche. Unfortunately, this edifice, which was surely the pride of the architects of the time, is nearly impossible to restore because of its nearly complete destruction, and because of the fact that many of its stones are broken or missing.

e). The Chenes Style

This style is easily distinguished from the others because it is heavy with ornamentation; no part of its facade is without relief work, and generally, its entrances represent the enormous mouths of monsters. This style is common in the state of Campeche and in the western part of Quintana Roo. It is also found in the fourth superstructure of the Temple of the Magician at Uxmal, and in the east facade of the Nunnery at Chichén Itzá. Photo 20.

Photo No. 20. The East Side of the Nunnery. Chichén Itzá. Photo by the author.

f). The Puuc Style

The only hills in the Yucatán are found in the southern part of the state, and are called the "Sierra Baja" or "Low Mountains". In the Maya language, they are called "Puuc", and archaeologists have given this same name to the architectural style created in this region.

This style is distinct in that the reliefs that adorn the facades of the buildings start from the central cornice, situated

122

on the level of the doors, and continue until they reach the upper cornice. The reliefs are made of small frames which simulate lattice work, Greek lines, masks of the God of Rain, serpent motifs, etc., and were nearly always covered with stucco. This style is found at Uxmal, Kabah, Sayil, Labná, Xlapak, Chacmultún, and other places. (Photo 21)

Photo No. 21. Corbelled arch at Labná, Yucatán. Puuc Style architecture. Photo by the author.

g) . The Chichén Itzá Style

Archaeologists use this name for some of the architecture of the buildings in the Central Group at Chichén Itzá, but in reality, these buildings belong to the Puuc and Chenes styles. Archaeologists say that while the Chichén Itzá is similar to each of these styles, the Chichén Itzá Style has certain characteristics which single it out; these differences have never been satisfactorily demonstrated. These buildings are the "Church", and the buildings on the east side of the Nunnery group; the former corresponds to the Puuc, and the latter to the Chenes. It is convenient to add to these classifications the Northern Group at Chichén Itzá, which is of the Maya-Toltec Style.

h). The Maya-Toltec Style

This architecture is easily recognized by the angle or inclination at the base of the structures, by the colonnades, and by the ball courts, which resemble those of the cultures on the high plains of México. In the relief decoration of this style one sees plumed serpents, jaguars walking one behind the other, eagles devouring hearts, skulls carved in relief, and the figures of reclining idols called Chacmools, (Photo 22) in which the idols are supporting altars, called "atlantes" or "Caryatids".

Photo No. 22. Chacmool. Temple of the Warriors. Chichén Itzá. Photo by the author.

Until now, the original name and the real use of these structures by the ancient Maya was unknown, because the Mayan culture had disintegrated about 100 years before the time of the arrival of the Spanish and Chichén Itzá, Uxmal, and other ceremonial centers had been abandoned for almost 300 years before this time. The natives lived in thatched huts with their civil and religious buildings (constructed of the same material) elevated on crude platforms as in the Formative Period.

124

Some of the names were given to the ancient structures by the Spaniards, and others by the archaeologists who were in charge of their restoration. Captain Francisco de Montejo el Adelantado and his companions were the ones who named "The Castle", the tallest pyramid at Chichén Itzá, when they arrived in 1527. The "Temple of the Warriors" was named by archaeologists from the Carnegie Institute in Washington, who restored it. Later, the name "Thousand Columns" was added. The "Adoratorio de Venus" platform received its name from the incomplete stars carved in relief on its four corners; these were interpreted as representations of the planet Venus. The name "Temple of the Jaguars" came from the carvings of these animals engraved on its four sides. In Uxmal, the "Nunnery" and the "Governors Palace" are said to have been named by the Franciscan priest Diego López Cogulludo when he visited the site after the conquest.

The situation was different at other sites. At Tikal, Guatemala, for example, the temples were classified by numbers. Hence, Temples number I, II, III, IV, etc.

Lamentably, the conquering Spaniards were dedicated primarily to the quest for gold and silver. Upon realizing that the few prizes they did find were ancient heirlooms which the Maya had inherited from their ancestors, and that the metal they contained had come from other places (as there wasn't any in the Yucatán), the Spaniards decided to settle, to work the land, and to raise animals brought from Spain, using the natives as slaves. They had little interest in the history of the Maya, and as a result lost the best opportunity to learn in detail the glorious past of these peoples.

i) . The Serpent in Meso-American Cultures

The snake, especially the rattlesnake, may be seen represented in great abundance in many Mayan areas, especially Chichén Itzá; some are carved in relief, while others are carved as entire bodies with enormous heads that weight nearly six tons. (Photo 23) They are also found painted on murals, in ceramics, in the codices, and on gold discs like those found in the "cenote", or sacred well, at Chichén Itzá. In several cases they are found with an open mouth, from which a human face emerges as if the snake was bringing man into the world. (Photo 24) Hence, the

Photo No. 23. Head of a serpent (weighing various tons) at the base of the Temple of Kukulcán. Photo by the author.

Photo No. 24. A head emerging from the mouth of a serpent. Temple of the Warriors. Photo by the author.

belief that the serpent is a symbol of life and fertility. Today's Maya confirm the fact that the land where rattlesnakes abound is the most fertile and gives the best harvests.

Many are the beliefs that persist among the natives. For example, the belief that if one puts a serpent's rattle inside a violin, guitar, or other musical instrument, the sound will be improved considerably. Another belief is that if one passes his hand over the snake's skin, he will easily learn manual skills.

The serpent was considered to be a sacred animal by the ancient natives, as it was in some ancient Asian cultures. In Meso-America, each culture represented it with their own stylizations; in the high interior plains it was primarily plumed. Since plumed serpents do not exist as such, it is believed that they were symbols representing the god Quetzalcoatl, a name which signifies "plumed serpent" or "Quetzal bird serpent" in the Nahuatl language. This name was also used as a title for priests and nobility.

The majority of investigators affirm that before the arrival of the Toltecs in the Yucatán (near the end of the Tenth Century A. D.), the serpents the Mayas used in their representations had scales, as can be seen in the balustrades of the "Caracol" or "The Observatory" at Chichén Itzá. However, upon the arrival of the Toltecs, immediate changes were made in the architecture, noticeably the use of plumes on the serpents.

These characteristics are seen principally at Chichén Itzá, and certain reflections can be seen in other sites, such as Uxmal, as well. This is not to say that the Toltecs were the creators of the architecture in the Yucatán, as some would suppose; the Toltec cultural influence came later than did the flowering of the Mayan culture. On the other hand, it is well known that among Meso-Americans, each culture had its own well-defined characteristics which identify its arts and sciences as products of the individual initiative and creativity of the members of that culture.

The learned writer and poet from the Yucatán, José Díaz Bolio, has done detailed and in-depth studies of the serpent, especially the rattlesnake, Ahau Can-Crotalus durissus durissus, which he says is typical of the Yucatán area and Central América. He states that Mayan art, like the Toltec, Aztec, and even the legendary Olmec, is based on the design of the serpent. In 1966, he also found that the Mayan geometry was based on the serpent.

He describes the "Canamayté-Cuadrivértice" of the serpent's skin, showing that using the four squares which form part of the design on the skin, one can draw, without a compass, the circle, the pentagon, the four-pronged cross of the moon and its phases, and in the center, the flower of lunar phases and the head of the spiral-solstitial. He also shows the way to draw, using the same four-sided vertex, the proportions of the human face, of the Maya profile, and of the human body, similar to the well-known drawings of Leonardo da Vinci. He also shows that the design of a pyramid, the dimensions of a straw hut, the false Mayan arch, the pyramid of nine bodies, and finally, the profile of the pyramid can all be drawn using this same pattern, as can be seen in the following drawings.

Crotalus durissus.

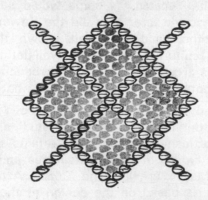

Courtesy of the
Yucatecan Researcher
José Díaz Bolio

The Four-Vertex Canamayte-diagram of proportions
in the Mayan rattlesnake

128

Hand-drawn circle,
without a compass.

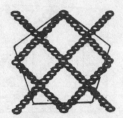

The pentagon, main form
in the Phythagorean Golden
Measure

The Moon's movements

A cosmogonic square at Uxmal
The 8 petals represent the
Moon's phases. The helicoidal
botton of the flower represents
the Sun's movements.

Proportion of a flower.

The human face.

The Mayan profile.

The human body.

A pyramid's plan

Courtesy of the
Yucatecan Researcher
José Díaz Bolio

129

Proportion of the pyramid.

The thatched-roof
hut-hosse.

Origin and proportion of the
Mayan vault. The Canamayté of
the rattlesnake provided the
proportions for architecture.

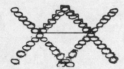

The profile of a pyramid.

Courtesy of the
Yucatecan Researcher
José Díaz Bolio

Díaz Bolio summarizes his theory: "We affirm, according to the Geo-Anthro Study of Rattlesnakes, which we created and published, that highly evolved cultures only existed where the durissus durissus rattler lived. Although there are other archaeological sites of importance in México outside of Central América and the Yucatán where there are no durissus durissus, there are none so highly evolved as were the Maya, inspite of the fact that there are some ten species of rattlesnake. In the Yucatán one only finds the durissus durissus rattler called Ahau Can (the royal serpent of the Maya)." [2]

Díaz Bolio has visited, on numerous occasions, almost all the archaeological zones in México and Central América on research trips in order to write his book **The Plumed Serpent; Pivot Point of Culture,** published in 1957, and consisting of 336 pages, an appendix, and numerous photographs and drawings. His conclusions have been deliberated pro and con, but his labors in research are worthy of the readers' time, inasmuch as they help clarify the mysteries of the ancient cultures.

2).— Díaz Bolio José, **Guía Instructiva a las Ruínas de Chichén Itzá,** México City, 1973; pages 8, 9 and 10.

CHAPTER EIGHT

SYSTEMS OF TRANSPORTATION

a) . **Highways**
b) . **Why didn't the Mayas use the wheel?**
c) . **Shipping**

a) . **Highways**

It has been suggested that almost all of the ceremonial centers in the Mayan country were inter-connected by good roads. A map of the Yucatán Península in the book **Sacbé de Los Mayas,** illustrated by the architect Luvel Lacoski, points out the routes that existed when the ancient Mayan culture was at its zenith. [1]

According to this map, the highway starts in Tulum on the Caribbean coast and goes to Cobá, from which one artery goes to Ekal and ends in Yaxuná. Another artery connects Cobá with Chichén Itzá, continuing on to Izamal then to Aké, which was also an important ceremonial center. From there it runs to T'hó or Ichcansihó, today's Mérida. From T'hó, one route goes to Mayapán, situated to the south, while another goes to Dzibilchaltún to the north, and a third to Uxmal. From Uxmal there are three more branches: one which ends at Champotón; another which extends to Kabah, Sayil, Labná, Nohcacab, Xtampak, Bacalar, Tipú, Uaxactún, Tikal, and ending at Uolantún; while the last goes to Hopelchén and ends in Tayasal, after crossing the previously mentioned link between Tipú and Uaxactún. (See map number 3)

Carlos Echánove Trujillo observed that "these roads, whose numbers have been exaggerated at times. have only been found in certain areas of the Yucatán Península, and none are approximately the lengh of the Yaxuná-Cobá route". [2] This is true because of the fact that over the centuries, the vegetation has destroyed them, with the help of man, who, after the conquest, built roads and railroads between haciendas, villages, and cities.

1).— Bustillos Carrillo, Prof. Antonio, **El Sacbe de los Mayas,** B. Costa- Amic, México City, 1964; page 10.
2).— Echánove T., Op. Cit.; page 42.

Map. No. 3

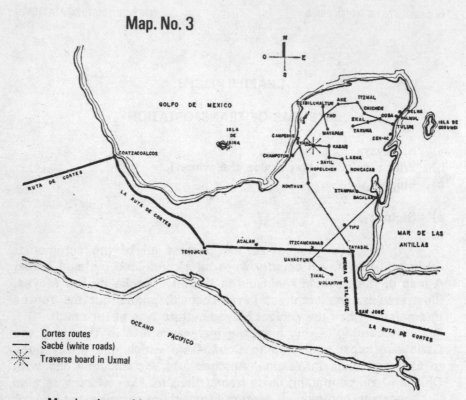

- ▬ Cortes routes
- ✳ Sacbé (white roads)
- ✳ Traverse board in Uxmal

Map by the architect Luvel Lacosky showing the main roads of the ancient Mayan

From the book "El Sacbé de los Mayas" by Antonio Bustillos Carrillo

Explorations up to 1975 show that the most extensive network of roads exists in Cobá, with forty-two coming from different directions. In that figure are probably included roads which lead to main buildings, but the longest are those to Yaxuná and Ixil, the latter being about twenty kilometers in length. [3]

The Cobá-Yaxuná route was well explored by the Carnegie Institute of Washington in 1933, at the same time they were restoring "The Market" area in Chichén Itzá, which was at the center of their operations. They had designated Professor Alfonso Villa Rojas as the man to go over the complete length of it, with the help of some fifteen peasants with axes and machetes. At the time, Professor Villa, now a Doctor of Anthropology, had to resign

3).— Sáenz César, **Boletín del I.N.A.H Epoca II,** México City, Octubre-diciembre, 1975; pages 55—56.

as director of the neighboring school at Chankom in order to join the Carnegie Institute, and the author was fortunate enough to land the vacant position at Chankom.

The exploration of this highway revealed it to be one hundred kilometers in length, four and one-half meters in width, and between sixty centimeters and two and one-half meters higher than the level of the natural terrain. There is some dispute as to the width of the highway, with some authors putting it at six meters; this variation, however, may be because of the fact that the road is wide at its inception, and narrows at goes along, as is the case at Kabah. At the arch which designates the entrance to Kabah from Uxmal, the road width is 6.42 meters, which increases to ten meters upon passing through the arch, where it connects with the most important buildings of Kabah before continuing onward. Photo 25.

Photo No. 25. The arch of Kabah. Photo by the author.

After exploring the Cobá-Yaxuná highway, it was supposed that it was nearly straight, with five very slight deviations. Its route correlated very closely with the location of several cenotes in the area, the locations and names of which are known today. The first is Chackne, which is two kilometers from Cobá; then

Oxkintok, at six kilometers; next, Caydzonot, at twelve kilometers. Continuing at intervals of between ten and fifteen kilometers are scattered a number of small populous areas and several small farms, all of which have cenotes of potable water; these extend all the way to Yaxuná. The date of construcction of this highway is put at some time betwen 633 and 731 A. D. [4]

In Ekal, a cylindrical stone which is four meters long, sixty centimeters in diameter, and which weighs five tons was found. It is believed to have been a road roller, used to compact the surface of the roads. Today it is exhibited in front of the Office of Communications and Transports in Mérida, as a relic of the ancient Mayan civilization.

Apart from these roads, smaller sections have been found in several ceremonial centers that link the most important buildings.

The Mayan name for these roads is "sacbé", and is derived from two Mayan words; "sac", meaning "white", and "be", which means "road". This name developed because the Maya surface the roads with white earth called "sascab".

Cobá was an important ceremonial center, as can be seen in the size, number, and extensiveness of its constructions. The architecture is poor, however, with an absence of aesthetics; the stones used in the constructions are crudely worked, and the stucco facing shows great unevenness. For some reason, which remains unknown to us, the architects and builders did not achieve the degree of perfection in Cobá as in other centers, such as Chichén Itzá, Uxmal, Palenque, Labná, etc. The number of highways in the Cobá area lead one to believe that it was an important commercial center, closely linked to Tulum, which may have been the most important Peninsular port on the Caribbean. Boats probably landed in Tulum, laden with goods from other coastal settlements, to be taken to Cobá, from which they would be distributed to the rest of the Península through operations of exchange.

It does not seem reasonable to believe that the Maya built another long highway from Cobá to Chichén Itzá (as per Lacoski's map) in a region without any apparent important population centers other than Yaxuná, which is only eighteen kilometers from Chichén Itzá. If in reality this road did exist, one possible explanation may be that it was used to transport harvests from the fields to some

4).— Bustillos C., Op. Cit.; page 49.

134

large villages in the area, which have long since disappeared. The existence of such a road would have made the long walk from the fields easier.

Urgent messages were probably sent along these highways by the use of runners in a relay-post system.

b). Why didn't the Maya use the wheel?

This is one of the questions most often asked by the public and by researchers. The Maya had an advanced knowledge of geometry, but did not possess the wheel, or rather, did not **use** the wheel. Some researchers suggest that the Maya believed that the sun, being round, and representing one of their most important gods, would have been offended at having its form used as an element of locomotion, and hence, such use would have been sacrilegious. Others believe that it was because the Maya lacked large beasts of burden. One historian of the past believed that the Maya intentionally did not use the wheel in order to more fully occupy the workers, and thus to reduce the chance for rebellion. None of these theories is convincing, however.

This author, through simple logic, is convinced that the Maya did indeed use the wheel for carts, but that they discarded it shortly thereafter because it was impractical. The wheels broke easily because they were not protected with a metal rim which would have helped to withstand the weight of the load. If one selects even the hardest wood to use in making a wheel, it will still split in the direction of the grain under pressure. Even if the Maya were ingenious enough to put two wheels together, with the grains perpendicular to each other for reinforcement, they would still be faced with another problem: the friction between wheel and axle would not only rapidly wear out the wood, but might actually heat the wood to the point of combustion. Carts built in such a way could never be used to transport enormous monoliths of stone, weighing tons, and/or large amounts of construction materials. It must be added that the making of wooden wheels with stone tools is extremely difficult.

The proof that some Meso-American cultures had knowledge of the wheel is evident in the small wheeled toys that have been found, especially in the Totonac culture. The movement of big stones or monoliths was actually accomplished through the use of wooden logs as rollers.

If a reader wants to test this reasoning, let him make a cart as described above and use it with a good deal of weight in it.

Some historians object that no one knows when or where the wheel first came into use. The wheel is such an indispensable and necessary element in today's world that if the wheels of all of our different vehicles (trains, buses, automobiles, airplanes, and all of our many other machines) were paralyzed, we would be subject to a chaos which would completely upset our activities, and be obliged to carry on a primitive lifestyle. The same historians say that sometime around the year 3000 B. C., the Egyptians drew scenes from their lives on the walls of their tombs, and in these scenes, rudimentary vehicles with wheels can be observed, and these historians suppose that this indispensable element in locomotion was invented some place near the Nile Valley or in nearby Mesopotamia. [5]

Other investigators observe that the study of the origin of the wheel, however important it may be, is very obscure. They believe that the first inhabitants of the world with knowledge of the wheel were the Sumerians, in the year 3250 B. C., because they found in Ur an inscription of a wooden wheel, shaped like a disc, on a tablet in which the grains of the wood can be seen, but which does not mention the details of the disc's use. Nevertheless, in the tablet representation one can observe around the wooden disc a cinch or ring, and in the center, a type of cap or bushing, which may have functioned as the hub of the wheel, and it is possible that both are made of bronze.

It is known that man began to use gold, silver, and copper as early as the year 7000 B. C., but it wasn't until the year 3000 B. C. that the alloy of copper and tin which produces bronze was discovered, a metal which is much stronger than are its two component elements separately.

The discovery of bronze virtually coincided with the Sumerian's knowledge of the wheel.

The first wheel with spokes was invented in 2000 B. C. in Eastern Iran, and the Egyptians obtained it in 1500 B. C. Even

5).— **Nueva Enciclopedia Temática**, Editorial Richards, Vol. 6, 1973; page 359.

though it was made of metal, it could not be used to transport stone blocks weighing several tons. To do this, they continued their use of wooden rollers.

The Greek wheel, with several spokes, appeared about 400 B. C., and the Roman wheel made its appearance about 100 B. C. Leonardo da Vinci was the man who first designed a wheel with spokes forming a 7 pointed star in the 15th Century. The pneumatic tire came in 1907. [6]

Perhaps the reader will remember that when the Statue of Tlaloc (the God of Rain of the Nahuas) was moved from its original location to the patio of the Museum of Anthopology in México City, it was necessary to use a special truck to support the enormous weight of the monolith. Modern technology eliminated the metal bushings at high rotation, as they produce heat and wear out rapidly, and used bearings instead, which avoid direct friction.

c). Shipping

We have seen that the Mayan territory is very extensive, covering an area of approximately 325,000 square kilometers and forming a Península, bounded on the north and west by the Gulf of México and on the east by the Caribbean Sea.

In this vast territory there were products that abounded in one region, but were scarce or completely lacking in others. This required commercial trade which covered long distances. For example, salt is produced on the northern coasts of the Península, but is lacking on the Caribbean coasts. The same is true of cacao: it grows well, and produces large crops in certain areas of Tabasco, on both sides of Río Hondo (Deep River), in Belice, and also in parts of the Honduras. Jade exists in the high areas of Guatemala north of Zacapa; while obsidian can be found in the center of Guatemala, and near its border with the Honduras. Copper deposits exist near the River Botagua, Guatemala, and the Quetzal bird plumes that were used to adorn the nobles' headdresses can be found near the border of Chiapas and Guatemala, and in the center of the Honduras. (See Map number 4)

6).— **Historia del Hombre; Dos Millones de Años de Civilización,** Readers Digest, México City, 1977; pp. 310—311.

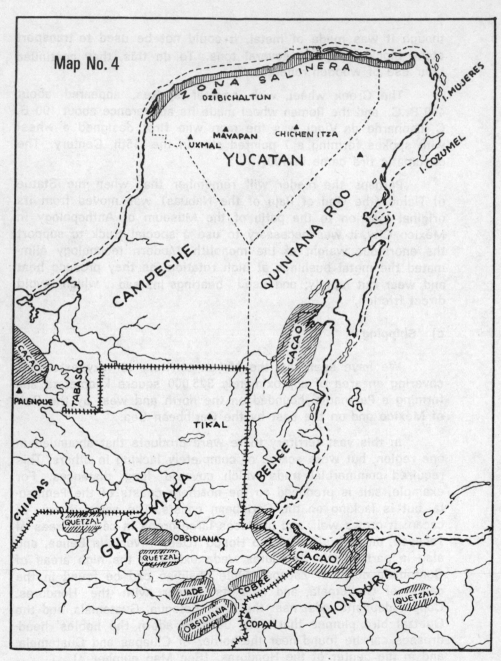

Map of the maritime routes (in dashed lines) and on the principle products of trade among the Maya.

Cotton, cloth, and dried and salted meats were indispensable goods which were taken to places where they did not exist in exchange for other goods.

Since commercial trade by land was difficult and labored because of the lack of vehicles and beast of burden, and in spite of the magnificent roads, it was necessary and far easier to use canoes to transport many products to towns along the coast, which were from there to be taken to towns in the interior. Canoes were carved, in one piece, from enormous tree trunks. The ancient sailors would stay close to the coast with the most distant journey probably being to the Island of Cozumel.

This method of transport was being practiced at the time of the arrival of the Spanish. Another proof of the existence of this maritime means of communication was related by Bartolomé Columbus (the brother of Admiral Christopher Columbus) in the report of his fourth and final voyage, as we will see in the final chapter of this book. The routes taken by these sailors are retraced by the broken lines on Map 4.

CHAPTER NINE

CERAMICS

a). **Generalizations**   d). **Ceramic of the Classical Period**
b). **Ceramic Styles**   e). **Post-Classical Ceramic**
c). **Formative Ceramics**

a). Generalizations

Ceramics have been the inseparable companion of man since he began domestic life, especially in America. Ceramics have been used as the key in investigating his evolutionary periods as the experts study the different styles created during the centuries.

The classification of ceramics has been a difficult task, especially when we take into consideration the fact that since the beginning, society has been divided in classes: the chiefs and dignitaries occupy the highest level and are the nobility, followed by the middle class, and finally, the lower class, who comprise the majority, and who also work to sustain the others. It is certain that the artifacts and domestic utensils which each class used were not the same; the nobility always had the finest, while those used by the middle class were of inferior quality, and the lower class used those of most humble quality, in most cases without decoration. The styles and quality of these utensils were not related to the time of their manufacture, but rather, related to the class in society which their owners occupied. The ceramic specialists have to be careful in classifying these objects, in attempting to determine the period of their manufacture.

Perhaps, at first, ceramics were uniform within the same time period, but later, upon the rise of social classes, the quality was varied. This phenomenon can be seen today; the wealthy have their showcases filled with fine china, the middle class use articles of average quality, and the lower classes use cups, plates,

141

etc., of zinc, poor-quality stoneware, and recently, plastic. If our civilization were to collapse today, and future archaeologists were to investigate, after several centuries, into our civilization, they would undoubtedly encounter similar problems to those who study the Maya today.

In the case of the Maya, archaeologists, upon making excavations, have encountered garbage dumps or midden heaps, in formerly inhabited places, at different depths (some several meters), where the Maya disposed of their articles of clay after they became useless, as well as other types and varieties of garbage.

The finding of these garbage dumps is very important, because they contain the secrets of the past. It is logical to assume that the articles on top are most recent, and that those below are older, providing that these heaps have not been previously disturbed. An undisturbed heap could give a sequence in history, but not an exact chronology. Researchers must rely on other sources to help interrelate the articles, and to help determine their approximate dates. The use of the Carbon-14 dating method, which measures the accumulation of organic matter in the artifacts, is of great help.

As the architecture had its own characteristics in each Mayan region, so did the ceramics. The artists in each place, according to their preparation and sensibilities, shaped their own creations — this is another reason why one does not encounter uniformity within the territory, even though the creators were from the same race and culture.

It is believed that ceramic commerce or exchange occured between one region and another, and also between countries. Professors Jiménez Moreno and María Teresa Fernández, in their work which is discussed elsewhere in this book, state that in Xochicalco, the Mayan influence was present near the end of the Pre-Classic Period and at the beginning of the Classic Period, or roughly around the years 200 — 300 A. D. Ceramic objects have been found at this site that correspond to the Chicanel and Matzanel Phases. It is believed that these ceramic objects came from the coasts of Oaxaca and Guerrero, where Mayan objects have also been found. These scholars affirm that the second phase of the Tajín Culture (650 — 1000 A. D.) spread its cultural influence to the Yucatán Península during the period of Puuc development.

One also notes in the Second Phase of Monte Albán the presence of ceramics, and of the general influence of the Maya from Guatemala. In Kaminaljuyú, Guatemala, one can find ceramics from Teotihuacan, which makes it evident that one can list in detail the many influences which were extended from one culture to another. [1]

Whenever one speaks of commercial trade in ceramics, covering many miles of distance without adequate transportation, it almost seems impossible. (At this point it seems timely to mention this well —known witticism— the means of transportation in those days was "the cart of San Fernando", or "sometimes on foot, other times walking"). Imagine, if you can, the manner of transportation which the ancient peoples used to take fragile ceramic pieces over enormous distances and rough roads, often encountering serious obstacles. What profit could there be for a merchant to carry this type of goods, ceramics, for several months? Perhaps the answer is that they were taken to other regions to be reproduced by artisans, or perhaps those artisans were commissioned to produce them in their own regions, as is being done today. Today, it is easier to buy foreign technology than to import the manufactured article itself. This may be the answer, without discounting the possibility of special cases in which fine ceramic objects were given as gifts by nobles to their peers in other countries, much as is done today. It is true that the Aztecs had commercial relations over great distances with other cultures, but their merchandise was not as fragile as clay. It consisted instead of items of precious metals: gold, silver, and copper, as well as products such as cacao, salt, rare feathers, fabrics of cotton, jade, obsidian, dried and salted meats, etc. In the case of the Aztecs, these trips were also spy trips which were disguised by their commercial aspects; commerce was an excellent ruse to disguise their true goals, because after they conquered a village, they became better informed collectors of tributes.

b). Ceramic Styles

Of the documents consulted in the research for this work, the one which best described the ceramic styles and their

1).— Jiménez M. Miranda, and Fernández, Op. Cit.; page 92.

evolution was Dr. Morley's book entitled, **The Maya Civilization.** Other authors offered limited commentary, and at times are over-generalized and disorganized in the form of their presentation, and for this reason, I have used this informative source to describe the ceramic styles.

The following is a summary of table Number 9 in Morley's book, including the warning that new information is changing some of the ideas which were previously held. For example, only months before the date of publication of this book, we received notice that in Miraflores, Guatemala, ceramic pieces had been discovered dating back to the year 2000 B. C.; until these new dates are published, we will continue to respect what is known offitialy for now.

From 1000 B.C. to 353 B.C. . Mamon ceramic
From 353 B.C. to 317 A.D. . Chicanel ceramics
From 317 A.D. to 633 A.D. . Tzakol ceramics
From 633 A.D. to 731 A.D. . Tepeu ceramics
From 731 A.D. to 987 A.D. . Mid— and Recent— Tepeu ceramics
From 987 A.D. to 1194 A.D. . Puuc — greatest development of ceramic "Pizarra de Yucatán" or "slate of Yucatán". The appearance of the fine orange ware imported from Tabasco.
From 1194 A.D. to 1441 A.D. . Mexicana, fine orange porcelain (phase 2). Appearance of the "plumbante" metalized) porcelain.
From 1441 A.D. to 1717 A.D. . Roja Basta (decadent). [2]

The description is brief, and relates only to the period since a full description would be complicated, tedious and appeal to only a few readers. For this reason, the characteristic of just a few will be described.

c). **Formative Period.**

Studies show that the ceramics of the Maya began in the high areas of Guatemala. Ceramics in the first Formative Phase

2).— Morley, S. G., Op. Cit. (1956 Ed.); Table No. 9.

144

(Las Charcas) have simple designs and are of one color. The cooking pots are shaped like a shoe, while drinking vessels are of the shape of a grater. Containers took the form of a vase with three long legs, and the use of these was continued in subsequent periods in various regions in Meso-America. In this same period an infinite number of hand-molded figurines appeared, as well as cylindrical clay stamps or seals, and whistles in the shape of animals.

In the two subsequent phases of this period (Sacatepéquez and Miraflores) came a change in form and color. In the long, final phase of the period, in the high plains of Guatemala, the development continued with the addition of the tripod base in the vessels with picture designs, and a general enrichment and variation in the forms, without, any external influence. The ceramics of this Formative Period are similar in all the Mayan region, from the lowlands to distant Huasteca, where Mayan was spoken. (3)

d) . Ceramics of the Classical Period.

Morley says that the stamp which is characteristic of this period is the evolution of the polychrome ceramic in the Central Mayan area, where the most elaborate and best designs are found in the New World. In the Tepeu Phase, the Maya painted naturalistic designs, some with a picture narrative, while in the second part of the period, small figurines appeared in the Central Mayan region; it seems that the place of origin of these figurines was on the coast of the Gulf of Campeche, in the state of Tabasco. The best examples come from Palenque and Jonuta. These figurines are made of clay, with a fine orange texture which was painted blue and other colors, and are mainly found in tombs.

The most distinctive vessels of the Florescent Phase are the pieces called "Pizarra de Yucatán" (the slate of Yucatán), which are characterized by a bath from gray to coffee colored. At times they are adorned with a pale gray painting, which is coarsely applied. In spite of the drab gray color, they have a smooth finish, carefully molded and showing excellent technique, which gives the impression of a competent, organized group of artisans. While in the Petén region, the polychrome vessels are created by talented individuals. Morley comments that the potters

3) .— Ibid, (1975 Ed.), pp. 385—386.

wheel was never used in pre-Columbian America, and that a proof of the industrialization of Mayan ceramics is still found in the use of the K'abal among the modern artisans in the Yucatán. The K'abal is a wooden cylinder which rests on a flat base, and which is worked with the foot. With this instrument the artisan is able to vary the process of making a vessel by using the simple technique for manipulation and extension of material similar to the potters of the Old World in the year 3000 B.C.

In some areas of the Yucatán, such as in the city of Ticul, the potters, rather than using the wooden cylinder, have a square or round pallet, in disc form. There is a hole in the center in which a thick nail fits which serves as an axle in the rotation of the pallet; this pallet is also called K'abal.

e). Post-Classic Ceramics

Morley says that the Post-Classic Style is most characteristic of Chichén Itzá, perhaps because this was the place of greatest activity in that period. This ceramic is a direct descendant of the Florescent Phase, and in its form and decoration is a copy of the fine orangeware imported by the Toltecs of Veracruz. After the Toltec period, there were changes in the preparation of the clay, and even in the color of the clay. Later came the introduction of a new form of kitchen pottery, incense holders, figurines, etc.; all of which indicates a surprising change in religious customs.

146

CHAPTER TEN

IMPORTANT CEREMONIAL CENTERS

a) . **Generalizations**   e) . **Uxmal**
b) . **Tikal**   f) . **Important Characteristics of**
c) . **Copán**   **Other Centers**
d) . **Chichén Itzá**

a) . **Generalizations**

The term "city" has not been accepted by some archae-ologists as accurate in reference to the places where the ancient Maya established their organized life. By virtue of the layout and the location of their most important buildings, these sites are not like our current, urban centers of streets and blocks, with houses in which the inhabitants live. Some of the central buildings are considered to be palaces where the nobility lived, while others were temples where the Maya organized and practiced their ceremonies and religious rites, and kept their idols. It is possible that the priests and some of their assistants lived in the temple annexes. Other buildings were used for administrative areas, schools, markets, observatories, etc.; hence, the entire cluster is called a ceremonial center. The balance of the population lived in thatched huts, much like the country people do today in the north of the Yucatán Península. This is proven by the description of Bishop Landa, and by the colored murals which still exist in the second chamber of the Temple of the Jaguars at Chichén Itzá, where one can observe a scene from the life of those ancient times.

In spite of the above information, some historians and archaeologists still call them cities. This name can only be accepted with respect to their number of inhabitants. It is certain that the common people had access to these centers when they were going to carry out important ceremonies, on market days (said to have been every five days), at times when they needed to transact important business matters, or for legal matters.

Some historians say that the middle class was made up of artisans, merchants, and workers, who lived near the ceremonial centers, while the others, according to their economic and social status, occupied more distant homes.

These ceremonial centers have been classified into four categories, according to their extensiveness, the number and size of their buildings, and to their inscriptions. First, and those that are considered as capitals: Tikal in Guatemala, Copán in Honduras, Chichén Itzá and Uxmal in the north of the Yucatán Península. Among those in the second category, we cite only a few of the best known: in Mexican territory, Palenque and Yaxchilan in Chiapas; Edzná and Calakmul in Campeche; Kabah and Sayil in Yucatán; Cobá in Quintana Roo; and in Guatemala, Uaxactún, Piedras Negras, and Quiriguá. Among those in the third category in the Yucatán are Labná (which could also belong to the second group for the number, size, and beauty of the buildings), Mayapán, Oxkintok, and Izamal. In the fourth group are mentioned Bonampak, Isla de Jaina, Acanceh, Dzibichaltún, Aké, and Ichpatún. [1]

a). Tikal

This ceremonial center is 304 kilometers directly north of Guatemala City, or about an hour by plane. It has an interesting museum, in which one can see many artifacts taken from the excavations; pieces of ceramics, bones, seashells, jade, stones with reliefs, etc.

The first European visitors to arrive at Tikal were the missionaries in the Seventeenth Century, and not until 1848 did an official expedition visit the site.

The work of restoration and exploration, called the "Tikal Project", started in 1956 by the University of Pennsylvania, after they signed a contract with the government of Guatemala. [2]

Because of its extensive area of about sixteen square kilometers, the number of its structures, about 3,000, and the size and majesty of the important buildings, Tikal is considered to be one of the most important archaeological centers in America. Some

1).— Morley S. G. Square 7. page 285.
2).— Coe William R., **Tikal, A. Handbook of the Ancient Maya Ruins**, Univ. of Pennsylvania Museum, Philadelphia, Penn., 1967; pp. 12—16.

experts have calculated that it had a population of 100,000 at the height of its epoch of splendor.

In the general map of Tikal, published by the University Museum of the University of Pennsylvania in 1967, the central part and its complexes are pointed out, as well as hundreds of smaller structures. The map also depicts several reservoirs where rain water was stored (some of which are still used today), as well as watering stations, and avenues which united the building complexes. Today these avenues carry the names of the men who explored them: "Mendez Causeway", "Maler Causeway", and "Tozzer Causeway".

The principle buildings consist of high platforms, superimposed one upon the other, upon which rest chambers with enormous combs. Photo No. 26

Photo No. 26. The Temple of Tikal. Photo courtesy of Professor Robert Turnbull.

Since little is known of these buildings, compared with those in the north of the Península, they are numbered Temple I, Temple II, etc., as we noted in the previous chapter.

149

b). Copán

Copán is another very important ceremonial center, situated in the valley by the same name, in the extreme western part of Honduras.

Nothing is known of the dates it was occupied, or of the origin of its name. However, it is believed that it was named after its abandonment in honor of a chief, Copán Calel, who fought the Spanish in 1530.

The Honduran government has converted the site into a beautiful national park by planting citrus trees and vines. They also allow the growth of wild trees in certain areas to give it greater beauty.

Some 1,500 meters from this ceremonial center, a small town was founded in 1870, named San José Copán, which continues to grow.

Many people and expeditions have visited this site since its discovery, some to observe and study, and others to restore the edifices. The Peabody Museum of Ethnology and Archaeology of Harvard University made the greatest contribution during their four expeditions. The first was in 1891—1892, under the direction of Marshall H. Saville; the second in 1892—1893, under John G. Owens; the third in 1893—1894, by Maudslay; and the fourth was directed by G. Byron Gordon. Each expedition was very successful in discovering new monuments, common tombs, and sepulchres of nobility. The most notable discoveries, however, were the hieroglyphic stone step mentioned elsewhere in this work. [3]

Beginning in 1935, the Carnegie Institute of Washington, together with the Honduran government, excavated and repaired various temples, twelve monoliths, the ball court, and perhaps most notably, they returned the Río Copán (Copán River) to its original course after a shift it its course threatened to destroy the acropolis.

In spite of its extensiveness and number of the structures, the buildings in Copán are inferior in size, aesthetic quality, and greatness, to those of other ceremonial centers at Uxmal, Chichén Itzá, Tikal, etc. However, the fine finish and beauty of its sculptures make Copán famous.

3).— Stromsvik Gustavo, **Ruinas de Copán, Guía**, October, 1967; pp. 3, 4, and 8.

Copán was also distinguished by its great scientific achievements, especially in mathematics and astronomy. Here was found the most exact calendar in the world, a plotting of the rotation of Venus, with a difference of only fourteen seconds from our reckoning, and the sequence of eclipses.

Copán was one of the sites to suffer great destruction, and it is not known whether it was intentionally destroyed when it was abandoned, or whether the destruction occurred through the forces of time, rain, or vegetation.

c) . Chichén Itzá

This is one of the most visited archaeological zones, not only in America, but in the entire world, owing to its magnificent buildings, the number of its constructions which are restored, and its geographic location. This together with tourist promotions, brought some 299,000 visitors from many different nations in 1977. This archaeological zone is situated some 120 kilometers east of Mérida, the capital of the state of Yucatán, on Federal Highway No. 180, which continues to the Caribbean coast.

Chichén Itzá is three kilometers by one and one half kilometers in area, and is divided into three parts: the Central Group, which is the oldest; the Northern Group, which is the newest; and the Southern Group, which has two periods, the new and the old, hence, some call it "Chichén Viejo" or "Old Chichén".

We mentioned in the previous chapter that the Toltecs had considerable influence in Chichén Itzá, especially in its architecture.

CENTRAL GROUP

In the Central Group are the following structures: (See Map 5)

1.— **El Osario, or Tomb of the Great Priest.** This small, unrestored pyramid shows Toltec influence. There, at the beginning of the 20th Century, Edward Thompson, Vice Consul of the United States, discovered six superimposed tombs, in each of which were found funerary vessels of fine clay, finished in polychrome ornamentation. In excavating toward the interior, Mr. Thompson found a stone floor which was, in reality, the cap or cover of

151

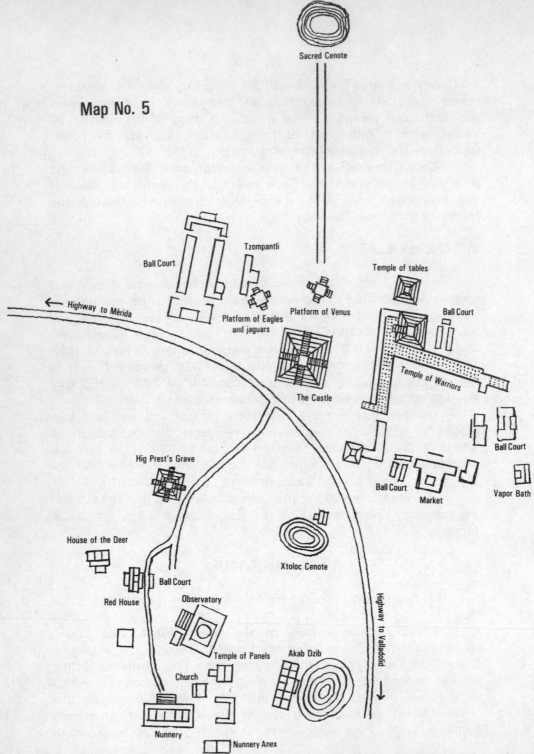

Sacred Cenote

Map No. 5

Ball Court

Tzompantli

Temple of tables

← Highway to Mérida

Platform of Eagles
and jaguars

Platform of Venus

Ball Court

Temple of Warriors

The Castle

Hig Prest's Grave

Ball Court

House of the Deer

Ball Court

Ball Court

Xtoloc Cenote

Market

Vapor Bath

Red House

Observatory

Highway to Valladolid

Temple of Panels

Akab Dzib

Church

Nunnery

Nunnery Anex

152   Map of the North and the Central Groups at Chichén Itzá, showing their most
       important buildings.

another large tomb which was built under the floor. Inside this larger tomb, Edward Thompson discovered lying with its head pointing eastward, a skeleton, surrounded by artistic incense burners, offering vessels of polychrome clay, a pair of low quality pearls, jewelry of copper, jade, and gold. [4]

Photo No. 27. The Red House or "Chichán Chob". Chichén Itzá. Photo by the author.

2.— **La Casa Colorada, or the Red House.** Photo 27 This structure is of purely Maya architecture. It was given this name because its interior was painted red, with a blue stripe. The Mayas of the Decadent Period called it "Chichán Chob", which means "small plate", according to Dr. Emilio Solís Alcalá in his **Maya-Spanish Dictionary.** There seems to be no reason for this second name. Perhaps when the site was abandoned, some of the inhabitants moved to the neighboring town of Pisté, after which they certainly frequented the ruins of their ancestors, and perhaps on such a visit, they found a small plate in the interior. This being the case, on subsequent visits, they would refer to it as "the place where the small plate was found", and over a period of time it was called in that way.

4).— Cirerol Sansores Manuel, **Chi Cheen Itsa,** Talleres Gráficos del Sudeste, Mérida, Yucatán, 1957; pp. 104—106.

Photo No. 28. The Observatory, Chichén Itzá. Photo by the author.

3.— La Casa del Venado, or the Deer House. This structure is also of pure Maya architecture. It is similar to the Red House, except that it was found in a state of ruin. The name was given to it because drawings of deer were found in its interior on stucco, which no longer exist.

4.— El Caracol, or the Observatory. Another structure of pure Maya architecture, the Observatory, is one of the most beautiful and important buildings at Chichén Itzá, and consists of a circular tower which rests on two superimposed platforms. Photos 28, 29 and 30.

Photo No. 29. The Observatory, Chichén Itzá. Photo by the author.

Some experts consider it to be of Toltec influence because it is of circular shape, and as such is similar to the round buildings found in Calixtlahuaca (Toluca), and in other areas of the Mexican Highlands. However, it is clearly of Mayan architecture, as can be seen in the balustrades of the stairs, with their intertwined serpents with scales; the serpents of the Toltecs were plumed rather than scaled. Some believe that the Observatory belongs to a transitional period. Its name is derived from its shape, and from the fact that at sunset, between 5:00 and 5:30 P. M., on the days of the equinox, the left outside edge of the window in the dome reflects on the right interior edge of the same window, which can

Photo No. 30. The Observatory, Chichén Itzá. Photo by the author.

be observed by a person standing within the tower. The structure consists of two circular rooms; the outer, which is the largest, has four doors which do not open exactly on the four cardinal points (they have a seventeen degree offset); the smaller inner room also has four doors, which are not in the same direction as those of the outer. The central part forms a thick column, and at about two meters of height there is a small window, through which one gains access to a staircase in the form of a "caracol" (snail); this is how it has gained it s other name. The building has an annex, which was added later in the Toltec Period, as is evident in its colonnades and in the plumed serpents which are carved on the balustrades of the stairs.

156

5.— **Baño de Vapor, or Steam Baths.** This structure is from the Toltec Period. On the south side of the Observatory's platform are seen the bases of columns and walls which once supported roofs of various rooms. There are also the remnants of a small construction which may have supported a stove, and some five meters away there is a circular font or basin with stairs leading into it. On the bottom of the font is a hole, which must have been used as a drain. This font is called the Steam Bath. When the hacienda Chichén Itzá was built by the Spanish southeast of the Observatory, (about a half kilometer) they used the stones from this edifice making it impossible to restore.

6.— **El Templo de los Tableros Esculpidos, or Temple of the Sculptured Tablets.** This partially restored structure is definitely influenced by the Toltecs, not only because of the slope of the building, but also because of its colonnades. There is relief work on both the north and south exterior which represents personages, plants, and animals, among them being monkeys, the heads of jaguars, birds, snakes, and people; from this it gets its name.

Photo No. 31. The Church, Chichén Itzá. Photo by the author.

7.— **La Iglesia, or the Church.** This structure is of purely Maya architecture. Photos 31 The name was given by the clergy

157

who visited the site after the conquest, thinking that it was a shrine to the natives' gods. The architecture corresponds to the Puuc style similar to Uxmal.

8.— **La Casa de las Monjas, or the Nunnery.** Near the Church one finds an architectural complex in the purely Maya style, which was given the name Casa de las Monjas (the Nunnery) by the Spanish who thought that this was the place where young girls lived who were being prepared for sacrifice in the cenote or sacred well, according to traditional information. This building has had various modifications; it can be clearly seen that nine chambers were built on the ground level, in rows of three, and near to the extreme west a platform was added, with a small temple on the upper part. For reasons unknown, the Maya filled in the central chambers, leaving a passage for communication between the other two chambers on the ends. Later they covered the platform with another larger platform, and built upon it several chambers whose lintels are inscribed with hieroglyphics. Later the platform was enlarged, and in order to support it, the three lower chambers to the extreme west were filled. On the east side they built another room with a fabulous facade in the Chenes style, with certain special characteristics. The Nunnery has four annexes, one of pure Mayan architecture, and three others of Toltec influence.

9.— **The Akab Dzib.** This construction of purely Maya influence, is about 200 meters east of the Nunnery. It is a building made up of seventeen empty chambers, and thought to be one of the oldest, owing to the lack of decoration on the facade, except for a cornice on the door level and near the roof. The name "akab" (night) and "dzib" (script) comes from one of the interior lintels which faces south, and on which are carved very fine and delicate hieroglyphs whose meaning is unknown; the name, thus, means "script or writing in obscurity".

10.— **The Cenote Xtoloc.** About 150 meters northeast of the Observatory is a large cenote, or natural well, which served as the principle source of potable water for the inhabitants of the area. The name comes from an iguana common in the Yucatán. The reptile comes out to sun bathe at certain times of the year and remains motionless like a statue; perhaps a large number existed in the cracks around the cenote, and the name was derived from this fact.

NORTHERN GROUP

In the Northern Group, all of the structures belong to the Maya-Toltec Period.

1.— **El Castillo or Templo de Kukulcán,** or the Castle or the Temple of Kukulcán, outstanding for its height, consists of nine superimposed platforms which decrease in size in conjunction with the elevation of the pyramid. Photos 32 and 33 On the summit is a square edifice with two chambers of different sizes which opens to the north and is the main entrance, and one more in the form of a U, which connects the three other entrances on the east, south, and west. Each side has ninety-one steps, not including the one corresponding to the platform. The total height is thirty meters (twenty-four meters of pyramid and six meters of temple) with the base measuring 55.30 meters on each side, and the width of the steps being 8.85 meters. Only the northern, western, and one-half of the eastern sides are restored.

Photo No. 32. The Castle or The Temple of Kukulcán, Chichén Itzá. Photo by the author.

This pyramid may have represented the civil calendar of the Mayas, with each step representing a day of the year. Each side

Photo No. 33. The Castle or Temple of Kukulcán. Photo by the author.

has ninety-one steps, making a total of 364 on all four sides; with the platform, there are 365 days. It has been said that each side of the pyramid represents a season of the year. Looking at only one side, the corners of the platform total eighteen, this being the months of the year, which consisted of twenty days plus a five-day month to total 365 days. Each side of the stairway has twenty-six sunken panels, which together total fifty-two, and as such, represent the number of years in the life cycle of the Maya, somethings similar to our century.

The pyramid is set at a seventeen degree angle off magnetic north, as is true of various structures among the Maya and other Meso-American cultures. The reason for the offset becomes clear when one sees the phenomenon brought about by the shadows on the day of the equinox. Several years ago, the caretakers of the buildings at Chichén Itzá, saw that from 5:00 P. M. to sunset, on March 21 and September 22, the corners of the superimposed platforms on the northeast projected, in succession, on the rim of the balustrade of the stairs on the northern, side, seven isosceles triangles, with the last forming the neck of the enormous serpent's head. This head rests at the base of the balustrade. It gave the impression of and undulating line of triangles which represented the body of the serpent. Photo 34

Photo No. 34. The Castle or The Temple of Kukulcán, Chichén Itzá, showing the effect or light and shadow during the equinox. Poto by the author.

Luis Arochi, a lawyer and a member of the Astronomical Society of Mexico A. C., and of the Mexican Society of Anthropology A. C., has paid particular attention to this phenomenon, and popularized it to such a degree that 14,000 people were present to see it on March 21, 1978. He has made detailed analytical studies of the Pyramid of Kukulcán, trying to relate its details with other buildings, not only at Chichén Itzá, but also of other cultures, trying to unlock some of the mysteries stored within them. Arochi's investigations have resulted in the publication of his book, **The Pyramid of Kukulcán: Its Solar Symbolism**, of some 207 well-illustrated pages.

One of his most notable discoveries made during the winter solstice, is described as follows: "At the solstice in December, looking at the pyramid from the southeast platform of the Ball Court, the sun, from the time it rises on the horizon, starts an ascent of the pyramid along the balustrades, until it reaches the apex of the pyramid, after which it continues its normal course... this in such a way that the pyramid of Kukulcán is an authentic solar stairway".[5] Arochi, with characteristic honesty, repeats that he is not the founder of the light and shadow phenomenon, even though he has been credited as such. His tenacity and love for archaeology frequently compel him to leave his native land, his work, and his comforts, to spend many days, at his own expense, to continue with perserverance and patience, his study of these phenomena.

The Maya, like other Meso-American cultures, were accustomed to covering their edifices with coats of rock and mortar, which later served as the foundations for other, larger structures. It is said that these ancient cultures covered their constructions every fifty-two years, adding another on top. Logic, however, tells us this may not be so, because if, for example, a structures was built in the Classic Period, by the end of the Maya civilization there would have been twelve periods of fifty-two years. The only building to have five superstructures is the Temple of the Magician at Uxmal. Nevertheless, the date of the first substructure in this complex is calculated, by means of Carbon-14 dating method, to the year 569 A. D., while the abandonment of Uxmal, according to new sources, occurred sometime in the 12th Century; hence, a

5).— Arochi Luis E., **La Pirámide de Kukulcán; Su Simbolismo Solar**, Editorial Orion, México City, 1976, 1976; pp. 39—46.

difference of 580 years, or eleven fifty-two year time periods. If they did, in fact, build a new superstructure every fifty-two years, the Temple of the Magician should have eleven superstructures.

In Chichén Itzá, the Post-Classic Period lasted some 219 years, or approximately four periods of fifty-two years. In this span, among the Northern Group, there is only one substructure in the Castle, and another in the Temple of the Warriors, which disproves the theory.

At first it was thought that the Castle or Temple of Kukulcán, rested on a base of stone masonry or rubble. However, it was found to have been built on a smaller pyramid. In 1931, local archaeologists made a tunnel in the south side of the pyramid toward the interior; in this way we learned of the existence of the inner pyramid. Taking many precautions, they opened a tunnel beneath the north stairway, putting up an angular roof as they proceeded. The tunnel began on the western side of the stairway and headed east, but upon arriving at the center point of the exterior stairway, they turned south where they found four wide stairs descending into the pyramid. At the base of the last stair was a stone box, which was found to contain human bones, two turquoise mosaics, two flint daggers, and a priceless necklace made of many pieces of jade of various sizes. The jade mosaics were taken to the Anthropological Museum in Mexico City; the flint daggers and the necklace to the Museum in Mérida. After removing the box, they encountered the stairs of a subterranean temple. Continuing the excavation, they dug upward, and after another sixty-two stairs, they arrived at the peak of the original pyramid, which the Maya had covered with rock and mortar in order to build an adequate foundation for the second pyramid. There they excavated the two chambers, and found in the first, a reclining idol called "chacmool". In the second chamber was found a masonry platform which, when broken, yielded a beautiful jaguar made from a single piece of stone painted red, with eyes and seventy-two spots made of jade, and flint teeth.[6] Some argue that the jade used for the eyes came from Asia, possibly China.

As to the exterior of the Temple of Kukulcán, I once had the idea that if the pyramid was indeed used as a calendar, perhaps the Maya had marked the passage of time as follows: a stone block was made which was slightly wider than the tread of the

6).— Cirerol S., Op. Cit.; pp. 64, 65, and 72.

individual step on the stairway, and slightly lower than the riser of the step. This stone had a hole in which to insert a brightly colored flag, which contrasted with the color of the stairway so that it could be easily distinguished. At the beginning of the year (some say this was July 16), a designated person would set the stone block with the flag on the first step, then it would be changed to the second on the following day, and so on. Anyone who wanted to know the date and season could easily see it from the location of the flag. Perhaps, so as not to need to count the steps one by one, a mark was made on the balustrade to separate units of twenty steps, which may have consisted of the hieroglyphic symbol for the month. As the pyramid was found in ruins, the plaster don't exist, so no marks were visible, this is difficult to prove, and as such remains merely a theory.

Photo No. 35. Panoramic view of the Temple of the Warriors. Photo by the author.

2.— The Temple of the Warriors, or the Temple of the 1,000 Columns.

This is one of the most beautiful structures at Chichén Itzá. (Photo 35) Its restoration was undertaken in 1925 by the Carnegie Institute of Washington, under the direction of Sylvanus G. Morley.

Perhaps this building was chosen because of its importance, which is reflected in its dimensions.

This temple looks much like the so-called Temple of Venus, or Tlahuizcalpantecutli, of Tula, which some call the Temple of Quetzalcoatl.

Upon raising the columns, almost all of which had fallen, it was found that those in front were square, and carved with pretty reliefs of people, each with a unique facial expression. For this reason, it is believed that these are not only decorative, but represent important historical figures, similar to the figures on the "Monument to the Country" on Avenida Montejo in Merida. The majority of the figures on these columns have lances in their hands; hence, the name "Temple of the Warriors". In its restoration, another temple was found beneath it, called the "Temple of the Chacmool", because in one of its chambers, a reclining idol, or Chacmool, was found. In the other chamber, they found a stone urn which contained a priceless turquoise mosaic, as well as murals, which are described in the chapter on clothing.

The uppermost part of the second construction consisted of two large chambers, the roof of which were supported by walls and columns, on which were carved reliefs representing people. In the rear is an altar of paving the form of plumed serpents, with the heads resting on the floor, the bodies forming the columns, and the tails and rattles at right angles, forming the crest. Photo 36

Explorations have revealed that this structure has had several additions: first, the square columns in the front were added, and later a colonnade of cylindrical columns which continues to the south, and ends in a right angle. The other colonnade goes almost parallel to the south of the building joining a mound that is about 200 meters away. This mound is united with another larger mound by and unrestored colonnade, with the "Market" complex lying just beyond. This complex consists of a series of columns, resting on a platform about 1.5 meters high.

The fronts of the superimposed platforms of the Temple of the Warriors are adorned with relief work which portrays seated persons with lances held in a defensive position. The first person is in front of a jaguar which is devouring a human heart, the second is in front of an animal which resembles a bear, and the third portrays a person seated before an eagle. This same sequence of relief work is repeated around the pyramid, on three levels.

Photo No. 36. Plumed serpents in the form of columns. Temple of the Warriors, Chichén Itzá. Photo by the author.

The front columns clearly supported a roof of stone masonry with the classical Maya arch. Some guide books suggest that the columns to the south were covered with a palm roof. This idea is absurd, since a building of this quality would hardly have had such a rustic annex. Moreover, a covering of many-angled palm roofs resting on the columns would certainly have leaked water. Columns situated at the front of this temple, aside from their use as support for the roofs of wide passageways, the columns were probably used to preserve, in relief, a historical record. My personal observations of the persons on these columns has led me to discover that each person has a distinct facial expression; some faces show hate, while others sadness and worry. I finally discovered the reason for these expressions; the scene was one of prisoners. There are reliefs of thirty-two of them in which the prisoners have their hands tied in front of them with cords. Photos 37 and 38 These reliefs correspond with a total of eight columns — four near the stairs, and four others slightly in front of these. It would follow that the rest of the reliefs (those with lances), are representations of the guards of these prisoners. Photo 39

Photo No. 37. Relief on a column of the Temple of the Warriors, showing a figure with its hands tied together. Chichén Itzá. Photo by the author.

At the time of these inscriptions there may possibly have existed a very strong division among the governors of Chichén Itzá, which could have culminated with an uprising which had to be put down. The victors wanted to exhibit the rebellious leaders as an example, hopefully to never be forgotten by successive generations. The distinguished soldiers of the battle were also portrayed as such, being represented on the columns as heroes.

3.— The Ball Court

Ball games were played by various Meso-American cultures — the Teotihuacan, the Zapotec, the Totonac, among others — however, the details from each region are vague and incomplete.

Photo No. 38. Relief on another column, showing another figure with its hands tied together. Temple of the Warriors, Chichén Itzá. Photo by the author.

It is said that in Teotihuacan, "the City of the Gods", or "where the gods made the sun", the leading men (the nobles and the priests) played ball in the open fields, to entertain the gods.

Although there were some similarities between the ball courts of the various cultures, each court had its own characteristics, which leads one to believe that the games were not alike, and that each had its own separate and local rules.

In the **Popol Vuh**, the sacred book of the Quiché of Guatemala, the ball game is mentioned many times, but its form is never really specified.

Photo No. 39. Soldier with three spears carved in a column of the Temple of the Warriors. Photo by the author.

There is no record that the Maya of the Decadent Period had a similar game. Bishop de Landa, known for his detail, does not say one word about this game, nor is any mention made in the chronicles of Chilam Balam or other documents.

In spite of the fact that the original name of the game in Chichén Itzá is not known, Franz Blum says that it was called "pok-yah" or "pokta-pok"[7] It is possible that Blum meant to write "ppuctal-ppuctal", which, in the **Spanish-Maya Dictionary** by Dr. Solís Alcalá, means "to get in the squatting position" or "to squat many times". In another part of his writing, in which he comments

7).— Blum, Frans, **La Vida de los Mayas,** S. E. P., Biblioteca Enciclopédica Popular No. 25, México City, 1944; pp. 32—35.

on the game, Blum likens it to American football, in which the players begin play in a squatting position.

We are almost certain that the name was given fairly recently because, at the arrival of the conquistadors, both the medium-sized court at Uxmal, and the large court at Chichén Itzá had been abandoned for over three hundred years, and both were found destroyed and covered with dense vegetation. With such a long gap between the time when the game was actually played and when the Spanish arrived, there was certainly no traditional name for it.

Blum says that he got his information from the writings of the Spanish missionaries Durán, Sahagún, Molina, and de Oviedo, but the descriptions which these men make are undoubtedly referring to the ball games of Tenochtitlan and Texcoco, which were still being played at the time of the Conquest. At that time they called this games "tlachtli". He also states that the information provided by the Spaniards that attended these games were based on two important concepts: one religious, and the other, gambling. To these a third can be added: the primordial motive of relaxation or diversion.

In some of the pictorial representations of the game, made by people of other cultures, ball courts can be seen with high parallel walls bordering two opposite sides, with a ring of stone on each. On both ends of these walls, the court opens to form the letter "T". In the center of the court, two players are drawn, one standing in front of the other. The player appears to extend his hand toward the other player; in his hand is a ball, approximately as big as a present-day softball. In the other drawing, a number of players with small bats (similar to those used in modern baseball) can be seen, passing the ball from one to the other, using the bat without ever directly using the hands.[8]

Not many years ago, it is believed that the largest ball court was at Chichén Itzá. Photo 40 It measures 170 meters long, 40 meters wide, and 12 meters high. The large platform at the base of the walls are 1.72 meters high. However, several years ago, a publication showed that in Tula, the capital of the Toltecs, there was a ball court that measured 214 meters in length.

The court at Chichén Itzá becomes larger at its south and north extremes, taking the form of the letter "T", bounded by the

8) .— Arroyo Raziel García, Five Mexican Sports. Publicaciones Internacionales, S. A. México, 1969. pp. 49—152.

Photo No. 40. The Ball Court, Chichén Itzá. Photo by the author.

big platforms, which were always 1.72 meters high, and which had exits at each end. At the southern end there is a spacious structure with the roof in partial ruin. The roof is supported by walls on the back and sides, and by columns in the front, and is decorated with relief work of the images of well dressed people. This structure has been called "The Theater" because it is believed that this was where the nobles sat to watch the games. At the extreme north end there is a higher, but smaller structure where, it is believed, the king, his court, and the principle priests sat. From this theory it gets its name: "the Sacred Tribune".

In the center of each of the lateral walls, and near the upper rim, a stone ring is embedded in the wall. This ring is decorated with plumed serpents. On the western wall are found the bases of three booths, while there are the bases of two booths on the eastern wall; perhaps these booths were the places in which the officials sat to judge the game.

We know from the excellent pictorial work that there were two teams of seven players, including the captain. The scenes of the players are repeated six times, three on each side of the court on the face of the lower platforms.

The uniform of these ball players consisted of a short skirt, feathered crests on the back, a knee protector on the left knee, and another on the hip. The arms and forearms were also protected. From the ears phallic symbol were protruded. Caps with a crest of feathers, and a type of sandal completed the uniform. Each player had a plate in his right hand, which was in the shape of a serpent's head, and a bat or club on his belt. Photos 41, 42, 43 and 44. In spite of the fact that the dress of all of the players is similar, each costume has some distinguishing mark which separates it from the others. The game consisted of passing a rubber ball through the vertical rings on the wall. It was originally thought that the rubber was imported from the south of Veracruz, where it is plentiful, but we now know that the rubber plant grew much closer to Chichén Itzá. I became aware of this fact when I visited the ruins of Konhunlich. On this occasion, the archaeologist, Víctor Segovia, who directed the restoration of the ruins, pointed out to me some rubber trees growing around the ball court.

Konhunlich is situated in Quintana Roo, about 300 kilometers from Chichén Itzá. Perhaps the Itzas cultivated the rubber tree even closer.

In the scene which is carved on the base of the platform which was discussed above, there are seven players in a line, one behind the other. The seven members of the opposite team are in a line facing them. The captain of one team has a flint knife in his right hand, and in his left hand, a human head, with blood flowing out as symbolized in the corn leaves. Kneeling in front of him is the other captain, minus his head, and out of his neck come seven streams of blood. Six of the streams become serpents, and the seventh a vine covered with fruit and flowers. It is thought by some that the sacrificed captain's blood was a symbolic fertilizer, used to obtain better harvests.

Between the two captains there is a skull encircled with a forked scroll which is symbolic of words. Photo 45. At one time it was believed that the winner cut off the head of the loser. Recently, however, some have speculated that the winning captain lost his head as an honor to the gods; considering the strength of our instinct for survival, however, it is difficult to believe that under these circumstances, a captain would actually try to win. Possibly this decapitation was symbolic and simulated, since the victim could hardly remain kneeling, and the skull to speak as is out of life.

Photo No. 41. A ball player. The center of the eastern side of the Ball Court at Chichén Itzá. Photo by the author.

Some booklets have described the game as having been played without the use of hands. The booklets indicate that the players used their shoulders, elbows, knees, hips, and ankles; but without the use of hands, it would be virtually impossible to put a ball through such a small ring at that height. If no hands were used, wat use was the plate on the right hand and the bat they had on their belts?

The manner of play is a matter of speculation. However, the layout of the field, the dress and equipment of the players,

173

Photo No. 42. A ball player in the center of the west side of the ball court. Photo by the author.

and other items which are known, help to give us a rough idea of the method of play.

During my many years as a guide, the many questions I have been asked have caused me to think and ponder, and in this way, I came across the following hypothesis: without a doubt, each ring corresponded to one of the teams, and the platforms served as the place where each captain played. The remaining six players on each team were on the field in an east-west line facing the members of the opposing team. The referee, with some signal or whistle, started play by throwing the ball between the players, who maneuvered the ball with the parts of the body mentioned above,

Photo No. 43. A ball player. The center of the western side of the Ball Court at Chichén Itzá. Photo by the author.

as well as the wooden plate in their right hands and the bat in their left. The players, according to the rules of the game, would try to bounce the ball off their wall towards their captain on the platform, who would, using his wooden plate, move the ball by bouncing it along the wall, taking care not to let it touch the ground, until he was close enough to attempt a shot at the stone ring. If they dropped the ball, the play would start over. Perhaps they played for a certain number of points rather than on a time limit.

Possibly sometime before, during, or after the game, a ceremony was carried out to appease the gods.

175

Photo No. 44. A ball player on the south extreme, of the east side of the ball court. Photo by the author.

One of the most notable characteristics of this ball court is its acoustics. Two people standing at its two extremes, the Theater and the Sacred Tribune (some 170 meters apart), can carry on a conversation in a normal voice, or hear a coin drop, provided that there is little wind or noise. From under the rings, one can hear some twelve echos when the hands are clapped.

In Chichén Itzá four other ball courts were found which are much smaller. They probably had different types of play, number of players, and so on. The one behind the Red House has pictured in the bases of its platforms, teams consisting of two players each.

Photo No. 45. Ball players, showing a decapitated captain on his knees. In front of this captain is another with a knife in his right hand and a human head in his left and. The Ball Court, Chichén Itzá. Photo by the author.

In Uxmal there is a fairly small ball court that it was decorated with plumed serpents on its walls, and this together with the slope in the back side of the walls, indicates that the ball games in the northern part of the Yucatán Península were introduced by the Toltecs.

4.— **Temple of the Jaguars.** (Photos 46 and 47)

In the lower portion of this temple are the most beautiful reliefs in Chichén Itzá, representing, in various levels from floor to ceiling, rows of warriors. These richly dressed warriors, who still show some of their original colors, give the impression of marching from the extreme end to the center of the chamber. The perspective of the lines of warriors, and the extremely fine details, show the level of artistry achieved by the sculptors of that time. On some warriors, the wrinkles in their faces, and even their fingernails can still be seen. From the two columns in front of the building, the archaeologist Manuel Cirerol Sansores has interpreted an allegory of the origin of the world and life, which

Photo No. 46. Temple of the Jaguars. Photo by the author.

Photo No. 47. On the left, an extreme of the Ball Court - On the rigth the Temple of the Jaguars. Photo by the author.

will be discussed in detail in another work now being written. In the uper part of this Temple of the Jaguars, were located drawings, already described in the chapter number 3.

5.— Tzompantli

About 100 meters east of the Ball Court is a platform in the form of a "T". The two wings are covered with relief carvings of skulls. In the explorations of its interior, a reclining "chacmool", a large stone ring like that at the Ball Court, and two skulls were found.

It was a custom of the Aztecs to stack the skulls of four prisoners, especially prisoners of high rank, on a stake, and in this way making a sort of trophy. Perhaps this is how the platform Tzompantli got its name.

6.— The Platform of the Jaguars and Eagles

This platform has been unduly called the "Platform of the Tigers and Eagles", for as was mentioned in another part of this work, tigers did not exist in America, only jaguars. A jaguar and an eagle, each with a heart clenched in its claws, are carved in an exquisitely artistic manner on the corners of the platform. Scrolls which are considered to symbolize speech are seen coming from the mouth of the jaguar and the beak of the eagle. Because there are no eagles in the Yucatán Península, and the animals of other species would not be able to understand one to the other, occurred to me that the eagle actually symbollically represents an important Toltec chieftan who is setting up the regulations for the introduction of human sacrifice at Chichén Itzá with his Maya colleague, who is represented by the jaguar.

7.— The Sacred Cenote or Sacred Well

Aside from the Xtoloc Cenote which is described earlier as being found at Chichén Itzá, there is another cenote of almost the same size called the "Sacred Cenote" or the "Sacrificial Cenote". This cenote is located about 400 meters north of the Castle pyramid, and is joined with the ceremonial center by a path which is said to have been found paved. This cenote is oval-shaped; it measures 60.50 meters long, 59 meters wide, and from the ground level down to the water level, it mesasures 21 meters. The depth of the cenote is also 21 meters, 14 of which are water (the remaining six are mud). Photo 48 and 49

Photo No. 48. The Sacrificial Cenote, Chichén Itzá. Photo by the author.

Photo No. 49. The Sacrificial Cenote. Photo by the author.

Some historical sources affirm that this cenote was used exclusively for human sacrifices, but some authors and archaeologist allege that a civilization as advanced as that of the Maya would never have carried out such barbaric acts. Nevertheless, there is indisputable proof that testifies to the fact that there were human sacrifices; one of these is the descriptions of Bishop Landa. Another source states that the Xius of Maní asked permission of the Sotuta to pass through their territory on a pilgrimage in which they took their children to Chichén Itzá to be sacrificed in the Sacred Cenote. The historian Molina Solís states that the delinquents were brought along in the same procession, sometimes tied-up, and upon arriving at the Sacred Cenote, were also thrown in as form of punishment.

A mural was found in the substructure of the Temple of the Warriors (time has destroyed it), which depicted a person, or the figure of a plumed serpent, in the form of a table with other people fastening down its hands and feet. An executioner is depicted, waiting at the side with a flint hatchet in his hand, ready to open the victim's chest. A similar scene is carved in relief on a gold disk which explorers found in the Sacred Cenote. The most convincing proof, however, that human sacrifices did in fact exist is found in the large number of human bones recovered from the Cenote during three separate explorations. A large number of objects of gold, copper, jade, and jadite, wooden lances, idols, copal incense bowls, and pieces of cloth and basket weaving, among other things, were also found in this cenote. The bones found there are of individuals of different ages and sex, predominantly of younger children. We can conclude that the skeletons found in the Cenote ar not from people who accidentally fell into it.

Human sacrifice was introduced to the Maya by the Toltecs during the Post-Classic Period, and the Maya of the Decadent Period still practiced the sacrifices inherited from their ancestors even at the time of the arrival of the Spaniards. Unofficial reports from some recent explorations state that in Guatemala, and even as far away as the Honduras, massive burial sites exist in which remains have been found which show that the bones of the rib cages are many times either broken or show traces of being hit upon with a cutting tool. The explorers of these graves have deduced that these are the skeletons of sacrificial victims.

I obtained this information from a tourist who is very interested in the Maya, although he is not an archaeologist; he said he heard this information directly from the explorers of those burial sites themselves.

8.— El Adoratorio de Venus, or The Temple of Venus.

This is only one of many names given to this square platform which measures 18 meters long on each side, 4 meters in height, and which has a staircase on each of its faces. It is located approximately 100 meters north of the Castle. The name of this building comes from some incompletely carved stars found on its corners which have been interpreted to represent the planet Venus. This structure also has beatiful, plumed serpents carved as decoration on its cornice. On both sides of each staircase, two monsters are carved in relief; a human face can be seen coming out of each of the monster's mouths. These carvings have been interpreted in many ways. Part of the colors used by the Maya can still be seen in these carvings.

When Chichén Itzá was still unexplored and its great archaeological value still unknown, the authorities did not pay attention to it nor guard it as they should have, and it was very easy for any visitor to do any type of exploration he desired. During this time a foreing by the name of Augustus Leplongeon came to the Yucatán. As he was very uninformed about the ruins at Chichén Itzá, he went there in search of treasures. He began his explorations and excavations by hand, but realizing that this method was expensive, or perhaps simply too slow, he used dynamite to continue his search, and in that way, he destroyed many of the beautiful stones with relief carvings of the Temple of Venus. Within this structure he found the first reclining idol which he named "chacmool"; "chac" meaning "red", and "mool" meaning "claw", or "the red claw". The Maya of today still use the term "chacmool" in reference to the jaguar. Leoplongeon thought that this figure represented a jaguar knigth. Today, this same chacmool can be seen in the Museum of Anthropology in Mexico City. Twelve more of these idols were found in later explorations, and they were all given the same name. Later, similar figures with distinct physical expressions were found in Tula and other places where there had been Toltec influence; they too, were called "chacmool" [9]

Later, in the Temple of Venus, a stone idol, approximately the size of a person, was found. This idol is naked and in a sitting position with its elbows on its knees; perhaps it represents an important deity of those times. This idol can be seen today in the Museum of Archaeology in Mérida. This platform has also been called the Platform of the Cones, the Platform of the Pineapples, the Platform of the Rite of the Sun, and the Dance Platform.

Apart from these structures which are described above, there are others in the Northern Group which have not been restored; the Temple of the Tables, which is located to one side of the Temple of the Warriors, the Steam Bath (a partially restored edifice), and other mounds which have not been named.

SOUTHERN GROUP

This section, still called "Old Chichén" by some people, is made up of various groups of buildings located at different distances from one another, which are, for the most part, in ruin.

The first group is located about one kilometer southeast of the Nunnery. The base of a small room can be seen on top of a small platform of about four meters in height; this platform appears to have undergone many modifications over the years. The room measures 2.85 meters in length, and 2.77 meters in width. In the front of this room, serving as part of the doorframe, are two anthropomorphic idols which measure 1.95 meters in height. These idols are called "atlases", and are very similar to those found at Tula. Eeach of these idols is supporting a large, flat stone which is carved with hieroglyphics marking the date 879 A. D. (in correlation with Goodman-Martínez-Hernández-Thompson), or 619 A. D. (in correlation with Spinden). It has been deduced that because of the fact that the Toltec influence arrived at Chichén Itzá in the year 975 A. D., these flat stones do not correspond to the construction date of this building. Nevertheless, this structure has been named **"The Temple of the Date"**.

About 80 meters from this small temple, there is a series of rooms in a double row, four of which are still in good condition.

9) .— Cirerol S., Op. Cit.; page 17.

In these four are found low platforms of about 42 to 54 centimeters in height which could have served as seats or altars. Phallic symbols of about 25 to 29 centimeters length and 23 centimeters in diameter. This is how this structure got the name **"Temple of the Phallic Symbols"**. It can be seen that on the patio on the eastern side of this building, a number of rooms were added whose roofs were supported by walls and columns. To the north of this structure more "atlases" can be seen in the form of doorframes, similar to those on the Temple of the Date.

Close to this group of buildings is a small structure called the **"Temple of the Eagle Owl"**, named thusly because some of these animals are carved on its columns.

There is another group of buildings a half of a kilometer further to the south which are in a state of ruin, distinguished by the height of one of the structure called the **Castle of Old Chichén"**. This building measures 15 meters high, and the base of its rooms can still be seen on its upper part.

There are two constructions located another half a kilometer to the south; a small one with finely carved reliefs known as **"The Four Lintels"**, and another structure 100 meters away from the first. This latter structure has been completely reconstructed by archaeologists of the Carnegie Institute of Washington. It seems as if by magic that this beautiful building of the Puuc Style (similar to those of Uxmal), rose from a pile of rubble. Above each of its doors is a stone lintel carved in relief with hieroglyphics; it was named **"The Temple of the Three Lintels"** because of these adornments. Photo 50

Aside from all of the restored structures at Chichén Itzá, a number of mounds, which are buildings in ruin, can be seen all about at regular distances. This tells us that Chichén Itzá was a very large and important ceremonial center.

d).— Uxmal

Because of the number, size, and beatuy of its buildings, Uxmal is considered to be the second capital of the Maya in the Northern Yucatán Península, which flourished during the Classic Period.

(The location of Uxmal and the date of its foundation will be detailed in the sixteen chapter).

Photo No. 50. The Temple of the Three Lintels. Chichén Itzá

Photo from the Official Guide of Chichén Itzá of the I.N.A.H.

A great deal is still unknown about Uxmal because archaeologists have dedicated the majority of their work to the restoration of the buildings rather than to sufficient investigation of Uxmal's history. Perhaps too, the investigations done there reveal little information about Uxmal's past. Although the indigenous cronicles found at the region after the conquest, mention Uxmal superficially, a large part of its history is still unknown.

It can be affirmed without equivocation that there was no rival among the civilized areas of America to the fine finish and the delicateness of the smooth lines of Uxmal's architecture.

The efforts of the Mexican government to restore the buildings of Uxmal have not been sufficient; everywhere, one can still see mounds of considerable size waiting for the archaeologist and his pick and shovel.

The first thing that a visitor to Uxmal encounters upon nearing the archaeological zone is a nucleus of unrestored mounds to the right, and he then sees the majesty of the impressive oval-shaped pyramid given the name "Temple of the Magician" (Templo del Adivino) on the left. Photo 51

Photo No. 51. Temple of the Magician in the back Nunnery Quadrangle. Photo Courtesy of José López Nájera.

186

This ceremonial center flourished in a region where the earth is very fertile, even though no rivers, cenotes, or lagoons are found in the area. The inhabitants of Uxmal solved this important problem of a lack of water by ingeneously constructing underground reservoirs called cisterns ("chultunes" in Maya), of different sizes, in which they captured the rainwater. Hundreds of these cisterns have been found in the Uxmal area, and there are probably thousands more in the surrounding jungle.

Pieces of pavement or stone were found at the bottom of some ravines which the Maya used as recepticles for rainwater. The water gather in this manner was then used for irrigation, in the preparation of mortar for the construction of buildings, and other secondary uses.

In Uxmal, and in the neighboring site Kabah, the Maya adopted the system of constructing some of their buildings in groups in the form of a square, similar to the European monasteries of the Medieval Period.

Perhaps the multitude of masks identified as "yum chaac" (God of the Rain) seen on the facades of the buildings is due to the fact that the ancient Maya of this area were basically agricultural workers.

The most important buildings at Uxmal are: 1. the Temple of the Magician, 2. the Nunnery, 3. the Governor's Palace, 4. the Great Pyramid, and 5. the House of the Tortoise. (See Map No. 6) There is another square of buildings called the Cemetery Group; its East, South, and North sides are completely fallen down, and on the West side, resting on an elevated platform, is a recently restored house. This name was given to this square because of the fact that the reliefs of skulls and crossbones are found on four small square platforms of eighty centimeters in height. This square could very well have been a worship site where rituals were performed upon the death of a noble, a priest, or some other important person, similar to the religious temples of today. These people were later cremated or buried. We known that the Maya practiced cremation by the clay recepticles which have been found in some excavations, full of ashes and burned bones.

To the West side of the Great Pyramid is another cuadrangle, the front part of which faces north. This cuadrangle is known by the arbitrary name of the House of the Doves. It was given this name because of its triangular-haped crest, which is

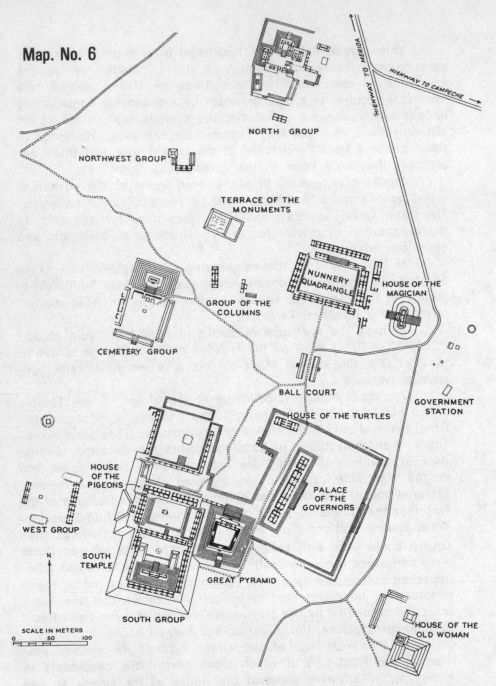

Map. No. 6

HIGHWAY TO MERIDA

HIGHWAY TO CAMPECHE →

NORTH GROUP

NORTHWEST GROUP

TERRACE OF THE MONUMENTS

NUNNERY QUADRANGLE

HOUSE OF THE MAGICIAN

GROUP OF THE COLUMNS

CEMETERY GROUP

BALL COURT

GOVERNMENT STATION

HOUSE OF THE TURTLES

HOUSE OF THE PIGEONS

PALACE OF THE GOVERNORS

WEST GROUP

N

SOUTH TEMPLE

GREAT PYRAMID

SCALE IN METERS

0   50   100

SOUTH GROUP

HOUSE OF THE OLD WOMAN

Map of the Central Section of Uxmal   From The Book "The Ancient Mayans" of Sylvanus G. Morley

composed of many little square windows which resemble a pigeon house.

Between the Nunnery and the House of the Tortoise is situated the Ball Court, which is of average size. The restoration of this structure has just recently begun. Some specialists calculate that the construction of this building took place in the Seventh Century A. D., basing their estimate on the hieroglyphics found on the court's rings. The author feels that their calculations are probably incorrect in that the fraction of the rings which remain —less than half— is certainly not enough whit which to calculate the period of its construction. The plumed serpents found on the walls of the Ball Court seem to indicate that the building was constructed under a Toltec influence, or in the late Tenth Century A. D. Unless these serpents were only added as decoration during the Tenth Century, this building could not have been constructed in the 700's.

1.— The Temple of the Magician

This oval-shaped pyramid —certainly an unusual form— was given this name in relation to a Maya legend of the Decadent Period which was still known at the time of the arrival of the Spaniards. The Spanish wrote down the legend, and it was passed on from generation to generation until it was included in the history texts of the primary schools, and later, in some tourist guides. This is the reason why, when visitors ask why the building bears this name, the following description is obligatory.

The Legend of the Magician — Many version of this legend exist, each writer accomodating his own criterion, perhap in order to make the legend more interesting. Basically, the legend is as follows: At one time, an old woman named "La Bruja" (the witch) who lived in Uxmal, wanted to have a son; unfortunately, she was not able to conceive one because of her old age. Nevertheles, she prayed with fervor to the gods for a son, always below the ceiba tree, the sacred tree of the Maya. To her great surprise, on one of these occasions she saw an enormous bat, of proportions which had never been seen before, fly out of one of the branches of the tree and begin to fly around her. This bat then asked her what she desired; the bat was the voice of the gods. The old woman was paralyzed with fear, and could hardly believe what she heard and saw. The bat repeated the question, saying: "This is your only opportunity to have your prayers answered". Then, with a voice broken with nervousness, she was at last able to say: "I want to have a son". The bat answered: "You will have your son if you do what I order. Follow that path until you reach a cave. In its interior you will find an enormous egg. Take it to your house and there, keep it warm, because from that egg will be born the son that you so desire". Finishing with these words, the bat disappeared in rapid flight. The old woman did as the bat said, putting the egg a prudent distance from the cooking stove during the day, and between her breasts at night. After seven days, her son was born. He was a curious child who grew rapidly; upon completing nine years of age, however, he stopped growing, and as such was considered a dwarf. This dwarf had extraordinary skills for fortelling the future; he knew ahead of time when the inhabitants of Uxmal and the surrounding area were going to have good or bad harvests, when there were going to be long droughts or abundant rain, epidemics, plagues, and storms. For this reason they called him "the Magician". His mother took very good care of him, as he embodied her lifelong dream.

Under the stove in her house, this old woman had hidden a copper disk which she inherited from her ancestors, who had recommended that she keep it secretly guarded. For this reason, the old woman frequently reminded her son not to go near the stove nor to touch the ashes. The woman reminded him so often that the clever dwarf began to suspect that something very important was hidden there, so he began to plot a way to keep his mother away from the house for a longer time than usual, so that he could investigate. It finally occurred to the dwarf to make some perforations in the pitchers which his mother used daily to fetch the water. When the old woman went for water and noticed that the pitchers were not filling up, she saw the perforations. Instead of getting angry, she shook her head, smiled at the mischevious ways of her son, and began to repair the vessels. While she was away, the dwarf had time to push aside the fire in the stove, and while digging through the ashes, to his surprise, he came upon the copper disk. After looking at it for a while, he hit it with such force that its sound could be heard for miles around. According to the prophesies and the laws that ruled during that time, the person who struck the disk, and made its sound reverberate throughout the region would obtain the throne of Uxmal without any excuse from the governor who was in power at the time.

The king, aware of these sacred arrangements, upon hearing the sound, became entranced and worried; he became filled with anger and ordered his soldiers to find the person who made the sound and to bring him to him immediately. The soldiers asked the neighbors of the region where the sound had come from, and in a short time they arrived at the old woman's house just as she was scolding the boy for his disobedience. After hearing this reprimand, the soldiers said: "This is the one we are looking for", and without consideration of his age or his size, they took him away, pushing and shoving him along until he was before the king. The village people hated the king because he was and ambitious and evil despot, and they were happy because they thought that a change in government which would better their lives had finally come. They joined in procession behind the dwarf, and crowded around the palace cheering the prodigious young boy.

The indignant king wanted the public dispersed, but the soldiers were unable to carry out his order. Seeing that part of his army was against him, he agreed to give up the throne under the condition that the dwarf undergo three tests to which the king would subject him. The dwarf accepted the challenge with a smile, but the village people were worried and doubtful because they knew the tests would be difficult.

For the first test, the boy was to guess the number of leaves of the enormous tree which grew in the plaza; for the second, both the king and the dwarf were to make and idol to be thrown into the fire; the maker of the idol which would resist flames would win. For the third test, the dwarf would allow a basket of coco-yoles (fruits like nuts) to be broken on his head, and if he survived the test, the king would be obliged to undergo the same test. The date of the event was set, and the village people were asked to attend.

The old woman spent the next few days worried and crying, praying to the gods under the same tree under which she always prayed. Suddenly, the same bat appeared again at the old woman, saying: "Do not worry. Your son will pass the tests if you do what I am going to tell you. I know how many leaves that tree has, and I will tell you the amount, but be careful not to forget it. Tell your son to make an idol of clay, since fire cannot destroy clay; I saw that the king is making one of very hard rock, but it will break. Go to the cave where you found the egg, and there you will find a wig reinforced with a strong helmet that will fit your son's head exactly. The rest, leave up to me". The bat then flew away and entered the jungle.

The entire village filled the great plaza on the day of the event. They were all impatient, as they doubted that the dwarf would triumph. The king, with great arrogance and in a disrespectful tone, said to the boy: "Miserable dwarf, as you figure, tell me how many leaves are on that tree". After remaining thoughtful for a few minutes, the boy answered the king, with great poise, the number his mother had told him. At this same instant, the enormous bat appeared and flew around the king saying: "The amount that the boy stated is correct, and I know because I bring the voice of the gods." It then flew away, disappearing before the amazed crowd. The crowd then shouted jubiously and enthusiastically to the king that there was no need to count the leaves, and that they believed that the bat was a messenger of the gods, even though animals do not talk. The king resisted at first, but the pressure from the shouts of the crowd gave him no other choice but to accept this decision.

It was time for the second test, and both contestants put their idols into the fire. The king's idol resisted the heat for a while, but later it broke apart and the dwarf was declared the victor.

The boy, with the protection of the helmet, was able to support the breaking of the cocoyoles in the third test. When the king realized that there were only three cocoyoles left to break, and that the smiling boy had passed all three tests, he was frightened and wanted to flee. It was now the king's turn to pass the third test, and the executer (whom he had treated so badly) was ready to administer his test. The first cocoyole was broken with all the force that the soldier could muster, so that when it hit upon the king's head, it split his skull and killed him inmmediately.

This is how the dwarf became the new ruler of Uxmal, governing with great knowledge from a temple built especially for him. That temple now bears his name — "The Temple of the Magician"

192

We know that legends are fantasies which rise from the imagination of people, but often times, at the bottom of each legend, lies an element of truth. Perhaps, at one time, there was a king of Uxmal who was very short and who ruled his people with great prudence and intelligence, although he was not born from an eggs nor did he need to pass the difficult tests mentioned above.

In the explorations of a number of years ago in the Temple of the Magician, it was discovered that the building consisted of four substructures. One can see the facade of the first substructure on the temple's West side, resting on a low platform. The East side of this temple was explored by the National Institute of Anthropology and History of Mexico, under the direction of the archaeologist César Sáenz. In 1968, Sáenz dug an inlet or a tunnel on the East side and found the facade of this side almost completely intact; it was of the Puuc Style, which is characteristic of that region. The second, third, and fourth structures of this pyramid begin at the level of the first oval-shaped platform; the Maya later covered the second and the third structures with the second oval-shaped platform. On top of this oval-shaped platform, the Maya built another cuadrangle using it for the base of the Temple of the Magician. The fourth structure faces to the west, and is of the Chenes Style. The facade of this structure represents the enormous face of a monster whose open mouth forms the door. (Photo 52 Each side of its steep staircase is ornamented with twelve masks of the God of Rain.

2.— The Nunnery Quadrangle

To the west to the Temple of the Magician is situated an incredibly beuatiful group of buildings; this group is truely a filigree made of stone. One can see that the Maya architects executed their most expert art in the construction of these buildings.

We are almost certain that there is not another architectural construction in all of Latin America which compared to this one.

The name, "The Nunnery", is attributed to the Franciscan priest Diego López Cogolludo who, upon seeing the buildings, thought they looked similar to the religious convents in Spain.

Photo No. 52. The Temple of the Magician, the fourth superstructure. Uxmal. Chenes Style. Photo courtesy of Francisco Góngora.

This group is constructed four meters above the level of the plaza, where the Ball Court is located.

The buildings which make up this square are at different heights or levels, arranged in a harmonious manner. The South side is the lowest and rests at the level of the floor of the patio, while the East and West sides begin at the level of the middle cornice of the Southern building. The North side begins at the level of the central cornice of the East and West sides, and at the height of the roof of the Southern building. The decoration carved in rock on the Southern building consists of eight straw houses, with a God of Rain, without the long nose, above the door of each house. The framework of this decoration forms small squares which appear to be little lattice work. The length of the Southern building is 69 meters; the building is divided into two rows of individual rooms, eight with their doors facing the interior of the square and eight with their doors facing outward. In the central point of the Southern building is situated the principle entrance to the entire group of buildings; this entrance is in the form of an angular arch. (Photo 53)

Photo No. 53. The South Side of the Nunnery Quadrangle at Uxmal. Photo by the author.

The West side o fthe Nunnery is possibly the most richly ornamented; its decoration is varied, as can be seen in Photo Number 54 and 55. This building rests on top of another, and the author was able to observe in a small boring on the platform the top part of a corbeled arch and the rock and mortar which were used to close it. When the sound and light show was installed at Uxmal, this inlet was covered up. The Western building measures 53 meters in length and 10.50 meters in width, and is divided into seven rooms which face the front and a number of interior rooms which are connected to the front rooms by wide doors. These interior rooms have no rear exit. (Some of the rears roof are down fallen)

The Northern building is the longest, measuring 82.70 meters in length and 10.50 meters in width. It has eleven rooms in front, and eleven more rooms on the rear without exist at the exterior (back side) each one of these are connected to one of the front rooms by a doorway. At both ends of this building are located another room, each which has an exit on the side of the building; the decoration of these rooms rivals that of the others. Above each door is a row of masks of the God of Rain which are alternated with thatched roofs carved in the stone. A number of other designs compliment this pattern as can be seen in Photos Numbers 56 and 57.

Photo No. 54. The West Side of the Nunnery Quadrangle at Uxmal. Photo by the author.

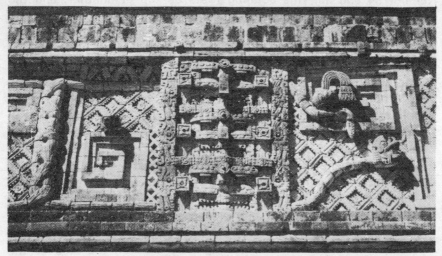

Photo No. 55. Detail of the west side of the Nunnery Quadrangle at Uxmal. Photo by the author.

Photo No. 56. The North Side of the Nunnery Quadrangle at Uxmal. Photo by the author.

Photo No. 57. Thatch roof house carved on stone. Detail of the North side of the Nunnery Quadrangle at Uxmal. Photo by the author.

The Eastern building is 48.50 meters in length and 10.50 meters wide. This construction has five doors which provide access to a number of interconnected double rooms, which have no rear exit. The decoration of this building consists of six trapezoids which form the heads of serpents. In the center of each trapezoids is a precious carved face which is ornamented with a variety of symbols. Between the central and the top cornice of the building is a lattice decoration which appears to be small lattice work. (Photo 58)

Photo No. 58. The East Side of the Nunnery Quadrangle at Uxmal. Photo by the author.

The reader may have noticed that each building in this group has an odd number of doors; the Eastern building has five, the Southern one has nine, (including the central entrance), the building on the West side has seven, and the Northern one has eleven. Some people believe that, perhaps for religious reasons, the Maya did not represent even numbers in their constructions, but the real motive on the part of the Maya was simply one of aesthetics: the Maya always gave distinction to the central room, and because it was the most important, it's entranceway or door was always larger and specially decorated. It seems only logical for reasons of construction harmony to build the same number of rooms to the left of this central room as to the right. In this way, with the inclusion of a central room, there were always and odd number of rooms in these constructions.

3.— The Governor's Palace

Just as the Nunnery is considered to be the most beautiful group of buildings in all of America, so is the singular Governor's Palace, unrivaled in its size, its proportions, anf its rich decoration. (Photo No. 59).

The name of this building is also attributed to the Franciscan priest Diego López Cogolludo, who so named it upon first sight.

Twenty thousand stones were used to ornament the four sides of the facade of the Governor's Palace; this shows us the persistence, strength, and tenacity of the Maya. (As the posterior side of this building is not reconstructed, it was necessary to count the number of stones on the front and on one side, double each of these figures, and then add the two resulting products together to arrive at the total number, or 20,000.) This building is 97.5 meters long, 12 meters wide, and 9 meters high. There are eleven doors on the front part of this building which give access to sixteen rooms; each side of the buildings also has a door which provides entrance to two rooms, making a total of twenty rooms.

At each end of this building (before the last door of each end), is an arch which at one time was a corridor which connected the front and the back of the building. It is possible that the Maya needed more rooms and had planned to convert these corridors into two rooms, divided in the middle by a wall with a small porch in the front.

This beautiful edifice is decorated with a large number of masks of the God of Rain, with greek lines arranged in harmony with them. The top cornice is carved in the form of a chain, but it reality this design consists of undulating serpents whose heads and tails, which were at one time on the corners, have disappeared. Recessed within the front wall of the Governor's Palace are a number of incomplete idols that could possibly have been representations of important people.

The three platforms upon which this buildings rests are calculated to encompass 500,000 cubic meters in area.

4.— The Great Pyramid

There is very little known about this building, but present evidence suggests that it rests on top of earlier constructions.

Photo No. 59. The Governor's Palace, Uxmal. Photo by the author.

The restoration of this enormous pyramid took place between the years 1972 and 1973, a project realized by the National Institute of Anthropology and History of Mexico under the direction of César Sáenz. This magnificent structure arose from what seemed to be a pile of rubbish.

This pyramid is composed of nine superimposed levels, with sixty-five stairs. Its facade is ornamented with greek lines and little parrots in different positions; some of these are facing straight forward while others are looking to the west or to the east, flying to the east or to the west, or flying either up or down.

The facade of this building juts out in its central portion; this is because of the fact that the Maya added some narrow rooms which cover part of the bottom structure. The reliefs of this addition are not as finely finished as the others, a fact which suggests that they were carved during the begining of Decadent Period.

5.— The House of the Tortoise

This rectangular-shaped building measures thirty meters in length from east to west, and eleven meters from north to south, and has an approximate height of seven meters. The East and West sides each have three doors, each door giving entrance to two rooms. In the center of the North and South sides, there are three rooms which have been restored, and two more rooms which are still without a roof. The name of this structure comes from the tortoises that are embedded around its uppermost cornice. Along the side walls of some of the rooms ar small platforms of about 30 centimeters in height; their purpose is still unknown.

e). Important Characteristics of Other Centers

We have seen that Chichén Itzá was determined to be the chief religious city or ceremonial center of the Maya because of the large quantity of jewels that were offered to the God of Rain in its sacred cenote, by the people of Chichén Itzá as well as by religious pilgrims who came from other regions of the Maya area. We have also seen that Uxmal was exceptional in its beautiful architecture, Tikal in the extensiveness, the number, and the height of its buildings, and Copán in its function as a scientific center.

201

Palenque

Just as Uxmal stands out because of its magnificent exterior carvings, Palenque is exceptional in its excellent and elaborate interior reliefs which are carved both in stone and stucco. Dr. Morley attributes the quality of these reliefs to the lime stone of that region, which has a very fine grain; a superior quality stone in comparison with that of other regions. This is why the reliefs appear to be so similar to those of lithography.

Everyone who visits Palenque marvels at the extraordinary artwork of the artists of that time. The most notable reliefs are found in the Temple of the Cross, the Temple of the Foliated Cross, the Temple of the Sun, and the Temple of the Inscriptions. A tomb of one of the most famous nobles of Palenque is found in the substructure of the Temple of the Inscriptions.

Piedras Negras

Piedras Negras is another important ceremonial center in which twenty-eight stelae are found in uninterrupted sequence, marking the end of hotuns, or periods of five years. Also found here is the most beautiful sculpture in all of the Maya area. This sculpture is an exquisitly carved tablet of stone, the stone being of such a fine quality that it resembles ivory. The quality sculpture work found at Piedras Negras is similar to that of Palenque, and considering the short distance between the two, it stands to reason that there was contact between the artisans of that time.

Calakmul

In spite of the fact that Calakmul is a ceremonial center of the second category, it is distinguished by the 103 stelae found there, seventy-three of which are sculptured (the other thirty are smooth).

Cobá

Cobá is noted for the five lagoons which surround it, for its size as well as for the number of ancient Maya roads or causeways which are located at the site.

202

Quiriguá

Quiriguá is exceptional in that the largest, elaborated stele in the Maya area was found there; it measures 10.67 meters high, 1.50 meters wide, and 1.27 meters thick, and weighs sixty-five tons.

Mayapán

Although the architecture of Mayapán is very poor, found there is a wall of eight kilometers in length inside of which are 3,600 basically small structures.

Mayapán was an important political center in the Northern Yucatán Península, for it was there that the Maya established a Confederation which lasted for about two hundred years. Mayapán was one of the few ceremonial centers that fell in the final stages of collapse of the Maya culture.

CHAPTER ELEVEN

SOCIAL ORGANIZATION

a) . **Political Aspect**
b) . **Religious Aspect**
c) . **The Organization of Construction Work**

a) . **Political Aspect**

The Mayan culture had been disintegrating for a number of decades when the Spanish arrived at the beginning of the sixteenth century. The Maya of this Decadent Period lived in thatched huts of either straw or palm leaves, in small villages, similar to the way they lived in the Formative Period. Photos 60 and 61 Their political organization at this time was perhaps only a pale reflection of that of their ancestors during their years of splendor.

The conquistadors found the territory of the Yucatán Península divided into nineteen sectors or districts, each one controlled by a cacique who governed it in his own manner. Some of these districts were also under the higher authority of one chief who lived in the most important population center or the capital of his district. This supreme chief was called "Halach Uinic", which translated means "powerful man" or "he who reigns"; he was also given the title of "Ahau" which means "king" or "sir".

The power of the Halach Uiniques (Halach Uinicoob) was unlimited. They willfully controlled the destiny of their territory; hence, they were in charge of studying the problems that existed and coming up with adequate solutions.

The position of Halach Uinic was hereditary rather than determined by popular election; this hereditary position fell upon the shoulders of the oldest or the most competent son. If there were no competent sons, a council elected one of the close relatives of the family to govern.

205

Photo No. 60. Thatch roof house in where some of the actual mayas still live.

Photo No. 61. Thatch roof house in where some of the actual mayas still live.

Under the Halach Uniques, in heirarchical order, were the Batabes (Bataboob), who were designated by the Halach Uiniques to govern the areas outside of the capital. This position was similar to that of our town president.

The Halach Uinic also assumed the position of Batab in the areas where he lived; in this way he actually had two positions or tittles. Perhaps it is for this reason that some historians mention the highest position as that of the Batab and that of the Halach Uinic as a secondary position.

Among the powers of the Batab was that of administrating all of the business related to his community, always looking for the best solution to any problem which may have arisen. He had judicial, executive, religious, and even military power. He zealously watched over the distribution of land, and saw that the land was cultivated in the best way to yield sufficient harvests for all of the inhabitants.

The Batab was also in charge of collecting small tributes to send, in part, to the Halach Uinic, and in part to use to sustain his own administration, and to cover his family and personal needs, citizenry tended to his parcel of land.

Continuing down in hierarchical order, under the Batabes were the Ah Cuch Cabes (Ah Cuch Caboob) who were equivalent to our aldermen of today. Two or more people of high moral character were appointed to this position, and it was their job to help their superiors with the administration of public affairs. Following the Ah Cuch Cabes were the Ah Kuleles (Ah Kuleloob) who were delegated by the Batabes. Under them were the Holpopes (Holpopoob) who acted as assistants to the aldermen. Finally, following the Holpopes were the Tupiles (Tupiloob) who were to carry out the orders of their superiors. [1]

b) . Religious Aspect

Aside from being respected for their knowledge and their position, the priests indirectly occupied a very important position in public administration. They served as counselors to the political leaders, greatly influencing their decisions. The priests had the most scientific knowledge, especially of astronomy, and for this reason, they were able to predict celestial phenomena. The priests

1) .— Canto López A., Op. Cit.; pp. 194—195 (Capítulo 11).

207

also kept track of the passage of time in a very admirable way, and likewise, they knew, in part, the mysteries of the complicated writings of their ancestors. Apart from their rigid preparation, the priests were known to have lead a very chaste life; they never married or had any association with women. They subjected themselves to very strict disciplinary ways; they were known to abstain from things, they assumed self-sacrifices which consisted of long fasts, bleeding the nose and the ears, piercing holes in their cheeks and their tongues, and various other things. The priests took an active part in the execution of human sacrifices which included tearing out the heart of the human victims and offering it to the gods. It is now known that the Maya practiced human sacrifice as far back in their history as the Classic Period. However, in the northern part of the Yucatán Península, human sacrifice was introduced at a later date by the Toltecs.

During the Decadent Period, the political organization of the Maya was as described above; however, the conditions of the life of the Maya during the Classic and Post-Classic Periods were completely different. During Decadent Period it was not necessary to work intensely on the construction of large edifices, nor was it necessary to educate and technically prepare a large group of artisans and professionals, nor to employ a large number of people to sustain the public administration which was well-organized and very active. This leads one to ask: What was the religious political organization of that brilliant epoch? The answer to this question still remains unknown.

The specialists, after long, in-depth studies and investigations, have proposed that the Maya of those periods had a theocratic government with a system similar to that of Ancient Greece; a system of city-states, united under a Confederation.

The author believes that the government of that epoch, in many ways, did not differ much from our own political organization, since our organization progressed and evolved from the villages of those times. Modifications and changes in the political organization were made as new societal demands and problems arose which required careful planning in order to avoid economic and political imbalances which lead to collapse and recession.

We know perfectly well that one single person cannot run a complex country.

During the Classic and Post-Classic Periods, the Maya were governed by a supreme chief, or Halach Uinic, who controlled a very extensive region, perhaps the size of a small nation. His position would be comparable to our President of the Republic (México). Below the Halach Uinic, in hierarchical order, were his most esteemed collaborators; one who was in charge of studying and finding solutions to the agricultural problems, another who programmed and planned the construction of buildings, another who studied and found solutions to political problems, another who studied and calculated the economic state of the region to determine whether there was a deficit or a surplus in the production of food, and so on...

Each of these administrators had his own group of collaborators who made up the bureaucracy of that time.

This theory is based on the belief that the history of mankind repeats itself in each civilization, with the natural variations resulting from the special circumstances of the time.

Perhaps the Palace of the Governor in Uxmal was, in reality, an administrative building where the collaborators or "Secretaries" carried out their business in a practical and simple form, without the great number of complications that we know of today. It is possible that the Temple of the Warriors at Chichén Itzá served the same purpose.

Perhaps the areas of secondary importance to the capital were governed by Batabes, as in the Decadent Period. It is also possible that in the smaller, less populated areas of the region, that other authorities of lesser power governed. They may have filled a position similar to our town presidents, with their own respective group of collaborators.

Because of the fact that the Maya were able to realize such incredible accomplishments with less than adequate materials, their civilization often appears to be something of a fairytale to us, or an impossibility. Nevertheless, it is a reality that we continue searching for, a reality that has been discovered to have been based, without a doubt, on an admirably formed political and religious organization.

c) . **The Organization of Construction Work.**

Some studies assert that it did, in fact, take a long time for the Maya to build each one of their buildings, because during

209

the summer growing season, especially during the rains, all of their time was dedicated to their fields. Once they were sure they had enough crops to sustain themselves, they worked on constructing the buildings. Many of the visitors to the Mayan archaeological sites have a similar idea, believing that the construction of one of the large buildings, without metal tools and without adequate means of locomotion, would have employed thousands of workers and hundreds of years.

This idea is not acceptable, however, if one keeps in mind that the entire Northern Group at Chichén Itzá is very extensive and includes many buildings (some of which are as large as the Castle and the Temple of the Warriors and its substructures), yet it had an active life of only 219 years, (which was the duration of the Toltec period there, between the years 975 to 1194 A. D.), including the time the buildings were in use and not only the time required for their construction. In the year 1194, Chichén Itzá was partially destroyed and abandoned, as will be seen in more detail in the following chapter.

These dates prove that the time it took to construct these buildings was relatively short, and that it did not take thousands of workers to build them as many people suppose.

Another authentic proof which contradicts the great time and manpower theory, was verified by an unforeseen happening; a few years ago (1967), in order to celebrate the Worlds Fair in Montreal, Canada, the Mexican government decided that in their exhibit they would construct a replica of the east side of the Nunnery of Uxmal. In order to complete this task, they designated fourteen workers, five of them were experts in the art of sculpture, five of the others were artisans with a lot of experience, and the last four were young, inexperienced apprentices. These workers began to carve the stones, making exact copies, piece by piece, without leaving out even the most minute detail, until they finished the mosaic. They also constructed four "chacmooles" which are reclining idols which have a plate resting on their stomachs, made completely of one piece of stone (these human figures are characteristic of the Toltec influence as was stated in the previous chapter.) They also carved some two-headed cougars, one of which was modeled after the actual one which is found on the platform situated in front of the Palace of the Governor at Uxmal. They also built a stele, elaborated with fine reliefs, which measured two meters in height, and one and one quarter meters in width, forming a pointed arch. This entire construction job lasted four months (120 days). It is necessary to say that the stones were transported by truck and that they were excavated with metal pickaxes and chisels). I thought that this work would serve as a base by which I could calculate the time of construction of the buildings during the period of the ancient Maya, and therefore prove my argument.

Taking into account the primitive tools used, and assuming an eight hour work day, everyday, the same east side of the Nunnery would have been constructed by the Maya in the following manner:

20 workers for the excavation of stone
15 workers to transport the rock
40 workers to carve the mosaic (instead of the fourteen used in 1967)
20 workers to produce the lime
15 workers to excavate and transport the "sascab" or the white earth used in the preparation of mortar.

110 workers in total.

The addition of the number of workers is to compensate for the difference in the tools used by the ancient Maya and the workers today.

The portion of the Nunnery reproduced for the exhibit in Montreal represents approximately one fifth of the entire building. (Photo 62) It was stated that the work done by the artisans took 120 days, plus an additional 25 days to assemble the building in Montreal, making a total of 145 days. To figure the time it would have taken to construct the entire building, it is only necessary to multiply 145 days by five, or 725 days.

To be a little more expressive, and taking into account a possibly poor estimate in the work force, one can add twenty workers to the above estimate. Skeptics can even add one year to the construction time, and still the calculations demonstrate that it was not necessary to employ thousands of workers, nor did it take a long time to construct the buildings. To construct the east side of the Nunnery at Uxmal, according to the above calculations, the Maya needed only 130 men and three years.

Photo No. 62. A reproduction of the architecture of Uxmal, using as a basis for this reproduction the East Side of the Nunnery Quadrangle. Photo taken from the magazine Montreal 67, published in French. Canada.

Using this as a base, one can go on to calculate the construction time of other Mayan buildings.

The following are some examples which further demonstrate the validity of the above stated calculations. The first example is the restoration of the front part of the Great Pyramid at Uxmal directed by César Sáenz. Sáenz began his work in September of 1972 employing only twenty-four workers who were mayan masons, all of whom were familiarized with this type of job. They finished at the end of April of the following year. They did not carve new stones; rather they used the originals that were found, for the most part, at the base of the mound which was to be restored.

The materials they used were; cement, powdered stone, and lime transported by dump trucks, and the tools they used were the same as those used by the actual masons including one-wheeled carts similar to a wheelbarrow.

In review: the work as it is seen, was done by twenty-four workers in approximately eight months. (See photos 63 to 69).

Photo No. 63. Sequence Number 1 of the restauration of the Great Pyramid at Uxmal. Photo by the author.

Photo No. 64. Sequence Number 2 of the restoration of the Great Pyramid at Uxmal. Photo by the author.

Photo No. 65. Sequence Number 3 of the restoration of the Great Pyramid at Uxmal. Photo by the author.

Photo No. 66. Sequence Number 4 of the restoration of the Great Pyramid at Uxmal. Photo by the author.

Photo 67. Sequence No. 5 of restauration of the Great Pyramid at Uxmal. Photo by the author.

Photo 68. Sequence No. 6 of restauration of the Great Pyramid at Uxmal. Photo by the author.

Photo 69. Sequence No. 7 of restauration of the Great Pyramid at Uxmal. Photo by the author.

The construction done today offers another comparative example to support the calculations: in eight months, five masons can construct a two-story house with seven rooms of average size (4.5 x 4 meters) without machine.

Another convincing comparison can be found in bees; these tiny insects, in an incredible way, can collect a number of pounds of honey and store it in their hive in a short period of three to four months, or the period of time when the flovers are in bloom. That amount of honey could not be transported at some distance by one man.

The organization of these insects is truely admirable; some collect the nectar from the flowers, others the pollen, others transport water, and the rest, who cannot fly because of their age, do the work inside of the hive, consisting mainly of feeding themselves, so that later they can flap their wings like electric fans, which produce the necessary ventilation. They also expel tiny bits of wax from their outer abdomen, which they mix with saliva in order to form the geometric cells, of exact milimetrical in size which make up the walls of their honeycomb.

216

Other bees direct the honey and the pollen to an interior compartment, or "papo" in Spanish, with which they make a nutritious drink which is the foodstuff of the larvae.

Why don't flies behave in the same manner?; simply because they do not have an organized society.

To reaffirm my theory, one can note the difference between India and Israel. India is a very old country, densely populated, but very poor with a great number of beggars. On the other hand, there is Israel; a very small, young country, but extremely industrious and well-organized whose struggle has seen great results, results which are the astonishment of the world we live in.

These examples plainly demonstrate that rapid evolution and success of a country is not based on the number of its inhabitants, but rather in its spirit of work, its ingenuity, and its organization.

It is almost certain that the Mayan workers had an organization similar to ours in that each worker was a specialist in one certain activity which he did all of his life; some excavated stone, others transported it, others produced lime for mortar, others excavated "sascab" (white earth) also used in the production of mortar, the engineers calculated the weight of the buildings in order to assure that adequate foundations were built, and the arquitects (who were perhaps the engineers), drew the plans for the complicated mosaics which were to adorn the facades. On the buildings where the drawings or designs are repeated many times (called "celocías"), some sculptures did the crosses or x's individually. The fabulous Palace of the Masks of the Gods of Rain at Kabah (the only one of its kind in the Mayan area), is completely covered with effigies that number into the hundreds. In this case, it is almost certain that some workers carved the eyes, others the noses, others the ears, and so on.

Some people think that the Maya first put the stones of the facades in place and then carved them. This is illogical, however, because, if during the carving, a wrong tap of the chisel ruined the drawing, they would have to take out that piece and replace it with another, a task which would have been very difficult if not impossible to do.

It is probable that the farmers worked their fields all year round, the potters produced ceramics to satisfy the needs of the region, the weavers of cotton wove cloth, the hunters tried to kill the largest quantity of animals for having enough meat and so on. The government then imposed a tribute consisting of part of the laborer's product, which was used to sustain the public administration and to eralize the greatest works of the government.

CHAPTER TWELVE

RELIGION

The **Popolvuh,** sacred book of the Quiché Maya of Guatemala (and previously mentioned in other chapters), has been cited by some as a book which contains the true religious sentiment of the Mayan people; in reality, this literary work by one of the earliest known Mayan ethnic groups is a lyric narrative which does not abound in religious information. Others have tried to use the Codices to determine the most important Mayan gods, and even though the experts have given names to each one of these gods, their work is still of a hypothetical nature. The **Relations** of the Franciscan Bishop Diego de Landa describe the ceremonies practiced by the Maya of the Decadent Period, mentioning a great number of details about the deities, but de Landa wrote with the idea that all of the Mayan deities were really bad spirits and Pagan demons; hence, we are left without a completely dependable, unbiased source of religious information about the Mayan culture.

There is no doubt that religion, as a worship of divinities, existed among the Maya in an interpretive form from the beginning of their civilization, and that this religion was based primarily on natural phenomena. With the passing of time, the Mayan priests organized the religion, and developed the ceremonies and rites from which the hierarchy of the gods later evolved. These gods were grouped into categories, according to their polytheistic consequence.

According to generally accepted research, the Maya believed that the earth was flat, and that the heavens were supported by four brothers, called Bacabs (Bacaboob). Each of these brothers was thought to be situated in one of the four cardinal directions, each with a ceiba tree and with his own particular color; the color for East was red, the color for West was black, the color for South was yellow, and the color for North was white. Green as designated as the color of the center of the earth.

219

The firmament was considered to be divided into thirteen levels, with a different god dwelling in each level. These gods not only ruled in their own levels or worlds, but also had power in all of the other levels as well. These were the gods of light and good; their worlds were called "Oxlahuntikú" by the Maya, or "the region of the thirteen gods". The Maya believed that below, and in juxtaposition to, these thirteen levels were nine other levers, in which lived nine different gods; hence the name "Bolontikú", or "the region of the nine gods". The thirteen upper-level gods were thought to be workers for the good, while the nine below were believed to work against the good. The ancient Maya believed that these latter gods were responsible for all of their calamities, such as sicknesses, plagues, prolonged droughts, wars, etc. These two groups of gods embodied moral positions similar of the Christian symbols of Heaven and Hell.

The ancient Maya also believed that the world was supported by an enormous alligator that lived in the water; this belief, like many others, was probably held predominently among the lower-class, uneducated people, since it is scarcely likely that the Mayan scientists of the Classic and Post-Classic Periods, with their advanced knowledge of mathematics, astronomy, etc., would have accepted such an outlandish notion as feasible.

It should be noted that some of these absurd beliefs, like the alligator myth listed above, still exist in the minds of many of the present-day Maya. For example, when there is a solar or lunar eclipse visible in their hacienda or village, the Maya ignore the real causes for these phenomena, they believe that the sun or moon is being attacked. In an attempt to aid the endangered celestial body in question, the Maya make a great deal of noise, and fire their rifles at the eclipes.

Some investigators assert that Hunab-kú (in Mayan, "hunab" means "only", and "kú" means "god"; hence, "Hunab-kú" is "only god") was considered by the ancient Maya to be an omnipotent, world-ruling god, and that Hunab-kú was followed in their religious hierarchy by various deities of lesser importance. In spite of this, the **Popol Vuh** lists Tepeu and Gugumatz as the progenitors or creators of the plants, animals, and most importantly, of man himself. Their first two attempts at the creation of man, employing mud and wood, were failures; only when the gods used corn were they ultimately successful in this endeavor.

Among the celestial deities were the Gods of the Sun (Kin) and of the Moon, (Uh) the God of the Planet Venus (Noh Ek), and the God of the North Star (Xaman Ek), to name just a few. [1]

There were also gods for a variety of natural phenomena, such as Yum Chaac, the God of Rain, Ik, the God of the Wind, and Yum Kak, the God or Fire.

Almost all of the activities to which the Maya were dedicated had their own particular deity. For example, Yum Kax was the God of the Fields and of Agriculture, and the God of War was Ek Chuah. The God of Knowledge and Wisdom was Itzamná, the Goddess of Suicide was Ix Tab, and the God of Death was Ah Puch. In addition to these there were many others.

As has been previously mentioned, there were also gods for each of the twenty days of the month, and nineteen more for each of the different months of the year.

Investigators say, with respect to the God of Rain (Yum Chaac), that it is represented by the large, nose artistically decorated, which adorns the facades of many of the temples in the Mayan area, especially in the Northern part of the Yucatán Península. None of these authors, however, can give a satisfactory explanation of the identity of the long nose figures as rain gods. In light of this fact, Villacorta intelligently designates this symbol as simply "the gods of the large nose". These representations are all very similar, but not exactly alike in composition, except for those of the so-called Palace of the Codzpop in Kabah. The four facades of this temple are totally covered with the nose, effigy. (Photos 70 and 71) Almost all of the effigies are similar, with very minor variations, except for those on the base of the doors, which are wider. The Maya of the Decadent Period must have confused these symbols with rolled "petates", or mats; "Codz" means "rolled" in Mayan, while "pop" means "mat".

There is another mask of Yum Chaac in the Central Chamber of the Great Pyramid of Uxmal which also has the wide rolled nose. This symbol of the Rain God differs from the others in that it depicts Yum Chaac with closed eyelids, stylized ears of corn in the ears, and different ornamentation on the forehead (Photo 72). On both sides of the stairway of the Temple of the Divine, also at Uxmal, are found twelve masks of the Rain God, all with eyes

1).— Canto López A., Op. Cit. pp. 142—143 (Capítulo XII).

Photo No. 70. The Palace of the "Codzpop", Kabah, Yucatán. Photo by the author.

Photo No. 71. Another view of the Codzpop at Kabah. Photo by the author.

Photo No. 72. The God of Rain found in the central chamber of the Great Pyramid at Uxmal. Photo by the author.

in the form of a spiral. Which was surely intended to represent them as eyes which are markedly crossed. We know from the writings of Bishop Landa that the Maya often changed the position of their childrens' pupils by placing a little ball between their eyes, as the Maya believed that having crossed eyes was a sign of nobility. These masks also have noses which are peculiarly curved upward, in an opposite direction to the noses of other Yum Chaacs, as can be seen in Photo 73. There are Yum Chaac masks, with their own unique stylizations, located some thirty kilometers to the southeast of Kabah, in Sayil and Labná. Eight houses of straw are etched in stone on the South Side of the Nunnery Quadrangle, with a mask of Yum Chaac carved above each; in these depictions of the Rain God, however, the large nose is replaced by a curving triangle, similar in manner to a shield in the shape of a pointed arch, in the center is a drawing of a flower similar to an iris in form. In the Northern part of the same Quadrangle, above each door over which reliefs still exist, are found superimposed masks which are different in the formation of the mouth, the number of teeth, the ornamentation on the forehead, etc., from the other existing Yum Chaac masks.

223

Photo No. 73. A mask of the God of Rain on the lateral parts of the Temple of the Magician; the West Side, Uxmal. Photo by the author.

Some historians affirm that the ancient Maya represented their deities in groups, much in the same manner as is the Christian Holy Trinity, except that the Maya, as polytheists. had groups of three, four, five, as only one. These make me to believe that these masks are meant to represent various groups of gods, rather than just Yum Chaac; these stylizations can be seen in Photos 74 to 81.

According to Bishop Landa, in his **Relacions,** the ancient Maya believed in the immortality of the spirit, and that the quality of life after death was determined by life in this world; the vicious and evil would receive a bad afterlife, while a good and pleasant afterlife was reserved for those of noble acts and customs. The good souls were said to repose in the shade of a ceiba tree, or "yaxché" in Maya, where peace and tranquility, along with an abundance of food and drink, reigned supreme. The evil souls, in contrast, were believed to be condemned to an inferno of exhausting demands: hunger, cold, fatigue, and sadness, coupled with the constant torment of demons. The chief of these demons was named Hun-hau. (2)

2) .— De Landa, Op. Cit.; page 60. (Capítulo XII).

Photo No. 74. A mask of the God of Rain on the Palace at Labná, Yucatán. Photo by the author.

Photo No. 75. Gods of Rain in the facade of the main house of Xlapak.

Photo No. 76. God of Rain in the facade of the second level of the Palace of Sayil.

Photo No. 77. Gods of Rain on the west corner of the Great Pyramide at Uxmal.

Photo No. 78. Gods of Rain on the east corner of the Great Pyramid at Uxmal.

Photo No. 79. Gods of Rain in the Palace of Codzpop of Kabah.

Photo 80. Gods of Rain on the facade of the north side of the Nunnery Quadrangle at Uxmal.

One living testimony to the Mayan belief in the immortality of the soul can be seen among the present-day Maya; on the anniversaries of the deaths of their relatives they prepare succulent dishes consisting of diverse meats, fruits, and drinks, all to be placed on the religious altars in their homes (these altars are now dedicated to the Catholic saints). After prayer, the house is left vacant, so that the relative's spirit can partake of the essence of the foods and drinks.

On October 31, and November 1 and 2 of each year, in almost every home in the Yucatán Península and in parts of the rest of the Republic of México, people celebrate ceremonies

Photo 81. Gods of Rain on the south-west corner of the east building of the Nunnery Quadrangle.

dedicated to all of the saints (November 1 and 2 is the official date for All Saints Day, with this date designated as an official day of vacation); in reality, this day is dedicated to the dead. All classes of people respect this day as special.

It is generally believed throughout the area that God puts the spirits of the dead people in different places in Heaven, from which they cannot escape during the course of the year. On the 31st of October, however, God grants liberty to the souls of all the children, and on the 1st and 2nd of November, he grants liberty to the adults and others, respectively. These liberties are understood to be a sort of vacation for the dead — time for them to enjoy with their loved ones here on earth. This "spiritual visit" is said to begin on the appropriate day (October 31, November 1 or 2) and to last throughout the month of November, when the spirit returns to his reclusion in Heaven. During the three abovementioned days, the best foods, fruits, and beverages are prepared in virtually all of the homes, with which to entertain the visiting spirits. These foods are placed on the religious altars, and prayers are made in much the same manner as on the anniversary of a death. It is also customary to place a small table to one side of the altar, on which are placed smaller portions of the same foods (these for the souls which have no living families, or whose families cannot or will not provide for the souls). A separate prayer is made for these souls as well.

After prayer, the altar rooms are left vacant for a period of one hour, so that the souls will not be disturbed in their "banquet". After this period, the family and guests dispose of the food which had been left on the altars, as they believe that the only thing left after the spirits have eaten is the waste pulp (the spirits have eaten the essences of the different foods).

This process is repeated on each of the next eight days, with the main dishes changed on each day; this ceremony is called "bix" (besh) in Maya, and "Ochavario" in Spanish. It is also a custom during these eight days to celebrate "matam-pixán", a celebration which consists of hanging "chuyubes" in front of the doors of the houses; these are filled with succulent dishes, drinks, and sweets, all for the spirit to enjoy.

In other parts of the Mexican Republic, such as in the states of Morelos, Toluca, Hidalgo, Guanajuato, and in the city of México, the families of the dead clean the area around the tombs, and spread beautiful tablecloths or colored papers over the tombs. Upon these coverings they place the favorite dishes of the deceased, which generally consist of tamales, sweets, corn drinks of different flavors, etc., for the young; soup, mole sauce, rum, beer, etc., for the adults. After celebrating the rosary, the family members attend to the ceremony of enjoying the food and drinks.

In the state of Michoacán, these offerings are put in the cemetaries in late afternoon, and the family members spend the night of the 1st of November with the dead, circling the tombs with great torches.

In Pátzcuaro and Janitzio, also in the state of Michoacán, the spectacle is impressive; hundreds of people are transported to the island of Janitzio, throughout the evening, in boats lighted with torches and candles. They disembark on the beaches of the island, and go to the cemetaries, where they leave their offerings. Then, they proceed to the church to hear mass, after finally returning to the tombs after midnight, where they enjoy the offerings. The people remain in the cemetaries until dawn.

CHAPTER THIRTEEN

DRESS

How did the Maya dress?

Before we can answer this question, we must first determine to which class — working, middle, or nobility — and to which period of Maya history — Classic, Post-Classic, or Decadent — the questioner is referring. Investigations have demonstrated that the Maya were historically divided into the three social classes which have been mentioned previously. We also have to accept the fact that in any civilization, the styles of dress change over a period of time.

Now we know that in this world, customs have changed a great deal, and the economy of the people is very much improved; styles change rapidly from year to year, especially in feminine apparel. Many different varieties of clothing are produced, not only for social demands, but also for the dressmakers and businessmen who promote the various styles for the sake of creating more business for themselves. All of this is a function of vanity, especially among the rich, who are always trying to "outdo" one another.

We have numerous sources which provide us with information about the dress of the ancient Maya. Some of these include the molded reliefs on the stelae, columns, and the facades of the buildings, the murals, the idols carved of stone and clay, drawings made on the ceramics, and also information cited in the Codices. The styles of dress found in these sources are so numerous and varied, especially the dress of the nobles, that their description would fill many pages.

One example of ancient Mayan dress dating back to the year 800 A. D. (or at the end of the Florescent Classic Period), can be found on the murals of Bonampak, a site distinguished by its marvelous paintings. Three social classes can be seen depicted in the same painting on some of the murals; one can see the nobles and the priests, the musicians (who were probably considered middle class), and the servants.

The Ahau or Halach Uinic can be seen richly dressed in a suit made of jaguar skin, colored cotton cloth, and numerous complicated adornments that reveal, on first sight, his high social stature. For the ancient Maya, the plumed headdress had a very important role; it was a distinctive part of the dress which indicated that the person who wore it was of very high social status. One can also see a number of servants dressed in simple tunics, and others in mere loincloths who are holding fans in their hands which were to be used to fan their superiors.

In another part of this same mural, three people can be seen carrying the rest of Halach Uinic's attire. There are other figures standing on a platform who seem to be awaiting the start of an important ceremony; they are richly dressed in very fine capes. It is possible that the dress of the nobles depicted in these murals, as it appears quite cumbersome, was only used for ceremonial purposes and not for daily activities. In another section of the mural one can see a group of musicians, consisting of trumpeters as well as a variety of persons playing the rhythm with maracas, rattles, tortoise shells, and a drum. Some masked dancers stand out among the musicians.

Another example of ancient Mayan dress, this from the Post-Classic Period of Chichén Itzá, is found on some murals excavated from the substructure of the Temple of the Warriors by the archaeologists of the Carnegie Institute in Washington. Reproductions of these murals have been published in many books.

On these colorful murals is depicted a small fishing village on the seashore, with a number of thatched huts which are similar to those used by the rural people today. The figures in these murals are the representations of people engaged in many different activities. Some seem to be travelling salesmen carrying their goods on their backs and holding canes in their hands to lean on. They are dressed as common people in simple loincloths. Fishermen are seen padling their canoes, some of whom are dressed in long shirts that do not quite reach their knees. In the water around them is drawn a variety of species of marine life.

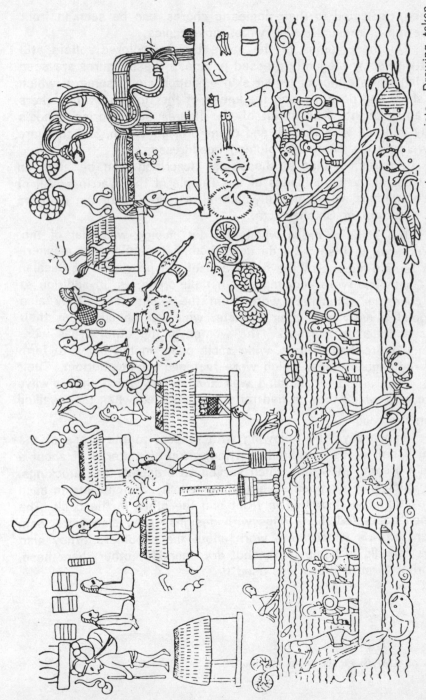

The mural painting of the sub-structure of the Temple of the Warriors, which no longer exists. Drawing taken from the official guide of the I.N.A.H.

Women, dedicated to their domestic chores, can be seen in front of the huts, dressed in very wide, loose tunics.

On the columns of the same temple, colored reliefs still exist that show elegantly dressed persons. These figures are seen wearing skirts either of jaguar skin or cotton cloth, some of which are short and do not reach the knees of the figures, while others are ankle-lenght. Almost all of the figures are wearing sandals richly adorned with tassels and other ornamentation, and they are all wearing the enormous plumed headdresses.

Figures, similar to those just described, can be seen on the front of the columnades of the Temple of the Warriors. All of these columns were colorfully painted, as were all of the interiors and exteriors of Chichén Itzá.

The style of dress which did not change was that of the workers, which Bishop Landa described in the following manner: "The female Indians of the coast and of the provinces of Bacalar and Campeche were very modest in their dress, as, in addition to the covering which they wore from the waist down, they also wrapped a sash over their breasts, which extended under their arms and tied in the back. The women in the other areas wore nothing more than a large, wide sack, open on the sides to form two rectangular flaps, which were fastened on the bottom. Their only other article of clothing was a shawl in which they always slept, and which they carried rolled-up or folded when they walked down the road".

Landa says the following with respect to the dress of the men: "Their dress consisted of a long strip of material of about a hand's breadth in width, which served as breeches and stockings, and which they wrapped several times about their waists in such a way that one flap hung in front and the other in the back. The women decorated these flaps with designs. They also wore long, square shawls which were worn about the shoulders. They also wore sandals of hemp or tanned, dry deerskin; other than these, no other form of dress was used. [1]

1).— De Landa, Op. Cit.; pp. 36—56 (Capítulo XIII).

CHAPTER FOURTEEN

AGRICULTURAL PRACTICES

(Note: As we lack information about the agricultural system of the ancient Maya, the method described in this chapter is the rudimentary method used by the majority of the present-day rural population of the Yucatán).

The soil of the Northern Yucatán Península is extremely rocky; nevertheless, dense vegetation springs forth from it in a rapid and inexplicable manner. Rich, deep soil can only be found in the southern part of the state, in the range of low mountains which are located there. These mountains begin near the state of Campeche, and take the form of a horseshoe as they enter the Yucatán and circle back again to the west. Another branch of the same mountain range extends in part of the state of Quintana Roo.

There also exist watering places of little more than one Península (with the exception of the lagoons of Cobá in Quintana Roo); the sources of water since ancient times have been natural wells, or "cenotes". These cenotes have different forms, dimensions, and depths, although all of their water levels are the same as sea level. The water contained in the cenotes is generally potable. Cenotes are commonly known by the names of corresponding underground rivers. Some of these cenotes are found in caverns with whimsical stalactites suspended from the ceiling, while others are contained within virtually vertical cones (stalagmites).

There also exist watering places of little more than six square kilometers which never become dry, but their water is turbid and unfit for human consumption.

In places which are vithout any natural sources of water, the inhabitants have resolved the problem by building cisterns, or "chultunes" in Maya, to collect rainwater; these cisterns have been found in many sites in the Península.

Some geography books describe the Yucatán as having nothing but scrub vegetation, because, for the most part, it lacks the trees of a true forest; this is not a natural phenomenon of the region, however, but can be attributed to the system of field rotation used by the native farmers, who plant a field for two follow ng years, then leave it and plant another field. After five or six years of abandonment, the field will be covered with natural vegetation to a height of six to eight meters, which will be chopped and burnetd down as the farmers return to use the field.

In places which are remote and not easily penetrated by man, fullygrown "selvas" or jungles can be found, in which live numerous wild animals.

Due to the rockiness of the soil, the present-day Maya still employ primitive agricultural methods similar to those used by their ancestors; the trees are cut and the branches extended uniformly, in medium sizes, across the ground, to be burned in the month of April before the coming of the rains. (Burning the branches is their only method for clearing the soil.) With this method, they destroy the humus of the soil, which is a valuable fertilizer, and in exchange obtain potassium in the ashes.

The rainy season usually begins sometime between the middle and the end of the month of May, and terminates near the end of September, although storms in the Caribbean sometimes find their way over the Yucatán and provoke showers in the months of October, Novermber, and even December. The average annual rainfall in the Yucatán is thirty-six inches.

Once the fields have been cleared by the fires, and after the first shower, the farmers begin to plant their seeds, especially corn seeds, using sticks with resistant points (the points are made of metal today). The farmers perforate the earth with their sticks, creating holes with a depth of about five centimeters, into which they deposit four or five corn seeds, which the farmers finally cover lightly with soil, using their sticks or feet. At times squash seeds are alternated with corn seeds within the same rows. In different parts of the milpa the farmers may plant several varieties of sweet potatoes, cassava plants, different kinds of chile peppers, watermelon, sugar melon, cucumbers, tomatoes, and "jícama", which is a white root similar to the beet, with a juicy pulp and agreeable taste (it is generally eaten raw). Where the soil is less rocky, they plant peanuts, achiote, and wild yucca, which are used to make starch.

To season the corn, the farmers bend the plants at a height slightly below that of the lowest ear of corn, in such a way so that all the ears rest with the points downward so as to protect them from the rain and birds. Sometimes beans are planted in the stems of the corn, and the vines are sustained by the corn stem.

Because the farmers do not have warehouses or storerooms in which to store their products, their harvests acording their needs — they harvest only that which they can consume or sell —. The mature beans are gathered with the corn that remains, and these crops are stored in small granaries which are improvised within the houses of the farmers.

If the rains do not arrive at an opportune moment, the effort of an entire year may be lost, which means a great loss in their economy.

With all labor done by hand, one man alone can cultivate, with a great deal of effort, one hectar of land, which is roughly 10,000 square meters.

We have already noted that the ancient Maya did not work with metal tools; the felling of trees must have been very hard work, and undoubtedly took a long time with axes of flint. Weeds were probably hoed with knives (also made of flint) soon after they germinated; in this way the weeds could be kept at bay with relative ease, as, if repeated frequently, this action could kill the weeds before they had a chance to produce seeds and propagate. When cultivated land is kept free of weeds, its plants grow luxuriant and production is abundant.

The Maya of today are not as industrious as were their ancestors, and each day a large number of them become less able to provide for their families' urgent daily needs. In ancient times there were no subsidies, and with the conditions of life and rigid discipline of the Classic and Post-Classic Periods, the ancient Mayan farmers were not only obliged to support their families, but also to sustain the nobility and the public administrators.

CHAPTER FIFTEEN

FOOD AND INDUSTRIAL PRODUCTS

a). **Vegetables and Their Preparation**
b). **Animals Which Provided Meat**
c). **Industrial Products**
d). **Colors**

a). **Vegetables and Their Preparation**

The Mayan culture relied on corn as their basic foodstuff, and from this basic grain they derived many rich and varied combinations, some of which have survived to this day. Below is a description of several of these: a) tortillas: the corn is boiled lightly with water and a dash of lime (the mineral lime — this is done to remove the cuticle from the corn kernel). Later, the corn is thoroughly washed, and then finely ground together with an amount of water which corresponds to the consistency desired in the dough. The dough obtained in this manner is then patted and pressed into thin tortillas (similar to North American pancakes), using banana leaves (which are today replaced by nylon papers). The tortilla patties are then cooked on a wood-fire griddle, and are finally consumed in place of French bread at mealtime. The preparation of tortillas requires skills which take a long time to acquire. b) pozole; the corn is cooked with water and lime until the grains swell, after which it is washed and coarsely ground. The Maya do three things with the resulting cornmeal: 1) it is dissolved in water with a bit of sugar or honey (to taste) to produce a refreshing drink, 2) milk is substituted for water in the above recipe, and this new mixture produces a drink which is tastier, and 3) coconut milk is used instead of water producing a drink which is downright delicious. c) Sacá; is a drink similar to pozole, but as cornmash is used which still has the cuticles of the kernels intact, it is of inferior quality to pozole.

d) choco-zacán; the tortilla mash is dissolved in water and cooked until a beverage is produced which can be consumed with or without sweeteners. This drink is used a great deal by mothers who are breast-feeding their babies, as it produces a large amount of milk. e) tanchucuá; this is actually identical to the drink just described (choco-zacán) except that chocolate is added as the beverage cooks, which produces a very appetizing drink. f) ak-zá; new or fresh corn (corn which has not been seasoned on the stalk) is lightly boiled in water, and the mash obtained in this manner is formed into a round ball with a cavity in the center. This cavity is filled with water and a little salt, and then the whole ball is left to sit in the night air. The following morning this mash is dissolved in water and cooked until it forms an appetizing drink. The Spanish name for ak-zá is "atole nuevo", or "new drink (of corn meal)". g) kah (pinole); the dry corn is toasted as if it were coffee, with tabasco grane added for having spetial taste and smell. This mixture of roasted grains is then finely ground and dissolved in hot water; as such, it is ready to drink, although some people later add chocolate. h) elote tierno, or "corn-on-the-cob"; the ear of corn is either roasted over charcoal, boiled in lightly salted water (in which case it is called "chacbi-nal"), or baked underground ("pibi-nal"); the later of these three methods produces a very delicious dish which is always in great demand. i) xton-lunch; this dish consists of young, tender corn, cooked in water until the kernals swell (but before they burst) as was the case with pozole, and tender squashes, with green and white stripes, which are called "x-ca". The squash are finely chopped after cooking with water, and mixed together with the cooked corn and a sweetener to taste. This dish is eaten as a dessert. j) pibi-uah; oil or lard with salt are added to the tortilla mash, and the mixture is shaped to form two large torts. Pieces of chicken and pork, stewed with tomatoes and onions which have been prepared with a red, achiote-base stock, are all ladled over the first tort(and the second tort is placed on top of the whole thing, with care taken in pressing the edges together to make sure that none of the "filling" leaks out from between. The torts and filling are then wrapped in banana leaves to be cooked underground by rocks which have been previously heated for this purpose (the more modern-thinking Maya now use ovens for this purpose, in order to make the whole process more simple). The dish is accompanied with chocolate which has been diluted in hot water or milk. This dish can also be fixed with beans called espelón instead of meat. k) x-tobiho- loch; the tortilla mash is mixed with lard and salt to taste, and flattened. Chicken or stewed pork is then placed on top, and then the outer tortilla-like shell is rolled about it, after rolled in corn leaves, and is also given the shape of a cob of corn, to be later steamed. Other similar dishes are called "dzotobichay", "papa- dzul", and other names.

We can easily see why the Maya appear to be the happiest people on earth when they have a good corn crop.

The Mayan people place their hopes in their gods, and before sampling the fruits of their harvests, they almost always celebrate a simple religious ceremony to give thanks to the gods of the fields for their benevolence. In these ceremonies, the first fruits obtained from the fields are used to make food and drinks like those described above. Containers of these dishes are then hung in special places in the trees which are located near the entrances of their fields, so that the gods can partake of the dishes. If these offerings are not given, the people feel uncom- fortable, as they believe that the gods will forget about them the following year and they will lose their protection.

After the harvest great parties are sometimes organized, which consist of prayers, in both Mayan and Spanish, followed by a superb banquet. Many people participate in these parties, especially family members, and there is no lack of liquor. These parties are called "hanli-col" (food of the milpa), and are also dedicated to the gods of the agriculture.

The ancient Maya's diet also consisted of a variety of fruits, some of which are: the fruit of the gum tree, which is either oval- shaped or is shaped like an apple. This fruit varies in size, with skin of a light brown color, and its pulp, when ripe, has the consistency of cantalope. It is a very sweet and juicy fruit, with an agreeable flavor. In Maya it is known as "yá". The ancient Maya also enjoyed the anona, or the "op" in Maya, and the Sara- muyo, "dzarmuy" in Maya, the pulp of which surrounds a bunch of black seeds, which are removed before eating the fruit. The saramuyo is still in demand today. The pitaya is the fruit of a cactus air plant which grows on the trees and on the stone fences of the Península. The pitaya is a bit larger than an orange, and its pulp is soft and covered with many black dots that appear to be seeds. The skin is either red or cream-colored when ripe. Historians say that the Spaniards had a preference for the pitaya over the other fruits, and even today, it is prefered by many because of its agreeable flavor. Another fruit eaten by the Maya was the "zapote negro" or the "black zapote", which in Maya is "ta-uch". It has a very black and smooth pulp when it is ripe. The wild guayaba, or "pichí" in Maya, is a small guava which was eaten by the Maya. (The larger guava was brought over by the Spaniards.) Among other fruits eaten by the ancient Maya are: the nance, or "chí" in Maya; the huaya or the mamoncillo, "huayum" in Maya; the piñuela, or "ch'om" in Maya; and the bonete, or the "kun-ché" in Maya. The "kanisté" was another fruit enjoyed by the Maya. The word "kanisté" in Maya means "tree of the yellow sweet potato" ("kan" means "yellow", "is" means "sweet potato", and "té" means "tree"). The kanisté is an oval shaped fruit with a very fine pulp. The Maya also ate the avocado, the papaya, and many other fruits. Among the edible roots known to the ancient Maya were the yucca, three types of sweet potato, and the jícama, among others mentioned in Chapter Fourteen.

b) . Animals Which Provided Meat

A large variety of wild animals have always existed in the jungles of the Yucatán Península. Some of these animals are: deer, wild boar, monkeys, anteaters, pizotes, rabbits or hares, racoons, armadillos, iguanas, tepescuintles (a type of undergroud dwelling animal), moles, fox, mico de noche (short tailed night monkeys), opposum, many varietis of snakes, jaguars, pumas, tapir, and many others. The majority of these animals are edible.

The Maya probably domesticated the wild boar, the rabbit, and the deer.

Among the birds of the jungle are: pheasant, wild turkey, partridge quail, doves, and a variety of different types of pigeons. They were always served as a source of protein for the Maya. Bishop Landa stated that the Maya raised hairless dogs that did not bark, which they sacrificed in their religious ceremonies, and then ate. In the zoo in Mérida, one can see Aztecan dogs without hair; however, these bark.

The variety of marine life fished from the extensive coasts of the Yucatán Península rounded off the protein-rich foodstuffs eaten by the Maya. The fish was often salted to preserve it, and then used as a form of exchange for other products from inland.

Aside from bartering, the Maya used cacao seeds, accounts of pebbles, and seashells as a simple form of currency. This normalized the exchange between different areas but was conventional into them, was not imposed by goverment.

Upon the arrival of the Spaniards, the Maya had an abundant flock of chickens and turkeys. The conquistadors always mentioned this fact because, on those occasions when they were received by the Maya in a peaceful manner, they were always fed with chicken or turkey.

c). Industrial Products

Cotton was one of the industrial products that the Maya cultivated, spun, and then wove into blankets and clothes, which they used to cover themselves. The Maya also knew the process by which to produce salt from the salt water of the coasts. The salt from the Yucatán is considered to be among the best, and the Maya used it to cook, to preserve meats, and also in their medicinal practices. The Maya collected the resin of the "pom" tree, which they burned as incense. In Mayan it is given the name "copal". Because the Maya always burned the incense in their religious ceremonies, it was an indispensable item. The resins of the "pich" tree and of the cedar tree produce a good quality glue which had a variety of uses for the Maya. The resin of the zapote tree produces chewing gum. The fibers of the henequén plant were also very important, as they were used to make cords of different thicknesses, purses, sacks, and many other articles.

The Maya of that time had not yet discovered sugar; they used honey as a sweetener. The bees which they raised were smaller than are those commonly used today (Italian bees) and had no stingers; as such, the bees were much easier to handle. These bees are called "xcole-cab" in the Mayan idiom, and can still be found today in the area.

The beehives used by the ancient Maya to breed their bees were very primitive. They consisted of carefully hollowed-out trunks of trees, of about fifty to sixty centimeters in length, and with a width of about thirty centimeters. A hole was chopped in the middle of the wooden outer wall to provide the bees with access to the hollowed-out center of the log. A nucleus of bees was placed in the interior, and the ends were covered with closely-fitting caps of wood and then sealed with clay. The beehives were stacked one on top of the other, with the stack resting on a sawhorse or a small wooden stand, in protective sheds with thatched roofs of straw or palm.

The honey produced by these bees is thinner than that of the Italian bees, and their wax is softer and stickier. With this wax the Maya made long, thin candles, using cotton strings as wicks. The cotton wicks were given many coatings of wax, until they were about as thick as a drinking straw, and then coiled into the shape of a disk. To use this candle, the Maya simply uncoiled twenty centimeter section of the coil, put it in a vertical position, and burned it in the same manner that we burn our candles today, after burning that section, they uncoiled another piece until lasting the whole coil.

Among other things, the Maya used the honey to make a type of liquor called "balché". This liquor was made by first dissolving honey in water, and then adding pieces of the bark of the balché tree to the mixture. The fermentation of this solution produced the balché liquor, which was consumed in both religious and secular celebrations.

Unfortunately, these bees are becoming extinct, and the primitive type of beehive is very rarely encountered in the region today.

d) . **Colors**

The dyes used by the ancient Maya were of vegetable or mineral origin. Among the vegetable-based dyes are listed: 1) the indigo plant, which produces the color blue, 2) the achiote, the fruit of which is a capsule almost round and is about the size of a plum. Harmless spines are found on the outside of the achiote. After it is dried, the outer husk is split open, and the small red seeds inside can be used to produce the color red. Today this fruit, which the Maya call "kuxub", is almost always used in the preparation of meats rather than used for its color, as it has a very delicious flavor. 3) In the area surrounding the state of Campeche, the "stick of color" grows in abundance; when the wood of this plant is cut in pieces and boiled in water it produces an aniline which the Mayas used in their paintings. 4) They also used the blackberry plant, the wood and bark of which give off shades of yellow, green, and brown. 5) Finely ground charcoal served as a source of the color black. 6) The "choch quitám", or "intestines of the wild boar" plant, which is about eigthty centimeters high, has roots which, when boiled, produce a yellow color.

Among the mineral colors, the Maya used a type of bright red earth, similar to the vermillion which is found in some places in the Península; for white they used lime.

Without a doubt, the ancient Maya mixed these basic colors to produce others, varying the tones with bright or dark colors. They also undoubtedly mixed these ingredients with others (which are unknown today) which gave the colors the resistance to endure over the centuries.

CHAPTER SIXTEEN

THE FOUNDATION OF IMPORTANT CEREMONIAL CENTERS IN THE NORTHERN YUCATAN PENINSULA

a) . Generalizations
b) . Discovery and Founding of Chichén Itzá
c) . Founding of Ekbalam
d) . Founding of Izamal

e) . Founding of Motul
f) . Founding of Ichcansiho
g) . Founding of Mayapán
h) . Founding of Uxmal

a) . Generalizations

Unfortunately, archaeological explorations can only supply us with the approximate dates of buildings and periods of cultural evolution. Most opinions are based on the type of ceramics and architectural styles of a given period. Even now, with the proof supplied through the use of Carbon-14 dating, little or nothing is known of what actually took place, or of the historical details.

In the specific case of the Maya, the most extensive and valuable information obtained has been from the Chronicles of Chilam Balam, reports written back to Spain after the Spanish conquest, the report of Bishop Landa (which has been quoted many times), and information reported by other people and religious leaders who took an active part in the life of that period.

Without these reports, however, we would be abysmally ignorant of the history of the Maya of the north of the Yucatán Península.

The distinguished Yucatecan attorney and historian, Juan Francisco Molina Solís, carefully and patiently arranged the most important details of the above sources and published an interesting, two-volume book, **History of the Discovery and Conquest of Yucatán.** He mentions in the begining of the first volume; the following: In the year 242 A. D., Holón Chan appeared from the southeast of Yucatán, and traveled in a northerly direction from what today is British Honduras (Belize), and the region of the

Chenes of the state of Campeche, founding in his passing numerous towns; these have come to be the ruins situated in these regions... the successors of Holón Chan constantly continued moving about until the year 442. In 462, it being necessary to explore new lands, they discovered the port of Ziyan Caan, Bakhalal (today Bacalar), and there established their capital. Settling there, they founded the caciqueship of the Chanes, which remained until the arrival of the Spaniards.

b). **Discovery and Founding of Chichén Itzá**

Between the years 462 to 522 A. D., the Chanes discovered Chichén Itzá; various other sources cite the years 455—452 as the approximate date of discovery), but did not settle there. It is very possible that the existence of the two enormous wells, or "cenotes", and the magnetism of the place bade them return, for on October 18, 514, Chichén Itzá was founded, a correlation of the work of Goodman-Martínez Hernández-Thompson. Some publications say that this site had been inhabited since before 2000 B. C., but these inhabitants were probably semi-sedentary people who did not develop culturally.

The priest Lakin Chan took part in the founding of Chichén Itzá. Lakin Chan, also called Itzamná, was a wise man, who also introduced hieroglyphic writing and architecture, and also bestowed names on several towns. It is also said that he cured the sick, and even brought some of the dead back to life.

Tradition says it is known that Itzamná had a typically hooked nose, and because of this, whenever some investigators encounter stone reliefs, or any other rendering of a person with the hooked nose, they identify that person as the legendary Itzamná. This is not necessarily true, of course, because the hooked nose is a very common physical characteristic among the Maya.

Most of the reliefs and depictions of people are located in the Northern Group in Chichén Itzá. Each of these images bears a different expression, and it is possible that each represents a picture of a person of historical importance to Chichén Itzá. Although some feature the above mentioned have acquiline nose, it is doubtful that they represent Itzamná, as they were carved during the later Toltec period. Some may, however, be commemorative works dedicated to him.

It should be noted that Itzamná was a legendary figure, and information as to his identification is usually vague and difficult to find.

"Chichén Itzá" is a composite of three Mayan words: "Chí", meaning "mouth", "chen", meaning "well", and "Itzá", which is the name of the tribes which settled there; hence, "Chichén Itzá" means "at the mouth of the well of the Itzas".

In **The Book of the Books of Chilam Balam,** the authors, experts in the Maya idiom, after detailed analysis, concluded that the word "Itzá" is composed of two elements; "itz", which is a synonym for "sorcerer" in the Cakchiquel dialect of the Guatemalan highlands, and "ha", "water".[1]Accordingly, "Chichén Itzá" would signify "the mouth of the well of the sorcerer of the water". This interpretation is not acceptable in that the region in which the Cakchiquel dialect is spoken is extremely distant from the Yucatán; hence, we are left with the "mouth of the well of the Itzas" definition. This name could not have been the original, however; it is illogical to think that an inhabitant, when asked, "What is the name of this place?", would use the third person in replying, "This is the mouth of the well of the Itzas", when they would, in fact, be referring to themselves. This name was certainly invented by the Maya of the Decadent Period, after the abandonment of Chichén Itzá.

Archaeologist J. Eric S. Thompson says that the original name of Chichén Itzá could have been "Ucyabnal" which is translated as "seven great proprietors".

c). Founding of Ekbalam

After Chichén Itzá was founded, another faction of the Itzas, or Chanes, settled in Ekbalam which is situated fifty kilometers due north of Chichén Itzá in the present day municipality of Calotmul.

Ekbalam means "black jaguar", which was also the name of its founder. Some historians translate Ekbalam as "black tiger", but this is doubtful, since tigers have never populated América, only jaguars.

Today the ruins of five buildings, dedicated to each one of the founding captains, are still visible. These buildings were

1).— **Chilam Balam,** Op. Cit.; page 31.

important enough to merit an exterior relief showing armed people workers, decorative moldings, and hieroglyphics. Cereal graneries and recepticals for rain water can also be seen at the site.

The chief of Ekbalam had four subordinate commanders who helped him govern with rectitude and knowledge. Since he was a highly esteemed and respected man, he was able to extend his government to distant places. This prestige of Ekbalam did not last, however. As the size of his domain increased, Ekbalam began to be seen as a supernatural being. He began to treat his subjects with scorn and arrogance, and, in order to satisfy his growing thirst for pleasure and enjoyment, Ekbalam burdened the people with forced labor. After a reign of more than forty years, the towns people, tired of oppression, rebelled and assassinated Ekbalam and his most dedicated cohorts.

With the death of Ekbalam came uncontrolled anarchy. One of his direct descendants, Heb-Lay-Chac, took hold of the situation and seized the throne. He governed with prudence and discretion and, as a result, soon became the subject of idolotry, of which he approved. He ordered the construction of rock and clay statues, in his own image, to be placed in the houses and streets of all his domain, and thus he was not only revered in life, but was worshiped as a deity after his death.

The descendants of Ekbalam continued to rule the city in peace. The dynasty was extinguished during the Confederation of Mayapán, and the family of the Cupules governed the region until the arrival of the Spaniards.

The people of Ekbalam adored the great priest Itzamná. As tradition says that they came from the east, it is concluded that they were a part of the Chanes. (2)

d). Founding of Izamal

After Ekbalam was founded, another Chanes group, lead by the captains Kinich-Kakmó, Kinich-Kabul, Cit-Ahcoy, and Cit-Ahcutz, founded Izamal, which probably became a dependent of Chichén Itzá. They (the captains) constructed temples and palaces, some of the ruins of which still bear the name of their founders. (3)

2).— Molina Solís Juan Francisco, **Historia del Descubrimiento y Conquista de Yucatán**, Ediciones Mensaje, México City, 1943, Vol. 1; pp. 13—15.

3).— Ibid, page 16.

In Izamal, originally called "Emal" and "Kinich-Kakmó", there is one of the greatest pyramids of the península.[4]The Spaniards, however, destroyed many of the buildings and used the rocks for their living quarters, civil buildings, and religious temples, such as the famous Franciscan Convent. This is one of the reasons why the restoration of Izamal's buildings is almost impossible.

e). Founding of Motul

Another group, lead by a captain called Zac-Mutul, settled in what is now the city of Motul, forty-two kilometers east of Mérida.

Zac-Mutul was a white man, and, like the other captains already mentioned, came from the east looking for an adequate place to live with his tribe. Although this site was rocky, it looked safe and hospitable and he decided to settle there.

It is thought that Zac-Mutul may be the man referred to as Zacmutixtun-Ah Mutul in the chronicle of Chicxulub, and as Mabun-Chan in other references. These references indicate that Zac-Mutul was a member of the Chanes family. His dynasty ruled for many years. [5]

f). Founding of Ichcansihó

Not long after Izamal and Motul were founded, another Chanes group migrated farther westward, founding Ichcansihó or T-hó, which was to become the present day city of Mérida.[6]

In **The Book of the Books of Chilam Balam,** the authors translate "Ichcansihó" as a composite of three Maya words: "ich", meaning "face"; "caan", meaning "sky" or "heaven"; and "sihó", "birth". Thus, "Ichcansihó" means "the face of the birth of the sky",[7] In Yucatecan Maya, "ich" has another meaning "inside, inside of, or interior", "caan" is sky, while "sihó" is the plural past tense of the verb "to be born". Using these definitions, "Ichcansihó" translates as those born from the sky. This name, which is more acceptable and sounds more poetic, was probably

---

4).— **Códice Pérez,** Solís Alcalá Dr. Ermilo (translator), Imprenta Oriente, Mérida, Yucatán, 1949; page 370.
5).— Molina Solís, Op. Cit.; pp. 16—17.
6).— Ibid, page 17.
7).— **Chilam Balam,** Op. Cit.; page 49.

given to priests and other important people related to the foundation of the city.

Undoubtedly, the second name, T-hó, was used after the collapse of the Maya culture when Ichcansihó was abandoned. "T" is a contraction of the Maya word "teet" or "telo" which signifies the expressions "right there" or "over there"; added to the word "hó", or "five", they form the phrase "there are the five". This refers to the number of the most important temples that existed in that place at the time of the arrival of the Spaniards.

It is thought that Ichcansiho's founder was Ah-Chan Caan, who built a temple over a mound situated on the east side of the city, (the ruins of the temple were discovered there when the conquistadors arrived).

The fact that another of the temples is called Baklum-Chan is another inequivocable proof that the Ichcansihó Maya group also stemmed from the Chanes of Chichán Itzá.

Another important fact is that upon the arrival of the Spaniards there existed, a few kilometers north of T-hó, a Maya village by the name of Itzamná (now Itzimná), where the cacique Itzam Pech lived with his many subjects. After the Spaniards founded Mérida in the place of T-hó, Itzamná was abandoned, and the Mayan residents moved to Chubulná (now Chuburná). [8]

The towns just mentioned — Ekbalam, Izamal, Motul, and Ichcansihó — were probably dependent upon Chichén Itzá, and perhaps were its tribuntaries or satellites. The extravagant ambition of Chichén Itzá's leaders, demanding more from their subjects each day, gave rise to a rebellion, in which Chichén Itzá was attacked, and then abandoned in 622 A. D. Most of its inhabitants went to Chan-Petén or Chan-Putún, which is thought to be the city of Champotón in Campeche. They settled there in 702 A. D., after a long and painful pilgrimage.

g). Founding of Mayapán

After the Itzas had lived in Chan-Putún for "thirteen twenties" (260 years), they returned to Chichén Itzá in search of their old homesteads, guided by the captains Kak-u-pacat and the agile Bilú or Bil Huh, in the year 982 A. D. The journey was difficult, and they lost their way several times. Finally they settled in a place

8).— Molina Solís, Op. Cit.; pp. 17—18.

they called Dzan, a town that still exists near the city of Ticul. "Dzan" means "arrival" in Maya.

After a time, most of the people went north and founded the city of Mayapán.[9] This occurred at the end of the Tenth Christian Century, a fact which indicates that Kukulcán was not the founder of Mayapán, as is stated by Bishop Landa in **Relaciones,** as this date precedes the dates of Kukulcán's arrival and his influence on Mayapán.

After some years of progressing and gaining strength in Mayapán, the Itzás undertook a war with Motul, in which they fought the decendants of Zac-Mutul until finally defeating them in battle.

It is believed the Xius of Uxmal joined forces with the Itzás in attacking and eventually defeating Itzamal, and in doing so, helped them to avenge earlier defeats suffered at the hands of the people of Izamal, Kak-u-pacat, the Itzá captain, distinguished himself in battle by always carrying a "shield of fire", which apparently gave him added strength. Bil Huh, the other captain, later established his residence in Izamal, and was ultimately deified and worshipped as a god throughout the Península.

Once Izamal and Motul were defeated, Chichén Itzá, the old capital, was repopulated. Later it took an active role in the Confederation of which Uxmal, Izamal, Mayapán, and possibly other cities in the region were members. Mayapán was the seat of the Confederation, which lasted almost 200 years, from 1007 to 1182 A. D.

There has been some disagreement among archaeologists as to whether or not the Confederation existed between these dates (1007-1182) since, according to some, Uxmal had already been abandoned. The archaeologist César Sáenz, in charge of the restorations of several archaeological zones in México, says that the Puuc region flourished from 600 to 900 A. D., and that the active existence of Uxmal lasted until the Eleventh and Twelfth Centuries.[10] This seems most reasonable, as it agrees with the existence of the Confederation, putting the abandonment of Uxmal in the same time period as that of the abandonment of Chichén Itzá (1194 A. D.); apparently the abandonments of Uxmal and Chichén Itzá were related.

9).— Ibid, pp. 20—22.
10).— Sáenz César, **Boletín del I. N. A. H. Epoca II,** México City, Julio-Septiembre 1972; page 38.

Mayapán is located 42 kilometers from the city of Mérida (to get there, one must pass through the towns of Kanasín, Acanceh, Tecoh, Telchaquillo, and various sisal or hennequin haciendas). In 1950-51, Morris Jones, of the United States Geological Survey, made a detailed map of Mayapán, revealing the remains of over 3,600 buildings, surrounded by a low, double wall, portions of which can still be seen. The wall is about eight kilometers long, with six entrances, and encloses an area of 4.14 square kilometers. Bishop Landa's account mentions only two doors and a half of quarter of a league perhaps because the information he received was merely an estimate.

J. Eric S. Thompson believes that Mayapán was a true city, and not exclusively a ceremonial center. Given the number of small constructions that seem to be living quarters, he calculates that 10,000 inhabitants may have lived there in Mayapán's time of splendor (Morley estimates 15,000). Thompson also supposes that its founding in excessively rocky terrain which is unsuitable for agriculture, was due to the fact that it was designed to function as a political center. It was strategically located, surrounded by important towns of the Confederation, upon which its economy would depend.[11] The most valid reason for Mayapán's location in such non-productive terrain, however, was the existence of numerous natural wells, or "cenotes", nearby; water was always of primary importance to the Maya.

Fausto Uc Flores, caretaker of the Mayapán ruins for more than twenty years, and an assistant in the explorations of Mayapán, showed me a map of Mayapán which was made by the Carnegie Institute, which locates nineteen cenotes within the original walls, and one other immediately outside of the wall. Almost all of the cenotes have Mayan names, with the exception of the San Joaquín, which is Spanish, and three others which have both Spanish and Mayan names: the Chen-Carro, Nacché-Burro, and Chen-Pié cenotes.

In general, the Mayapán ruins are difficult to examine, as they are covered with dense vegetation.

While it is true that the soil surrounding Mayapán is very rocky, this is not the case in the area in which the most important structures are located. It seems as if dirt from the outside was brought inside so that an even and fertile land was obtained for

11).— Thompson, Op. Cit.; page 132.

vegetable gardens, and ornamental and medicinal plants. Flores listened to my theory and agreed with me, showing me that the soil of the interior is so fertile that excellent crops are harvested from everything planted within the walls.

Within the perimeter of the wall are a number of smaller subdivisions of land, which were once enclosed by dry, unmortared walls. These subdivisions were probably alloted to each representative of the Confederation from outside of Mayapán, who in turn alloted smaller plots to his helpers, according to their class or rank.

Mayapán's architecture is ordinary, and lacks any feeling for the aesthetic. For the most part, the rocks are roughly worked and not on a par with the refinement and splendor of Uxmal, Chichén Itzá, Palenque, etc. The craftsmen tried to correct this deficiency by adding a thick coating of stucco to the walls. The same thing can also be seen in Dzibichaltún, Tulum, Cobá, Konhunlich, and several other ceremonial centers.

The ceramics of Mayapán, for the most part, reveal a marked decadence.

h). Founding of Uxmal

Uxmal, well known for its grand and beautiful architecture, is located 78 kilometers south of Mérida. Its name is a compound of two monosyllabic words; "ux", which means "to pick" (as fruit from plants), and "mal" one time or "the time when a good harvest was obtained there".

Some tourist guides say that Uxmal was originally named Oxmal. Translated, this means ox, three and mal, time ("three times"), and it is speculated that Uxmal fell under three separate incursions. This name is fine for the period of time after the third occupation of the city, it certainly could not have been called "three times" during the first and second incursions. Perhaps after Uxmal was abandoned, the later Maya, using historical data which they obtained from tradition, referred to the ceremonial center as Oxmal; nevertheless, "Oxmal" could not have been the original name.

Discrepancies exist on the dates of the occupation and foundation of this ceremonial center. Researchers base their work on the Maya chronicles which used the Katun Round or

Short Count systems of dating. The very nature of the way the Round works lends itself to errors in the correlation of dates with those of the European calendar, as is described in detail in the chapter on chronology.

One of the accounts that seems most valid says that when the Chanes settled in Bakhalal (now Bacalar), another group headed by the Ak Mekat Tutul Xiu headed out toward the southern part of the Yucatán, that was known at that time as Chacnovitan. The migration had begun in the west, passing through the area of what are today the states of Tabasco and Campeche, during the year 482 A. D. This group, like the Chanes, progresivly founded towns along their route, towns such as Tankuiché, Opichén, Ticul, Nohpat, Sayil, Labná, Sabacché, Kabah, Uxmal, and others, later coming in contact with the Chanes of Chichén Itzá. The same report says that Ah Suytok Tutul Xiu founded Uxmal before Mayapán."(12)

Although some historians affirm that the name Tutul Xiu was of Nahua origin, we know that the word "xiu" means "grass" or "herb" in Mayan, and that the combination of "tu" and "tul" is a gerund of the verb "to over flow"; hence, "Tutul Xiu" means "ower flow with grass" in Yucatecan Maya. This can be interpreted as either a dark or very grassy place. Even today the Maya use the names of animals, plants, and other similar expressions for first and last names, and long ago, they also used them as titles for priests and the nobility.

The Xiues belonged to the same race as the Chanes, but were a separate tribe. They spoke the same dialect and used basically the same architecture, writing, calendar, and costumes. Also, there is proof that one of the most notable chiefs of the Xiues was named Hunikil-chac, while others say that Hunikil-chac was a name also given to Tutul Xiu(13)The following statement can be found in the first part of the Maya chronicle called **Matichu:** "This is the order of the katuns from when they left their land, their home of Nonoual —

Four katuns they were the Tutul Xiu 10.2.0.0.0. — 10.5.0.0.0; 3 Ahau-10 Ahau (849-928 A. D.) to the west of Zuyua.
The land from where they came (is) Tulapán Chiconautlan.
Four katuns they walked until arriving here in the company of the leader (Holón) Chan Tepeuh and companions.

12) .— Molina Solís, Op. Cit.; page 9.
13) .— Ibid, pp. 9—10.

When they left the (Petén) region it was 8 Ahau (the equivalent of 928—948 A. D. ..." [14]

In the third part of the chronicle appears the following:

"In the katun 2 Ahau 10.9.0.0.0. (987-1007 A. D.) Ah Suytok Tutul Xiu settled in Uxmal."

(Note: The numbers which appear separated by periods or dots refer to the known order of the Mayan baktuns, katuns, tuns, uinals, and days, which, since they do not amount to a uinal of the Long Count, that in these cases were correlated with the Short Count and the Christian Calendar.

Comparing the two sources cited above, we find 482 A. D. noted in the first as the year of the beginning of Ah Mekat Tutul Xiu's migration, while the second indicates that it was between the years 849 and 928 A. D. when the Xius left the region of Nonoual, which supposedly extended south of the present-day state of Oaxaca to Tabasco. This contrast of the two sources shows a discrepancy of 367 to 446 years.

It should be noted that Tulapán, mentioned in the first quote from the **Chronicles** as the place of departure of the Xius, may have some relationship with Tula, or some other Nahua village.

As for (Holón) Chan Tepeuh, you will recall that another Holón Chan, minus the last name of Tepeuh, lead the first migration, and that descendants of this first Holón Chan settled in Bakhalal or Bacalar in the year 462 A. D. The name "Tepeuh" is of Nahua origin and belongs to the period which was 446 years later; this indicates that the discrepancy between the two calendars results from errors in calculation, but rather in the fact that the sources are reporting two separate migrations.

In our discussions of the Toltec culture, it was stated that Chief Mixcoatl started the Toltec migration, and that he was also called Totepeuh, a name similar to that of Holón Chan Tepeuh. It is also possible that some Nahuas migrated to Yucatán and intermarried with the Maya.

A third account of the occupation of Uxmal is provided by Bishop Landa: "...the Indians tell that people came from the south to Yucatán with their leaders, and that they appear to have come from Chiapas, although the Indians do not really know; yet this author agrees because many words and the composition of many verbs are the same in Chiapas as in Yucatán, and there are

14) .— **Chilam Balam**, Op. Cit.; pp. 35—36.

259

great indications in part of Chiapas of places that had been deserted; and they say that these people spent forty years in the uninhabited places of Yucatán which had no sources of water except that of rainwater; and at the end of that time they arrived at the lands that happen to be somewhat in front of the city of Mayapán, ten leagues from it, and that there they commenced to settle and made many good buildings in many areas; and that those of Mayapán befriended them, and they rested from their tilling the land like natives; and Tutul Xiu subjected them to the laws of Mayapán, and they became related by marriage with one another; and Xiu, for his gentleness, came to be very esteemed by all."

In this account, Mayapán appears to have existed prior to Uxmal, something on which historians do not agree; they do agree upon the origin of the migration, however.

A fourth account of Uxmal's founding is found in the work of Friar Alonzo Ponce. Ponce states that a well-informed, sagacious old man from the town of Maní had obtained information from his ancestors which indicated that Uxmal had been occupied for more than 900 years (since the man recounting this story said more than 900; for this more we can add 50 years to this total)[15] Since Ponce was in Yucatán in 1588, we can calculate that Uxmal was occupied in the year 638 A. D. by subtracting 950 years from the year 1588 A. D.

In summary, Ah Suytok Tutul Xiu was a descendant of Ah Mekat Tutul Xiu, but was not an occupant of Uxmal in 986-1007 A. D. The error may have occurred in the attempt to correlate the Katun Round and the calendar which is used today. Studies of Uxmal's architectural styles indicate that it existed long before the arrival of Ah Suytok Tutul Xiu.

A more accurate date has been yielded by the use of the Carbon-14 dating method. Yale University submitted a sapodilla wood lintel to the Carbon-14 test, and arrived at the year 569 A. D. (fifty years of error more or less).[16] The wood was taken from the first substructure on the west side of the Temple of the Magician. The advanced architectural technique employed in the construction of this structure indicates that it was not the first building at Uxmal.

15).— Foncerrada de Molina Marta, **Uxmal; La Ciudad del Dios de la Lluvia,** F. C. E., México City, 1968; pp. 12—13.
16).— Sáenz, Op. Cit. (Julio-Septiembre, 1972); page 39.

We can see from the first account that the migration of Ah Mekat Tutul Xiu began in the year 482 A. D. Allowing one hundred years for his descendants to arrive at Uxmal, we calculate Uxmal's founding at 582 A. D.; this time is close to both the results of the Carbon-14 test on the wood lintel, and to the time mentioned by the wise old man of Maní.

With these dates in mind, the date of the occupation of Uxmal can be calculated to the beginning of the Sixth Century, A. D. Of course, the buildings of elevated aesthetics were not built immediately.

CHAPTER SEVENTEEN

THE FINAL EPOCH OF THE MAYA

a). **Confederation of Mayapán**
b). **Arrival of Kukulcán**
c). **Abandonment of Chichén Itzá**
d). **Destruction of Mayapán and Decline of the Maya Culture**
e). **Discovery of América and Foundation of Mérida**

a). **Confederation of Mayapán**

When the Confederation of Mayapán was organized, at the beginning of the Classic Period (1007 A. D.), each member governor was accompanied by his most dedicated collaborators. Each representative had an assigned area within the walls of Mayapán, and from there he governed his respective dominions through subordinate caciques.

Those that did not belong to the nobility (the lower class) grouped themselves in living quarters ' around the wall. Soon numerous "suburbs" made up of farmers and artisans dedicated to working to meet their own needs, and to supporting, in part, the nobility of Mayapán. Even the stewards and trustees assigned to collect tribute lacked the right to live inside the walls of the center itself. The only access that the lower class had to the interior of the center was at those times when their superiors needed their services or reports.

The foundation of the Conferation produced a state of peace and tranquility among the people of the Yucatán, and progress was seen in all parts of the Península. [1]

b). **Arrival of Kukulcán**

Although some investigators say that Kukulcán was the organizer of the Confederation, while others believe that the ca-

1).— Molina Solis, Op. Cit.; pp. 24—25.

ciques of Uxmal, exercising great influence over the Península, persuaded the other caciques to form a league or confederation of mutual assistance, which would resolve, in peace and harmony, any problems which might surface. Still other authorities maintain that Kukulcán arrived during the federative period, and counseled peace, unity, and an "esprit de corps", encouraging the governors to preserve their alliance.

Kukulcán came from the southwest, from the direction of Champotón, accompanied by a large retinue. He wore full-length clothing, sandles, and a beard, and preached that the Maya people should create idols of rock, clay, and wood. He constantly asserted that the Maya people were obligated to worship the idols, and should offer sacrifices to them of vegetables, animals, human blood, and even the hearts of men and women.

Although tradition indicates that Kukulcán had white skin and blue eyes, he is not depicted in the native chronicles in this manner; perhaps the relationship that existed between him and Quetzalcoatl of the Toltecs — both names signify "plumed serpent" or "Quetzal bird", in both the Maya and Nahuatl languages — gave origin to this version of his appearance, since Kukulcán and Quetzalcoatl are considered to be the same person.

Landa says that Kukulcán reigned with the Itzás, and that the pyramid that bears his name is proof of this fact. Landa also states that Kukulcán had no wife or children, and that for his awe-inspiring characteristics he was taken as a god. Landa leads us to understand that Kukulcán was the organizer of the Confederation of Mayapán; in Mayapán he erected another temple, similar to the one at Chichén Itzá. Upon his return to México, he built another temple near the sea, in the style of Chichén Itzá, in order to leave a permanent memory of himself in the Yucatán.

Apart from these reports, there are not many more details of the existence of Kukulcán available today. The Pérez Codex mentions him only superficially. In some passages he is confused with Hunac-Cel, as if to suggest that the two were one and the same. In other passages, he is associated with the name Ah-Nac-Xiu-Kukulcán.

It is possible that when he left the Península, his name was used as a title for priests or nobility, as was the name of Quetzalcoatl in the Nahua cultures of other epochs.

264

I should mention that apart from Kukulcán and Quetzalcoatl, similar deities existed in other cultures, locations, and epochs in América, under other names. Among the Quiché of Guatemala the deity was called "Gucumatz"; the Mixtecs called him "Huixipecochi"; he was called "Votán" in the southeast of México and Central América; "Viracocha", in Perú; "Bochica", in Columbia; and "Sume", in Brazil. "Kon-Tiki" was also used in Perú, but at a different time than was "Viracocha". "Kon-Tiki" was given worldwide recognition by Thor Heyerdahl when he sailed from Perú on a raft bearing the same name.

c). Abandonment of Chichén Itzá

After Kukulcán left Yucatán, differences among the chiefs of the Confederation surfaced, and were finally brought to a head by a rather bizarre incident. The chief of Chichén Itzá, Chac-Xib-Chac, was to wed a maiden who, at the same time, was being courted by the king of Mayapán, Hunac-Cel, who was also in love with her. The maiden preferred Chac-Xib-Chac, much to the despair of Hunac-Cel. Hunac-Cel hid his anger, and outwardly displayed total indifference, while he cleverly engineered, and later, carried out the abduction of the maiden during the wedding festivities, taking advantage of the fact that most of the residents of Chichén Itzá were drunk. This action created unrest among the surrounding villages, which united with Chichén Itzá in declaring war on Mayapán. [2]

J. Eric S. Thompson relates a similar story, with Chac-Xib-Chac indicted as the abductor of the sweetheart of Ah Ulil, the principal chief of Izamal. Hunac-Cel, angered by the abduction, and acting on behalf of Ah Ulil, declared war on Chac-Xib-Chac and Chichén Itzá.[3] Soon Hunac-Cel realized that he was losing the war to his stronger foes, and in an attempt to avert defeat, sent emissaries to Xicalango, Tabasco, to convince the mercenary Nahuas to come to his aid; in exchange for some excellent "gifts" the Nahuas entered the fray on the side of Hunac-Cel.

The battle techniques and weapons that the Nahuas brought with them (some of which, like the bow and arrow, were unknown to the native Maya) played an important role in Hunac-Cel's

2).— Ibid, pp. 28—30.
3).— Thompson, Op. Cit.; page 130.

victory. In 1194 A. D., Chichén was defeated and abandoned. Part of its inhabitants left and settled in Tayasal, near Lake Petén Itzá in Guatemala, which had been their place of origin. Others were made prisoners and enslaved, while the rest spread out in different directions. The people of the city of Izamal and its surrounding area met with a similar fate as that of Chichén Itzá. [4]

With its victory over Chichén Itzá, Mayapán's dominance was made evident, bringing about a hegemony which lasted over two hundred years, from 1194—1441 A. D.

d) . Destruction of Mayapán and Collapse of the Maya Culture

During the period of Mayapán's hegemony, it was governed by the Cocoms dynasty. The insatiably ambitious Cocoms exerted constant pressure on their subjects, giving rise to a general discontent that predisposed the courage for the oppressed against their oppressors. The Maya familiarized themselves with the Nahuas, learning their battle strategies until the Nahuas were no longer feared.

Tutul Xiu managed to escape from the walled city of Mayapán, and supported the insurrection of almost all of the inhabitants of the Península, who could no longer tolerate the unjustness of the Cocoms. After a bloody battle, which saw great victories and defeats on both sides, Mayapán was finally overcome and totally destroyed. All of the Mayapán chiefs, especially those of the Cocom family, were slain, with the exception of a son, who was doing business in Ulua, Guatemala at the time, and another relative named Cocom Cat. When the son returned from Guatemala, he founded the town of Tboolom (which is now called Tibolón) in the caciqueship of Sotuta. Cocom Cat sought refuge with his friends in Tiab, which is now called Teabo. [5]

The remains of forty-one people were found in later explorations of the ruins of Mayapán, squeezed into a narrow, vertical hole that leads to a cavern under one of the pyramids. Inside of this cavern were the skeletons of a man and a women that are probably the remains of a chief and his wife. The skeletons were accompanied by some poorly made pots, and a huge pile of the bones of birds and other animals. [6]

4) .— Molina Solís, Op. Cit.;
5) .— Molina Solís, Op. Cit.; pp. 31—33.
6) .— Thompson, Op. Cit.; pp. 135 and 140.

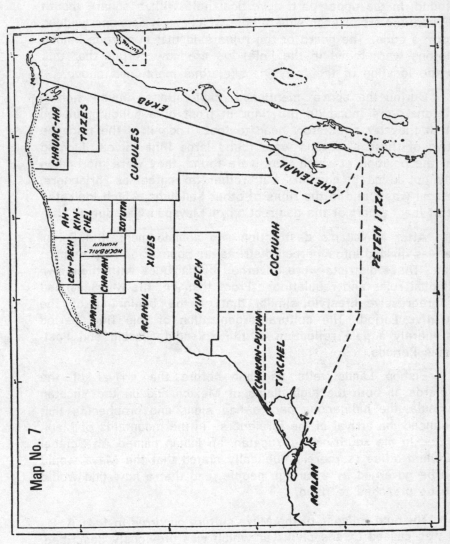

Map. No. 7. This map shows the approximate division of the Yucatán at the time of the Conquest, with the chieftainships which existed at that time. From the book "Relación de las Cosas de Yucatán". Editorial Porrúa. S. A. 1959.

During one of the last visits that the author of this book made to the ruins of Mayapán, upon ascending a small pyramid (of 12 by 15 meters) which is situated to the right side of the main entrance, and 200 meters northwest of the Kukulcán Pyramid, he found, in the upper part, a vertical hole with a square mouth of 65 centimeters on each side, a hole which, as it deepens, widens to form a cone. The guard of the ruins said that numerous human skeletons were found in the hole; we are now certain that this was the location of the forty-one skeletons mentioned above.

During the above mentioned explorations, seven human skeletons were found on the floor in front of a building, placed so that they lay alternately head to foot. Lodged in the ribcages of two of these skeletons were found large flint knives. Judging from the position in which they were found, they were more than likely not killed in combat, but rather executed as prisoners. Charcoal was found in the ruins of other buildings, which indicates that at least a part of the destruction of Mayapán was due to fire.

After Mayapán's destruction and abandonment, the Península was divided into nineteen districts, as appears on map number seven. These districts were governed by caciques with their own individual rules and regulations. From then on, the Maya carried on a regressive lifestyle, similar that of the beginning of the Formative Period. The cultural organization of this final period was merely a pale reflection of the splendid Classic and Post-Classic Periods.

Bishop Landa tells us that before the arrival of the Spaniards, in both the high plains of México and on the Yucatán Península, the indigenous people had signs and prophecies that announced the arrival of the foreigners. In the mountains of Maní, situated in the south of the Yucatán, an Indian named Ah Cambal of Chilam office (sorcerer) publically stated that the Maya would soon be governed by a foreign people, and that a new god would soon be preached to them.

The final collapse of the Maya culture occurred in 1441 A. D., and was caused by the civil war which was previously described. The arrival of the conquering Spanish destroyed any possibility of a resurgence of the once great Maya culture.

e) Discovery of America and Foundation of Mérida

On the twelfth of October, 1492, Christopher Columbus discovered the Americas with three ships that had sailed from Spain on August third of the same year. The Santa María, with a hundred-tons capacity, captained by Juan de la Cosa, and on which travelled Admiral Columbus, was the first; the Pinta, captained by Martín Alonzo Pinzón and with a 600-tons capacity, was the second; and the Niña, with a capacity of 400-tons and captained by Vicente Yáñez Pinzón, brother of the captain of the Pinta, was the third. All three crews combined totalled less than 100 men. After sailing for many days, they landed on an island in the Lucayne Archipelago, which Columbus named San Salvador which is not satisfactorily identified. [7]

On July 30, 1502, Barthalome Columbus, in the company of his brother, Christopher, discovered the island of Guanajas, surrounded by various smaller islands, in the Gulf of Honduras, and made contact with the indigenous people of the Yucatán Península. The Indians were travelling in a very long, single-piece, canoe, which was eight feet wide. The canoe held twenty-five people, the majority of which were men. It was a merchant canoe, and apart from its occupants, carried cotton blankets, axes, copper swords, pottery (which probably contained drinking water), and good quality cacao. The men in the party were covered with wide sashes, and the women with cotton blankets. To the Europeans, this suggested the possibility that a form of civilization existed in these regions. As they were unable to understand the Maya language, the Spaniards deduced through the use of sign language that the natives were from a rich country, which proved to be the Yucatán Península.

Columbus deviated from his course, but was unable to find the place he sought. Believing that the Península was an island, he named it "Isla Rica" (Rich Island), a name which enraptured other adventure some Spaniards. Among these were Juan Díaz de Solís and Vincente Yáñez Pinzón, who landed on the islands of Guanajas in 1506. Sailing west, the two traversed part of the coast of the Yucatán, and eventually discovered a bay, giving it the name Bay of Nativity; they were unable, however, to encounter the legendary land, and never actually set foot on Yucatecan soil! [8]

7).— Jiménez M. Miranda, and Fernández, Op. Cit.; page 192.
8).— Molina Solís, Op. Cit.; page 41.

In 1511, the mayor of Dairén, Núñez de Balboa, sent a caravel, under the command of Valdivia, to the island of Española, to deliver one thousand ducats of gold reals and some correspondence to Admiral Columbus, and to search for food and other provisions.

After travelling the first few days of the voyage with favorable weather, a storm appeared which carried the caravel and its crew into a place which they called "Los Bajos de las Víboras" (The Pit of the Vipers). Lashed by the storm's fury, the party crashed onto the dangerous reefs near Jamaica, which broke their vessel into pieces. The twenty people on board managed to save a small boat, in which they eventually drifted to the coast of the Yucatán. As they were not able to take provisions with them, however, seven of the twenty on board died of starvation.

Once they landed on the shores of the Yucatán, they were made prisoners by savage tribes (cannibals). Valdivia and four of his companions were sacrificed, and their flesh was distributed among the natives. The others, including Gerónimo de Aguilar and Gonzalo de Guerrero, were placed in wooden cages, to be fattened and later sacrificed. During one of the many nights of their captivity, the prisoners forced the door of their cage, and fled into the jungle. They travelled until they entered the territory of a more hospitable cacique, where, although they were taken as slaves, they were also given some consideration.[9] Later, Gonzalo de Guerrero was given to the cacique of Chetemal (today's Chetumal), where he gained the sympathy and affection of his owner by demonstrating his bravery and intelligence in clashes between Chetemal and its neighboring caciques. Guerrero, through his merits, eventually earned the rank of general-in-chief of the armies of the cacique. He later married a Maya princess, and from that marriage came the first mestizo children of the Yucatán.

For his part, Gerónimo de Aguilar, that was a priest of the highest order, was subject to tests of chastity, and, like Guerrero, conquered the affection and confidence of his superior, who latter named Aguilar to manage his estate in his absence.

One day, Aguilar received a letter of the Cortés Expedition, which had made a stop on the island of Cozumel in their journey from Cuba to Veracruz, from some of his Mayan friends. Aguilar travelled to Cozumel to join the party, and in doing so, gained his

9) .— Ibid, pp. 44—47 and 50.

liberty from the Maya, proved to be very helpful to Cortés in the expedition, as by that time he had become fluent in the Mayan language.

It wasn't until the month of March in 1517, when Francisco Hernández de Córdoba, on an expedition consisting of three ships and 110 men, sailed to the Guanaja Islands in search of natives for use as slaves in Cuba. A storm blew the party far to the west of its original course, and they were forced to land on a small island, which they named "Island of Women" (isla Mujeres). The name was derived from the fact that they found a number of idols with figures like women within a small temple on the island. The figurines appeared to be dressed in skirts, with their chests covered with cotton cloth.[10] (This island is now an attractive tourist center, with water so incredibly transparent that one can see up to twenty meters in depth from the surface, with sand as white as sugar.)

After abandoning the island, the party finally set foot on Yucatecan soil in the place known today as Cabo Catoche. Unfortunately for the Spaniards, while the natives greeted them with apparent hospitality, they secretly plotted an ambush. In the ensuing battle, the natives sustained many losses, and, in the end, were forced to flee. Hernández de Córdoba lost twenty-six men; in this situation, a disaster."[11]

After this incident, Hernández de Córdoba and his party continued their voyage westward; then, after many days of navigation, a coastal village of nearly three thousand thatched houses loomed on the horizon. This was the village of Ah Kin Pech (today Campeche). Many of the inhabitants of the village came out to greet the Spanish party, displaying a peaceful manner. The Spaniards were invited into the houses of the natives, to be regaled with a succulent banquet of corn tortillas, venison, turkey, partridges, rabbit, and fruit. During their two-day stay in the village, the Spaniards were entertained by the caciques and their priests; while the Spaniards were recieved with genuine friendship, the natives did not wish for them to stay in the village, and urged them to move onward.

The Spaniards, realizing that the natives were becoming hostile, resolved to abandon it, and continued their voyage, as always, to the west. After a few days, they found themselves in

10).— Ibid, pp. 52—53.
11).— Ibid, pp. 55—56.

a bay, into which emptied the river Potochán (today Champotón). One league from the riverbank they found a village of the same name, governed by the brave cacique Moch Couoh. The cacique waged a furious battle with the Spaniards for more than four hours, and in spite of the fact that the natives lost many warriors, they continued to attack with such courage that the Spanish were forced to retreat. The Spaniards suffered fifty-six casualties in the battle.[12]

Demoralized by these occurences, the Spaniards decided to return to Cuba, by way of Florida. In Florida, they lost another battle to the natives, and returned to Cuba beaten and discouraged. Hernández de Córdoba died a few days later of the many wounds he had recieved in the various battles.

With the news of the existence of rich lands of that area the governor of Cuba, Diego Velázquez, organized two more expeditions, one commanded by Juan de Grijalva, and the other by Hernando de Cortés. Both expeditions roughly followed the same course as that of Hernández de Córdoba, although Cortés eventually landed at Veracruz to realize the conquest of México.

Later, and after three successive attempts, Francisco de Montejo el Adelantado (the Older), and later, both his son, Francisco de Montejo el Mozo (the Younger), and his nephew, Francisco de Montejo, realized the conquest of Yucatán.

Francisco de Montejo (el Mozo) founded the city of Mérida on the sixth of January, 1542, an event which provides a fitting ending for our descriptive outline of the great Maya culture.

A fitting ending for our story is a fragment of a beautiful poem written by the unforgetable Yucatecan poet Antonio Mediz Bolio:

"Acquire wisdom and be those of Itza".
So says the Word that announced in its hour
the change from the old times.

I come to you singing in the middle of the night,
and I say to you with the voice of your brother:
Fly anew pheasant, through the fragrant air,
and leap again Deer in the happy plains!

12).— Ibid, pp. 57—59.

The gift of faith that enlightens might be distributed
among all without measure

of the hope that rages and of the love that makes life!
That will be the day in which, with all its beauty and its power,
the great Mayab shall be resurrected, that which to us seems dead!

Tac Tu Lak Kin

BIBLIOGRAPHY

1).— Acosta Jorge R. and Martínez del Río Dr. Pablo, **Guía Oficial de Tula.** Instituto Nacional de Antropología e Historia de México, México D. F., 1961.

2).— Acosta Jorge R., **Guía Oficial de Teotihuacan.** Instituto Nacional de Antropología e Historia. Edimex, S. de R. L. y Litoarte, S. de R. L. México, 1965.

3).— Arochi Luis E., **La Pirámide de Kukulcán; Su Simbolismo Solar.** Editorial Orión, México D. F., 1976.

4).— Blom Frans, **La Vida de los Mayas.** Secretaría de Educación Pública, Biblioteca Enciclopédica Popular No. 25, México D. F., 1944.

5).— Bustillos Carrillo Profr. Antonio, **El Sacbé de los Mayas.** B. Costa-Amic, México D. F., 1964.

6).— Calderón Héctor M., **Clave Fonética de los Jeroglíficos Mayas.** Editorial Orión, México D. F., 1962.

7).— Calderón Héctor M., **La Ciencia Matemática de los Mayas.** Editorial Orión, México D. F., 1966.

8).— Canto López Antonio, **Apuntaciones Sobre Mesoamérica.** Published by author, Mérida, Yucatán, México, 1973.

9).— Cirerol Sansores Manuel, **Chi Cheen Itsa.** Talleres Gráficos del Sudeste, S. A., Mérida, Yucatán, México, 1957.

10).— Cirerol Sansores Manuel, **Guía de Ushmal.** Published by author, Mérida, Yucatán, México, 1956.

11).— Cirerol Sansores Manuel, **El Arte Pictórico de los Antiguos Mayas.** Talleres Gráficos del Sudeste, S. A. Mérida, Yucatán, 1955.

12).— **Códice Pérez.** Solís Alcalá Dr. Emilio, (translator), Imprenta Oriente, Mérida, Yucatán, México, 1949.

13).— Coe William R., **Tikal, A Handbook of the Ancient Maya Ruins.** The University Museum of the University of Pennsylvania, Philadelphia, Pennsylvania, 1967.

14).— Cordan Wolfgang, **Secret of the Forest.** Doubleday and Company, Inc., Garden City, New York, 1964.

15).— Covarrubias, Miguel, **Indian Art of Mexico and Central America.** Alfred A. Knoph, New York, 1957.

16).— del Castillo Bernal Díaz, **Historia de la Conquista de la Nueva España.** Editorial Porrúa, S. A., México, 1962.

17).— de Landa Fray Diego, **Relación de las Cosas de Yucatán.** Editorial Porrúa, S. A., México D. F., 1959. (Eighth Edition).

18).— Duarte Magaloni Ignacio, **Educadores del Mundo.** B. Costa-Amic, México D. F., 1969.

19) .— Díaz Bolio José, **Guía Instructiva a las Ruinas de Chichén Itzá.** Published by author, Mérida, Yucatán, 1972.

20) .— Díaz Bolio José, **La Serpiente Emplumada Eje de Culturas.** Segunda Edición, 1957.

21) .— Echánove Trujillo Carlos A., **¡Esas Pobres Ruinas Mayas Maravillollosas!.** B. Costa-Amic, México, 1973.

22) .— **El Libros de los Libros de Chilam Balam.** Barrera Vásquez Alfredo and Rendón Silva. Fondo de Cultura Económica, México D. F., 1965.

23) .— Jimínez Moreno Wigberto, Miranda José and Fernández María Teresa, **Historia de México.** Editorial E.C.L.A.L.S.A. Constitución, 18. Librebría de Porrúa Hnos y CIA. S. A. México D. F., 1967. (Third Edition).

24) .— Foncerrada de Molina, Marta, **Uxmal; La Ciudad del dios de la Lluvia.** Fondo de Cultura Económica, México D. F., 1968.

25) .— Girard Rafael, **El Colapso Maya y los Nahuas.** Talleres Gráficos de Impresiones Modernas, S. A., México D. F., 1959.

26) .— González Blackaller C., and Guevara Ramírez I., **Síntesis de la Historia de México.** Editorial Herrero, S. A., México D. F., 1962.

27) .— **Guía Oficial de Monte Albán-Mitla.** Instituto Nacional de Antropología e Historia de México, México D. F., 1962.

28) .— **Historia del Hombre; Dos Millones de Años de Civilización.** Readers Digest México, S. A. de C. V., México D. F., 1977.

29) .— Iturribaria Jorge Fernando, **Las Viejas Culturas de Oaxaca.** Imprenta Valle, México D. F., 1952.

30) .— **La Aventura de México.** Ayala Anguiano Armando (Director General) Vol. 1, No. 2, Publicaciones AAA, S. A., México D. F., 1966.

31) .— Martínez Marín Carlos, **Los Aztecas.** Instituto Nacional de Antropología e Historia de México, México D. F., 1965.

32) .— Molina Solís Juan Francisco, **Historia del Descubrimiento y Conquista de Yucatán.** Ediciones Mensaje, México D. F., 1943. Vol. I y II.

33) .— Morley Sylvanus Griswold, **An Introduction to the Study of the Maya Hieroglyphs.** Dover Publications, Inc., New York, 1975.

34) .— Morley Sylvanus G., **La Civilización Maya.** Fondo de Cultura Económica, México D. F., 1956.

35) .— Morley Silvanus G., **La Civilización Maya.** Fondo de Cultura Económica, México D. F., 1975.

36) .— Pacheco Cruz Santiago, **Diccionario de Etimologías Toponímicas Mayas,** 1959, Mérida, Yucatán, México.

37) .— Proskouriakoff Tatiana, **Album de Arquitectura Maya.** Fondo de Cultura Económica, México D. F., 1969.

38).— Raziel García Arroyo, **Macutli Tlachtli.** Cinco Deportes Mexicanos. Publicaciones Internacionales, S. A. México, 1969.

39).— **Richards Topical Encyclopedia.** (Adaptación parcial) Printed and made in México. Copyright 1963 by Editorial Richard, S. A., Panamá, R. de P.

40).— Roys Ralph L. **The Book of Chilam Balam of Chumayel.** New Edition copyright 1967 by the University of Oklahoma Press.

41).— Sáenz César, **Boletín del I. N. A. H. Epoca II.** Instituto Nacional de Antropología e Historia de México, México D. F., Julio-Septiembre 1972. p. 38.

42).— Sáenz César, **Boletín del I. N. A. H. Epoca II.** Instituto Nacional de Antropología e Historia de México, México D. F., Octubre-Diciembre 1975. pp. 55, 56.

43).— Solís Alcalá Dr. Emilio, **Diccionario Español-Maya.** Editorial Yikal Maya Than, Mérida, Yucatán, México, 1949.

44).— Stromsvik Gustavo, **Ruinas de Copán, Guía.** Pedro Aplicano M. Editor. October 1967. Honduras.

45).— Stephens John L., **Incidents of Travel in Yucatan.** Two Volumes, 1963. Dover Publication, Inc. New York.

46).— Stephens John L., **Incidents of Travel in Central America, Chiapas and Yucatan.** Copyright 1969 by Dover Publications Inc.

47).— Thompson, J. Eric S., **Grandeza y Decadencia de los Mayas.** Fondo de Cultura Económica, México D. F., 1959.

48).— Thompson J. Eric S., **The Rise and Fall of Maya Civilization.** University of Oklahoma Press Norman. 1966 Oklahoma U. S. A.

49).— Thompson J. Eric S., **Arqueología Maya.** Editorial Maya. México D. F., 1978.

50).— Thompson Edward **Herbert. People of the Serpent.** Life and adventure Among the Maya. Capricorn Books Edition 1965.

51).— Watson Don **Indias of the Mesa Verde,** Mesa Verde Museum Association, Mesa Verde National Park, Colorado, U.S.A. 1961.

(40) — Pozas, Juan. *Juegos de Manos*. México. Cuban Importers Inc. México.
    Publicaciones Internacionales S. A. México, 1990.

(41) — *Britannica Junior Encyclopaedia*. (Adesso, En particular Chicago, and
    articles in México. Copyright 1984 by Educational Britannica S. A. Bartholome A. S.)

(42) — Roys Ralph. *The Book of Chilam Balam of Chumayel*. New Edition.
    copyright 1967 by the University of Oklahoma Press.

(43) — Sáenz César Adolfo del P. M. A. H. *Cuerpo Técnico de Antropología e
    Historia de México*. Diez Ángel Ciudad. 1967. pp. 26.

(44) — *Antropología e Historia de México*. Mexico D. F. Julio Septiembre.
    1984. p. 38.

(45) — Soto Alberto Emilio. *Enciclopedia Espasa-Calpe*. Tomo 30. Núm.
    Maya Guatemala. Yucatán. México. 1948.

(46) — Stephens John Lloyd. *Ruinas de Copán, Guat. Panorámica de los
    Ríos del Departamento de Honduras*.

(47) — Stephens John Lloyd. *Incidents of Travel in Yucatán*. Two Volumes.
    1843. Dover Publications Inc., New York.

(48) — Stromsvik John. *Incidents of Travel in Central America, Chiapas
    and Yucatán*. Copyright 1969 by Dover Publications, Inc.

(49) — Thompson Eric S. *Grandeur y Decadencia de los Mayas*. Fondo
    de Cultura Económica. México D. F. Fondo.

(50) — Thompson Eric S. *The Rise and Fall of Maya Civilization*. University
    of Oklahoma Press. Norman. 1966. Oklahoma. U. S. A.

(51) — Thompson E. Eric S. *Arqueología Maya*. Editorial Mayo. México D.
    F. 1975.

(52) — Tozzer Gerard Herbert. *Ruins of the Ancient City and silver.
    Maya's about the Maya. Computers History Editors*. 1952.

(53) — Waltzer Thor Index of the Maya Yucatán Maya Writing Studies.
    Research on Maya with National Geographic. Chicago U. S. 1960.

This book was printed by
LITOARTE, S. de R.L.
F.C. Cuernavaca 683, México 11520, D.F.
in July, 1985.